Praise for *Executive Stamina*

"Sage advice and practical actions for optimizing the effectiveness of your professional and personal life for the long haul."
> —Steve Milovich, Senior Vice President, Corporate Human Resources, Organization and Leadership Development, The Walt Disney Company

"Imagine sitting down with one of the best executive coaches after the world has drained the life out of you. Through this book, Seldman will bring you back and ready to face the world anew. It's an amazing mixture of insightful, thought-provoking ideas and practical, down-to-earth actions you can apply immediately. It's also one of those special books in which you'll come across a chapter that seems especially written for you!"
> —Kevin D. Wilde, VP, Organization Effectiveness and Chief Learning Officer, General Mills, Inc.

"Executive stamina is critical for success in any corporate environment. As executives we are constantly faced with challenges in managing our time, energy and productivity. In this book you will learn how to align your work and life goals, maximize your career contributions and build more positive personal relationships. This book shares essential insights about how to achieve peak performance and live a more fulfilling life."
> —Tamar Elkeles, PhD, Vice President, Qualcomm and Author, "The Chief Learning Officer"

"Executive Stamina: Because life is not a sprint but a marathon. The Seldmans' share a wealth of consulting and coaching experience that executives and entrepreneurs of all ages can put to use right away to enrich their lives."
> —Franke James, Author, *The OfficePolitics.com Guide to Winning the Game Everyone Plays*

"In work, as in life, people either charge or discharge their personal battery and vitality each day. *Executive Stamina* raises the bar on our understanding of how today's leaders and professionals can strengthen and sustain their energy and effectiveness. The perspectives and recommendations are practical, systematic and draw upon his unique integration of many different disciplines and approaches. I highly recommend *Executive Stamina* for anyone seeking professional and personal success and wellness."
> —Ed Betof Ed.D., Senior Fellow and Academic Director, The Executive Program in Workplace Learning Leadership, University of Pennsylvania

"Just as he does as an executive coach, Seldman provides insight, process and tools for each of us to maximize our potential in our personal and professional lives. *Executive Stamina* takes a holistic approach for each of us to construct a roadmap to success"
> —Mike Theilmann, Executive Vice President, Chief Human Resources & Administration Officer, JCPenney

"Like many senior executives, there are days when I feel I need to be an Olympic athlete just to keep up with the pace of business life. The physical demands of travel, long hours and packed schedules are matched by the need for faster analysis, decision-making and follow-through. 'Executive Stamina' is the ideal prescription for those who recognize there has to be a better way to manage the challenges of the roles we relish. This book will connect with anyone seeking to improve both their personal performance as well as their work/life balance."

    —Peter Gibbons, Senior Vice President, Global Manufacturing Operations, Starbucks Coffee Company

"*Executive Stamina* addresses issues of stress, health and career advancement in an extremely knowledgeable, holistic and compassionate way. It provides groundbreaking but straightforward tools to maintain your focus on your performance, your relationships and your well-being."

    —Jovita Thomas-Williams, President, JTW Affiliates

"This book is the 'holy grail' for corporate success. Seldman is one of the few who understand how long the corporate race actually is and how absolutely crucial executive stamina is to WINNING it".

    —Michael Feiner, Professor and Sanford C. Bernstein Ethics Fellow at Columbia University Graduate School of Business

"You can't read *Executive Stamina* without getting energized to make changes for a better 'you.' Marty combines his extensive executive coaching expertise with the Joshua's vital information on nutrition and fitness and makes it interesting and practical. *Executive Stamina* is a toolkit for work and life!"

    —Mary Eckenrod, Vice President, World Wide Talent and Organization Development, Lenovo

EXECUTIVE STAMINA

How to Optimize Time, Energy, and Productivity to Achieve Peak Performance

Marty Seldman
and
Joshua Seldman

WILEY

John Wiley & Sons, Inc.

Published by John Wiley & Sons, Inc., Hoboken, New Jersey
Published simultaneously in Canada

For general information on our other products and services or for technical support, please contact our Customer Care Department within the United States at (800) 762-2974, outside the United States at (317) 572-3993 or fax (317) 572-4002.

Wiley also publishes its books in a variety of electronic formats. Some content that appears in print may not be available in electronic books. For more information about Wiley products, visit our web site at www.wiley.com.

Library of Congress Cataloging-in-Publication Data:

Seldman, Marty.
  Executive stamina : how to optimize time, energy, and productivity to achieve peak performance/Marty Seldman and Joshua Seldman.
        p. cm.
  Includes bibliographical references and index.
  ISBN 978-0-470-22290-4 (cloth)
1. Executive ability. 2. Management. 3. Career development. I. Seldman, Joshua, 1977- II. Title.
  HD38.2.S457 2008
  658.4'093–dc22   2007051407

Printed in the United States of America

10 9 8 7 6 5 4 3 2 1

To Jyoti and Eliyahu Shaiyah,
Our future
and
In Loving Remembrance of
Ronnie Miller Hasday

Contents

About the Authors

Marty Seldman earned his PhD in clinical psychology. In 1986, he started his career as an international executive coach. At that point he had lived in many other cultures and worked in a variety of roles in the interpersonal skills training field. Eventually, coaching became his primary professional focus, and in the past 22 years he has conducted in-depth, one-on-one coaching sessions with more than 1,500 executives. He counts himself fortunate to have worked with a number of companies and clients consistently over many years, which has allowed him to track individual career paths and corporate procedures. This has given him a thorough understanding of why certain individuals reach higher levels of achievement, and others don't.

Joshua Seldman is a highly respected cycling and fitness coach, and through his experience as an athlete and coach, has become one of the foremost experts on endurance performance. During his career as a professional athlete, he was a 12- and 24-hour solo mountain bike champion, and competed in the Elite national championships, world championships, and international stage races, such as the Tour of Chile.

Joshua worked for many years as a lead coach for Carmichael Training Systems, one of the top coaching companies in the world. He has coached all levels of individuals including national and world champions, as well as members of the Leukemia Society's Team in Training, and riders who had survived cancer as they completed the Lance Armstrong/Bristol-Myers Squibb's Tour of Hope ride across the country from Los Angeles to Washington, D.C. in eight days.

Currently he specializes in corporate wellness and executive performance, working with individuals and companies to maximize their performance through the benefits of improved fitness, higher energy levels, increased stamina, and a balanced life.

Acknowledgments

Marty Seldman

I am very grateful for all the support and assistance I received in conceiving and completing *Executive Stamina*.

First of all, to Joshua, for our many brainstorming discussions, from which the book emerged, and for his expertise and writing throughout the process.

John Willig is a wonderful agent who was supportive at many key points where I needed his advice.

The John Wiley & Sons, Inc. editorial team provided so much help in making my ideas more accessible to the reader. Thank you, Matthew Holt, Shannon Vargo, Miriam Palmer-Sherman, Jessica Campilango, and Janice Borzendowski.

Jnana Gowan contributed her wide knowledge of yoga practice and flexibility exercises. Lisa Feiner of Feiner Health was an invaluable advisor for the Nutrition section. Kate Wharmby researched many portions of Stress Management.

I also want to acknowledge two people who helped me with their support but, even more, their patience.

Talia Amedi, my daughter, was my production assistant, and I was amazed at her calm in dealing with a technology-challenged writer like myself.

And thank you to Kelly Reineke, my wife, for enduring the ups and downs of the writing process, and skillfully delivering feedback when I need it.

To the executives, who allowed me to interview you and present your profile, thank you, and I hope that readers will learn from your examples:

Ed Betof, Nila Betof, Tamar Ekeles, Michael Feiner, Eric Foss, Melanie McDonald, Steven Milovich, Daniel Naor, Ramalinga Raju, Sam Su, Michael White, Kevin Wilde.

Franke James and John Cammack were kind enough to be early readers and give me useful feedback to enhance the book.

Joshua Seldman

This book was made possible due first to the wisdom, guidance, and dedication of Marty, who spent countless hours both in the vision and execution of this project. His passion for his clients was a daily inspiration, as is his life-long commitment to bettering himself as well as those he works with. It is an honor to have as a father someone who has lived the principles of *Executive Stamina*, and truly found something he is both good at and loves doing each day.

I need to acknowledge the contribution of the people who have supported and guided me in my development and tenure as a coach. First of all I would like to thank Jim Lehman, the first coach I had the pleasure of working with, for his immense wisdom, kind words, and helpful suggestions throughout the years. Next I would like to thank perhaps one of the most powerful individuals I know, Chris Carmichael, for his trust, leadership, and instruction in each of the stages of my becoming a coach. Lastly, a special thank you is necessary to James Herrera for both his role in researching and formulating ideas for this book, as well as his friendship, support and direction in this project and many others throughout my coaching career. His support, patience, and guidance were instrumental in many of the achievements I have had throughout my career; he is the true definition of a coach.

I want to acknowledge the many athletes and executives whose dedication, passion, and effort allowed me to enjoy what I do, learn tremendous amounts, and see the human spirit at its greatest. Thank you each for the time we spent working together.

Thank you to my sister Talia, for her ability and open-hearted care as she produced each page of the book. I am so grateful for and to you.

Thank you to our agent, John Willig, for his role in facilitating the publishing of this book, as well as the skilled staff at John Wiley & Sons, Inc. for their support and expertise from start to finish.

I am finally grateful for Roberta Seldman and her ability to give tremendous energy to support my choices and decisions. A huge thank you goes to her for helping me believe what is truly possible.

Introduction

Work smarter? Work harder?

If you read the surveys or listen to anecdotes about overworked executives, you know that many people have already exhausted the work harder option. *Executive Stamina* is a current, comprehensive exploration of the work smarter solution.

Working smarter is about:

- Understanding the commitments you make in your personal and professional life.
- Hearing what you say yes to and what you say no to.
- Dealing with people who distract you, waste your time, and drain your energy.
- Overcoming procrastination and perfectionism.
- Gaining control over your calendar.
- Using fitness to increase energy and improve execution.
- Recognizing your body's need for activity, nutrition, rest, and relief from stress.
- Finding your career "sweet spot."
- Reducing stress at the office and on the road.
- Noticing change and understanding the implications of change.
- Avoiding career mistakes of omission and commission caused by being too busy or stressed.
- Maintaining your personal relationships and living in alignment with your values.

1

I am going to focus on both short-term and long-term aspects of *stamina*, by which I mean the capacity to stay focused on, and energized about, the task at hand, as well as the stamina to sustain a long, balanced, and successful career.

My goal in this book is to equip you with the skills, techniques, and positive practices that will help you pave a sustainable path to your full career potential. You will be encouraged to focus on fitness, nutrition, time and stress management, positive relationships, and living in alignment with your values—not just for your well-being, but to optimize your effectiveness.

The skills and systems you will learn are no longer simply "nice to have." A glance at these trends and statistics indicate Executive Stamina skills are now in the "need to have" category to achieve career and personal objectives.

The Vanishing Vacation

Taking time off from work should not be viewed as a luxury or an option, yet every year fewer and fewer people make use of their vacations. The Conference Board found that at the start of the summer of 2006, 40 percent of consumers had no plans to take a vacation over the next six months—the lowest percentage recorded by the group in 28 years.

Mike Pina, a spokesman for the American Automobile Association (AAA), which has 50 million members in North America, says, "The idea of somebody going away for two weeks is really becoming a thing of the past." A nine-year study of 12,338 men, ages 35 to 37, all free of illness at the start, showed that those who took the most vacations were 29 percent less likely to be diagnosed later with heart disease—and 17 percent less likely to die of it—than those who skipped vacations.

In the last few years, many corporations have begun to encourage workers to take the vacation time allotted to them. Responding to the negative impacts of increased workloads, in 2005, PriceWaterhouseCoopers mandated vacations for all employees for five days during the Fourth of July holiday and 10 days during the winter holiday season.

The Blurry Line between Work and Personal Life

There are myriad reasons contributing to an increased focus on work life and diminished attention to our personal lives, but the number-one culprits are technology and the constant feed of information we are faced with as a result. E-mail, instant messaging, cell phones, pagers, and personal communication devices (PCDs) have all but erased the line between work time and personal time. Increasingly, an expectation or implicit agreement is that managers and executives will be available at all times to their employers.

Many of these technologies have an addictive quality, in that they cause people to feel obligated to respond to or repeatedly check their devices. This tendency, this behavior, is so widespread that treatment programs are developing to address them—for example, Marsha Egan's 12-step program for e-mail addiction and the web site CrackBerry.com.

Mike Song, coauthor of *The Hamster Revolution: How to Manage Your Email Before It Manages You* (Berrett-Koehler Publishers, 2007), surveyed 8,000 employees working in major corporations over three years and found that most say they spend about 40 percent of their workday on e-mail.

Some businesspeople become so dependent on their PCDs that they spend less time with their families and friends, get less sleep, and even begin to neglect personal health and hygiene.

Health-Related Implications

This increased focus on work has also led to increased incidence of medical conditions among the working population. For example, in 1980, almost 6 million people in the United States had been diagnosed with diabetes. By 2006, this number had risen to 20 million nationwide. An additional 54 million are living with prediabetes, a condition characterized by higher-than-normal blood glucose levels.

Maintaining a balanced diet and regular exercise routine are two factors that can help stave off such illnesses. However, Dr. Larry Cohen of the U.S.

Centers for Disease Control and Prevention reports that, based on a 2005 study of 305,000 people, fewer than a third of American adults eat the government-recommended amount of fruits and vegetables.

The increase in unhealthy lifestyles has become so pervasive within the workforce that progressive state and federal agencies have begun to create initiatives to help combat the problem. California's State Assembly is so concerned about employee health issues that it introduced a bill to give businesses a tax credit for money they spend to improve the fitness of their employees.

H.R. Magazine reports that more than half of employees say they have "high levels of stress," extreme fatigue, and/or feel out of control. Ronald Downey, a Kansas State professor quoted in the stress management article titled "Stress Management," (September 2006, vol. 51, no 9xz), stated that, "The consequences of excessive stress are straightforward: physical illness, increase in healthcare costs, heightened turnover, loss of productive employees, and loss of collegiality."

In addition to government initiatives, a number of corporations have responded to these issues by implementing and enforcing wellness programs. At Scotts Miracle-Gro, for example, employees who refuse to change unhealthy behavior know they can lose their jobs. Wal-Mart has instituted its Personal Sustainability Project, which focuses on helping the environment and improving personal health and family relationships.

Extreme Workloads

In an article in *Harvard Business Review*, "Extreme Jobs: The Dangerous Allure of the 70-Hour Workweek" (December, 2006), Sylvia Ann Hewlett and Carolyn Buck Luce estimated that in large global corporations 45 percent of managerial jobs are extreme. Professionals in these roles indicate they pay a large price in terms of their health and family relationships. In a follow-up survey, 58 percent of these men and 80 percent of these women indicated that they do not want to continue working at their current pace for more than a year.

Furthermore, many corporations today have moved to so-called flatter organizations, with less middle management, resulting in executives having more direct reports. The result is that each manager and his or her direct reports are tasked with more responsibility. In addition, there is often a strong reluctance to add head count until current employees are "maxed out." Often, even existing spaces in the organizational charts go unfilled, meaning that it is not uncommon to encounter executives who are doing two jobs.

Globalization

As the world's economy becomes global, and organizations increasingly compete on a broader scale, employees are forced to adjust to changing work models. Globalization contributes to most all of the trends just described in the following ways:

- Working across many times zones can dramatically lengthen the workday and, consequently, affect sleep patterns.
- Language and cultural differences add to job complexity, misunderstandings, and stress.
- The amount and pace of change are rising rapidly, and the increased threat of competition and loss of control adds to stress and anxiety.
- Individuals in roles that demand international travel often report increased strains in their personal relationships and increased feelings of guilt associated with missing key family events.

The World Bank found that 36 percent of international business travelers said their travel caused a high or very high level of stress.

What's the Solution?

The fact that you have picked up this book indicates you want to learn more about these trends; hopefully, it also means you are interested in developing concrete, practical ways of managing these issues and for achieving personal and career success. And that's the purpose of this book.

The methods I describe in *Executive Stamina* are based on insights I've gained through my executive coaching experience. I divide my approach into three categories:

1. Success factors
2. Derailment and "topping out" factors
3. Practical solutions

Success Factors

A success factor is an attribute or skill that is central to achieving your goals. Some success factors are subtle; others seem basic, like common sense. It is good to remember, however, that common sense is not always common practice. Therefore, one of my goals in explaining the success factors in later chapters is to make them as simple as possible to learn and adopt.

Here are some of the wide range of skills and practices I will discuss:

- Prioritizing and reprioritizing
- Relentlessly pursuing top talent
- Delegating effectively
- Taking control of your time
- Knowing the difference between nice to do, need to do, and need to do well
- Developing mental toughness
- Gaining organizational savvy
- Developing the ability to accurately "read" and evaluate people
- Becoming aware of one's strengths, weaknesses, and impact on others
- Learning emotional self-management skills
- Maintaining high levels of energy and enthusiasm
- Detecting trends, change, and the implications of change

- Developing listening skills
- Being open to feedback; being curious and a lifelong learner
- Learning to think clearly and strategically, and to make objective decisions

Derailment and "Topping Out" Factors

Derailing, or "topping out," means failing to reach your full potential. Topping out is costly to the individual involved, as well as to his or her company, in the form of severance fees and, subsequently, on-boarding fees for a new hire. In business, you sometimes hear the quip, "We all have to 'top out' somewhere." While this is true, in coaching, the goal is to prevent people from topping out prematurely or, even worse, derailing for reasons that might have been avoidable.

Many of my clients exhibited high integrity, functional competence, a drive for results, and were working extremely hard, but were in danger of ignoring two key laws: the Law of Diminishing Returns and the Law of Gradual Change.

The Law of Diminishing Returns

The Law of Diminishing Returns, as depicted in Figure I.1, indicates that for a considerable period of time, more effort, particularly if it is well focused, will lead to improved results. However, at a certain point, increasing the time at work will stop yielding incremental gains, and, at a further point, will actually jeopardize your objectives.

Translated into a business context, this means that working many hours without the proper support, recovery time, or an effective stress management system is actually a risky endeavor. Thus, even with good intentions, executives may undermine their effectiveness, make career management mistakes, and detract from their personal goals and values.

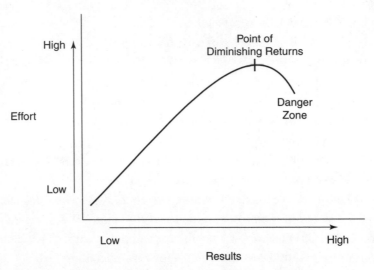

Figure I.1　Law of Diminishing Returns

Some of the negative impacts I have observed in clients who have moved past the inflection point and into the danger zone of diminished returns include:

- *Low energy and enthusiasm*: In business, especially in the United States, executives are often evaluated on their energy and confidence levels.
- *Decline in listening skills:* This hurts the executive in several arenas, including respectful relationships, teamwork, information gathering, and conflict resolution.
- *Weakened immune system*: The cumulative effects of travel, stress, lack of sleep, poor diet, and insufficient exercise lower our immune defenses, resulting in more illness and longer recovery times.
- *Impulsive, short-term decision making*: Executives are paid to make decisions. Quality decisions are the essence of their value to their organizations. Under stress, it is difficult to weigh alternatives and consequences objectively or to be patient when looking for a solution.
- *Inadequate emotional control*: When strong emotions are triggered, we are likely to say things we will regret or have to apologize for later. In

business, especially at the higher levels, it doesn't take much to get in trouble or alienate someone. Remember the saying, "Your friends come and go, but your enemies accumulate."

- *Narrowed focus and reduced flexibility*: Under stress, we tend to narrow our focus to the issues that concern us. When we begin using this tunnel vision, we revert to ingrained, habitual patterns. This can leave us vulnerable to important changes that may occur externally and internally. We may not pick up on these changes or have the capacity to respond to them.

- *Lack of organizational savvy and political awareness*: Organizational savvy is the ability to navigate politics, perception, egos, turf issues, hidden agendas, and power plays while keeping your ethical framework. It is a key success factor, particularly at higher levels of corporate life. Executives who are stressed or burned out may either make mistakes or fail to maintain the networks, awareness, and peripheral vision they need.

- *Work stress leading to family stress*: When we pass the point of diminishing returns and experience difficulties in the above-mentioned areas, it is very easy for these effects to carry over into our personal lives. This can trigger a vicious cycle (described in more depth shortly) in which our friends and family are no longer a source of rest and recovery, but become an additional source of stress.

- *Development of addictions*: Human beings have a tendency to form addictions. If something brings us pleasure, reduces our pain, or distracts us from our worries, we have a tendency to want to do it more often. As a result, most of us have at least some form of mild addiction, or something to which we are very attached. With most of us, this stays at a manageable level and doesn't interfere with our work or personal life. Some of us are smart or lucky enough to form positive addictions, like regular exercise. A build-up of stress and pressure without relaxation or recovery can add to the compulsion to find something that takes away pain, gives pleasure, or distracts from worries. Some of these addictions can lead to serious problems in and of themselves. Others simply waste precious time.

The sources of addiction are constantly growing. In addition to nicotine, caffeine, alcohol, and street and prescription drugs, now we also have eating disorders, and addictions to gambling, sex, Internet pornography, and shopping. People are also beginning to display addictive behavior when web surfing or using their "Crackberries." In *Executive Stamina,* I will discuss the signs of addiction, how it can derail an executive, and how to prevent it from forming.

Overcoming the Law of Diminishing Returns

As you can see, the consequences and risks to both our careers and personal lives begin to pile up after the key inflection point. Of course, we are all flesh and blood, and each of us has our limits, but Executive Stamina practices will help you substantially extend those limits. You will be able to achieve much more before you start "hitting the wall." You can accomplish this by:

- Building your capacity and stamina.
- Learning to focus your time and effort on the highest payoff activities and success factors, and eliminating nonessential tasks.
- Finding your career "sweet spot," which increases your effectiveness, resiliency, and satisfaction while simultaneously reducing your stress.

The Law of Gradual Change

If you ask people about their highest priorities and what they value the most, most will list their health, their commitment to a romantic partner, a desire to be a good parent, spiritual or religious values, personal principles, and so on. If you then ask, "Would you trade these precious priorities or put them at risk to gain incremental success in your organization?" most would respond with a vehement no. Yet, in my experience as a coach, I have routinely seen executives make these exact sacrifices, without realizing the damage it was causing, until the damage was done. The major reason is that they did not notice the gradual deterioration that was occurring in these areas.

Marriages don't fall apart overnight. We don't usually lose our health, become alienated from our children, or drift away from religious practices all of a sudden, either. Even individuals who have strayed from their principles and compromised their integrity often report that they took gradual steps before falling down the slippery slope.

The Law of Gradual Change states that most people do not notice slow deterioration or change and so fail to take timely corrective action. An analogy of the Law of Gradual Change that most of us, at some point, have learned is that of the "boiled frog": that is, if you put a frog into boiling water, supposedly it has the reflexes and leg strength to immediately jump out. However, if you put a frog in warm water over a low flame and increase the temperature very slowly, the frog may remain in the water. By the time it starts to feel uncomfortable, it has lost strength in its legs and cannot escape, hence becoming a boiled frog.

A more recent business example is the very late, and so far ineffective, responses by American auto manufacturers to the multidecade shift in the consumer's perception of the quality of Japanese cars. Many of Detroit's executives grew up in an era when "Made in Japan" was associated with shoddy work. They did not notice the slow but consistent improvements Japanese manufacturers were making.

Author Fyodor Dostoevsky captured this phenomenon as it relates to our personal lives when he remarked that if a man "lost his soul" overnight he would immediately be aware of his loss and desperate to regain his values. He went on to say that this is not how a man loses his soul; rather that he loses it so slowly and gradually that by the time he realizes it, it is often too late.

In *Executive Stamina*, you will learn about two systems—Scheduling Minimums and the Shifts and Drifts Tracking System—that will help you prevent the Law of Gradual Change from impacting your business or personal life.

When the Law of Diminishing Returns and the Law of Gradual Change are considered together, it is easy to understand why executives need to be equipped with skills and systems to negate the impact of these two forces. In some cases, I have coached people who are full of regret, remorse, or guilt because they realize they have traded off something precious to "climb the ladder" another rung. In many other instances, the effect is ironic, because the drive, ambition, and extra dedication actually triggered derailment factors that undermined those career goals.

The pressure of juggling demanding, complex executive roles, personal priorities, and other obligations can impact us in a variety of ways. You may be reading this book because you are concerned about the state of your health and well-being, or your relationships, or staying aligned with your values. Each of these is a valid and realistic concern that I will address in future chapters. The point I want to emphasize here is, even if you don't care about your health, relationships, or values, even if all you want to do is maximize your career progression, you still need the skills and systems to understand and work within the parameters of these two laws. If you ignore them, you risk making mistakes of both omission and commission that can undo years of hard work.

Practical Solutions

In order to help my coaching clients (and maintain my practice), I needed to develop simple but effective ways for them to improve. Any techniques or skills or new behaviors I recommended had to be easy to learn, easy to use, and easy to practice. They had to fit within the existing framework of the executive's workday routine and organization's culture. In addition, the new techniques, skills, and behaviors had to lead to visible improvement and be sustainable. In *Executive Stamina*, you will learn hundreds of methods that have been successfully implemented by my clients.

In addition, I combine the techniques that have proven so successful in my executive coaching practice with the methods Joshua has found so effective in endurance coaching. Although the endurance coaching program was designed for athletes, Joshua has found it works well with executives, too, in raising their endurance and energy levels and strengthening their cognitive performance. That is why you'll find that each section of *Executive Stamina* places equal emphasis on the supreme value of fitness, nutrition, and stress management systems, and how they connect to our effectiveness, career progress, and personal values.

Optimizing Time and Energy

Every recommendation I make in the book is based on my belief that time and energy are, or should be, very precious commodities in your life. You will learn many techniques that increase the odds that your schedule is aligned with your highest priorities. Equally important is to learn to master the ways to protect yourself from being diverted to tasks that are not advancing your goals.

Executive Stamina will help you maximize your energy levels in three ways:

- *Increasing energy:* By raising your fitness level, eating the right foods at the right time, and developing a personal stress management program, you will develop greater endurance and resiliency and improve your sleep and overall immune system.
- *Preserving energy:* Significant attention will be paid to teaching you to protect yourself from activities and, sometimes, people who drain your energy. Poorly run and/or unnecessary meetings, interruptions, "toxic" people, and even your own thinking and emotional patterns are a few of the things that can trigger a loss of energy. It is more important than ever to have tools to handle such situations.
- *Renewing energy:* A reporter taking his first meeting with Mahatma Gandhi in the midst of the campaign to depose the British from rule over India was surprised to see the great leader so relaxed, youthful, and energetic. He remarked, "I have heard that you have worked 15 hours a day, every day, for years, without a vacation." Gandhi replied, "I am always on vacation." Gandhi's life was a convergence of his higher values, what he was effective at, and what he enjoyed.

He also walked, prayed, and meditated regularly. Many of us have had the experience of working extremely hard on a project or activity while maintaining high energy and enthusiasm. We will examine how to create more of these situations in your life, by finding the "sweet spot" of your competence, your enjoyment, and your values.

Overview of the Book

Executive Stamina is organized as follows. Although you will learn specific techniques in each section, throughout, I often point out how the various parts of our lives, and thus these techniques, are connected.

Part I: Work/Life Alignment

Aligning work and life involves an investigation into your core values, commitments, current priorities, and long-term goals. This section, therefore, is designed to help you identify what is truly important to you and to give you a realistic view of your current commitments. You will learn the core systems for ensuring that your schedule align with your top priorities and values. In addition, you will learn to focus on the characteristics and qualities of your career "sweet spot."

Part II: Health and Wellness

Health and wellness must be linked to your career goals. This section will help you establish the fitness, nutrition, and stress management systems necessary to sustain the energy, enthusiasm, and focus you need to be successful. You will learn how to integrate key practices into your daily life, along with tips for applications at the office, at home, and on the road.

Part III: Job Performance and Business Results

Most executives have an intense desire to achieve, coupled with a strong sense of responsibility. This section focuses on how to stay in control of both by optimizing time and minimizing distractions and unnecessary stresses. You will learn how to consistently make the best use of your time to maximize your effectiveness.

Part IV: Career Management

The chapters in this section are targeted on the key proactive and protective skills that, in addition to consistent performance, maximize career progression. You will learn to avoid the most common mistakes of omission and commission that can derail careers.

Part V: Positive Relationship Maintenance

The chapters in Part V are designed to ensure that you do not sacrifice your most precious relationships because of a hectic workload. Particular attention will be devoted to preventing vicious cycles that can impact health, stress levels, and job performance.

An Executive Stamina Role Model

Bill George, in his recent book *True North* (Jossey-Bass, 2007), states, "Integrating their lives is one of the greatest challenges leaders face. To lead an integrated life you need to bring together the major elements of your personal life and professional life, including work, family, community, and friends so that you can be the same person in each environment."

It is with those wise words in mind that I want to conclude this introduction with the profile of a man who has managed to do just that—integrate his work and personal life. I use Steve Milovich as a positive example, not because he is perfect or never goes past the point of diminishing returns, but because he is thoughtful about his energy and balance on a regular basis, which is what I am encouraging you to be.

Steve Milovich, an executive I have worked with, is an excellent example of how to make effective use of many of the Executive Stamina methods. Steve is a 52-year-old executive at the Walt Disney Company, a complex global media and entertainment corporation with a wide variety of businesses, including theme parks, movies, television channels, and consumer products. His role is Senior Vice President for Corporate Human Resources, Organizational and Leadership Development. On any given day, Steve might deal with executives in any or all of the Disney businesses, the senior management team, and, informally, with any company employee who sees him walking through the corporate headquarters complex. He is just as likely to be seen going into CEO Bob Iger's office as to be chatting with the film crew on the production lot for a scene from, say, *Pirates of the Caribbean*.

As an executive, Steve stands out in a variety of ways. He is highly credible, trustworthy (he deals with highly confidential and sensitive situations), candid, and very agreeable. He is one of the most well-liked people at headquarters, despite the fact that he is charged with giving people feedback (positive and negative) and delivering messages not always easy to express.

I've known Steve for 20 years and have tracked his development as a leader in various positions at PepsiCo, Allied Signal, and, now, Disney. Over those years, we've had many discussions about the various career paths he could have taken, and the trade-offs involved with each. Throughout, the major factor affecting his decisions has always been the impact of his choices on his family. Without stating it precisely, his attitude seemed to be, "It is easier to get a new job than it is to get a new family."

Although I knew about some of his positive practices with regard to work/life balance, fitness, and stress management, I decided to conduct a detailed interview with him to find out some of the specifics that might not be obvious to an outside observer. Here are some of the things I learned:

- He has a spiritual practice that is very important to him. It includes a period of contemplation and centering each morning (and some evenings).
- During the day he maintains a high degree of awareness of his body, mind, and emotions. This enables him to take quick, simple, and timely actions to restore his equilibrium when necessary. In particular, he uses particular breathing patterns to become centered and calm.
- He has designed his office to double as a sanctuary. Personal, meaningful objects and pictures make it a good environment for thinking and reflecting and for taking restorative breaks.
- Steve controls his calendar, never forgetting to factor in stress when planning his day. For example, if he knows that he will be dealing with difficult people or situations for parts of the day, he will purposely schedule meetings at other periods of the day with people he enjoys working with or on projects that are energizing for him. In sum, he plans his schedule with attention to balance.
- True vacations are a priority for Steve. Recently, he took a vacation with his daughter to Rome during which he had almost no contact with the office. He planned in advance with his direct reports and key clients to "go off the air." His philosophy is that if an executive can't leave for a week, it is a negative reflection on his or her leadership and delegation skills. Months later he was still glowing from the experience, during which he traced his roots with his family and lived a European lifestyle.
- Five years ago, Steve renewed his interest in music and has a home studio. Since then, it has become an important avocation, and he believes it helps him be more creative at the office.
- He hired his personal assistant for qualities that match his own. She is of vital importance in helping him achieve his goal to have more control over his calendar. She understands him extremely well, is

updated on his priorities, and is willing and able to "bench" people who will divert his time and energy.

- Steve's conscious intention is to be genuine, authentic, and candid. He tells his colleagues, "I bring who I am to work." In this way, he can be congruent in his communication, "comfortable in his own skin," and honest about who he is at all times.
- He has found his corporate life "sweet spot." Although he has opportunities to take on a variety of human resources roles, he clearly recognizes his strengths, as a coach, adviser, and designer of organizational structures; he loves to see people reach their full potential.
- He finds time to do aerobic exercise and weight training several times a week, in spite of his 12-hour days and occasional weekend work.

There are many executives like Steve Milovich who are achieving career success and organizational impact using these principles. You can be one, too, so let's get started learning about the Executive Stamina methods and finding out which ones will make the most effective difference to you.

A Disclaimer

This book is intended as a reference volume only, not a medical manual. The authors and any contributors mentioned within this book are not engaged in rendering medical, legal or other professional advice. It is not intended as a substitute for any treatment or advice that may have been prescribed by your doctor or other professional. If you suspect that you have a medical problem, we urge you to seek competent medical help. Please consult a physician or other appropriate professional before using the fitness and nutritional information and advice that you may find in this book.

PART I

WORK/LIFE ALIGNMENT

1

What Is Most Important to You?

Occasionally I am asked, "From a coach's perspective, what is the most important practice that executives neglect to make time for?" I always answer, "reflection." Other coaches and management consultants who are asked the same question often give a similar response. In this chapter, I address the importance of reflecting on your core values, commitments, current priorities, and long-term goals, in order to achieve a proper work/life balance.

The Importance of Reflection

While there are many methods to prepare you for thoughtful reflection, I have found the series of exercises I present here to be most effective in helping you to evaluate your core values, commitments, current priorities, and long-term goals. I want to point out from the get-go that it is very important to focus on each of these areas individually while never losing sight of the big picture—that is, how they affect one another.

These exercises will become the foundation of your Executive Stamina system and will help you by answering three crucial questions:

1. *What is already on your plate?* To avoid passing the point of diminishing returns, first you need to have a realistic idea of what you are already committed to in your life. By understanding the current demands on

21

your time and estimating accurately the effort that certain activities require, you will be able to make better decisions about what to say yes or no to. Only when you fully understand your current situation can you decide wisely whether to take on additional responsibilities or change your life in a significant way, such as by:

- Becoming the president of the Parent Teacher's Association at your child's school
- Remodeling your house
- Accepting a new job or position that will require more travel
- Caring for an aging parent
- Adding head count to your organization
- Putting your daughter on the Select soccer traveling team
- Studying for an MBA
- Starting your own business

In none of these cases is there one "right" decision; the objective is to become better at making the decision that is right for you at a given point in time.

2. *What is precious to you?* The reflective exercises will highlight for you what matters most to you: the values, priorities, goals, and relationships that are the most meaningful and the most important to maintain. These activities will help you answer questions such as, "What is the best use of my time?" In addition, by ensuring that what is most important stays at the top of your list, you will be taking an important step to countering the Law of Gradual Change. You will be able to view future commitments and revisit current ones with a keener eye toward their impact on these vital areas.

3. *Are you living your stated priorities?* This exercise puts your stated values, priorities, goals, and so on to an acid test. Match your actual schedule—how you *really* spend your time—against your avowed business, career, and personal priorities. This, for most of us, is a very difficult thing to do because, often, there are at least some key areas of life where we are not spending our time and energy on that which we state is most important.

As you complete the reflective exercises, remember that each of us is in a unique circumstance, due to a combination of a number of factors. There are many permutations of specific values, commitments, relationships, and long-term goals. In addition, our lives are fluid, dynamic, and changing (sometimes daily) due to circumstances or simply phases that shift our priorities.

For example, in my career, I've worked with people who felt that being in a romantic relationship was not an important priority for them. They preferred to dedicate themselves to their careers or to public service, and as a result attained a significant amount of reward and recognition and so were comfortable with their decision. I've also coached parents who felt they were doing the right thing by making their careers a lower priority for a period of time while their children were young or had special needs. Another client, an executive from India, made a commitment to stay in the same city as his widowed mother, and so turned down a promotion that would have taken him to the United States. Each of these individuals was clear about what mattered, and so were able to establish a personal order of importance.

Derivation of Core Values

Most of us derive our core values from our family, cultures, and society, coupled with significant experiences and other people who played an part in our development.

In terms of family, we tend to model ourselves after someone we admire; or we simply absorbed, hence mimic, the values we saw demonstrated on a regular basis. Someone growing up in a blue-collar or union household, for example, might retain strong values about how front-line employees are treated, even after he rises to senior management. Another person who heard her parents say very negative things about people who "blow their own horns" may come to regard modesty as a very important part of character.

Needless to say, our early familial experiences often influence our values later in life. For example, individuals whose parents were absent a lot, or didn't attend school or sporting events, may decide that, when they become parents, they will be more active in supporting their children in their activities.

Cultural norms and values also have a significant influence on what we feel is important. Whether we value individualistic, bootstrap-type behavior or cooperative, team-based behavior probably has a lot to do with how and where we grew up. Many other values, such as patriotism, religion, family, entrepreneurship, education, and respect for elders, are also culturally determined.

The Reflection Exercises

My suggestion to you in approaching the upcoming exercises is to reflect on key experiences of people you've met or read about who have inspired you. If, say, a religious or spiritual person has inspired you, his or her values may rise to the top of your list. Also consider significant experiences in your own life. If you've been the victim of discrimination or been exposed to a group of people who were treated unfairly, you may have developed a heightened sensitivity to fairness and justice.

As you complete the values exercises, it's important to keep in mind that your values can shift. I don't mean that in the way Groucho Marx did when he said, "Those are my principles. If you don't like them, there are others I can show you." I'm referring to the fact that the significance we attribute to our values can become heightened due to events in our lives or society in general. For example, let's say that the Smokey the Bear public service announcement "Give a hoot, don't pollute" you saw as a child gave you an early awareness about the environment. As an adult, reading about global warming has made you gravely concerned about the impact of climate change, leading you to donate money to certain organizations, to volunteer, and/or to alter your lifestyle. Similarly, a person who regards integrity as a core value may become even more conscious of its importance in the wake of learning about corporate scandals. In the face of conflicts of interest, this person would be reminded of the crucial role that integrity plays in his or her own role at work.

Values Exercise 1: The Pleasant Path

In this first exercise, please take time to reflect on your core values. Don't concern yourself with how many you list or about the exact words you use; just be sure the meaning is clear to you. To get started it is often useful to think about messages you received from your family in your formative years:

- What values did your parents encourage or deem important?
- Think about the society (or societies) you grew up in. What were the commonly held values? Our religious values can often mirror family and society, so it is definitely worthwhile to think of the key values emphasized in your denomination.
- What grabs your attention? Where do you direct your energy and emotions? These are useful guides to what matters to you. Think of movies, books, or media stories.
- Who are the people that inspire you?
- What makes you angry?

These are all clues to your deeper values.

My Core Values

_____
_____
_____
_____
_____
_____

Values Exercise 2: The Unpleasant Path

A less pleasant but equally effective way of determining your true values is to focus on negative emotions: regret, remorse, guilt, and loss of self-respect. Though these feelings are the results of some of our worst experiences, they can be important to us in a couple of ways. One is that they tell us we have a conscience and a code of behavior we want to follow. Recalling these feelings, and memories of the incidents that prompted them, can help us avoid certain behaviors or motivate us to improve. Think about it—would you want to have a business partner, romantic partner, or friend who had no capacity for healthy remorse? It is hard enough to change habits or correct behavior when we are motivated. Without remorse, there is little or no motivation to correct the mistakes, intentional or unintentional, we all inevitably make.

The second benefit negative feelings can deliver to us is in the form of greater awareness of what is important to us. These uncomfortable feelings are valid indicators of which behavior we hold in high regard. When we are disappointed in ourselves or feel we have come up short on our own standards, it is a sharp reminder of the path we *do* want to follow.

In later chapters, my goal is to give you methods for living in alignment with your values, as well as for minimizing feelings of regret or remorse. Employing these methods:

- Leads to peace of mind, self-respect, and a congruent self-image, because your "talk" will match your "walk."
- Prevents negative emotions from hurting your career, by draining energy, chewing up time, and depleting our confidence.
- Ensures that others respect you because you will be acting in accordance with the values you espouse.

Although the ultimate goal is to reduce these negative experiences in your life, I want you to reflect on them now, in order to gain additional insights into your core values.

- Think of times when you experienced regret, guilt, or remorse.
- What do those experiences indicate about your core values?

Core Values

Making Commitments

Next I want you to take a broad, comprehensive view of your current commitments. While our commitments are often closely related to our values, it is important to concentrate on these separately, as well. The goal here is to list everything that you (or in some cases your family) are already committed to.

In our business lives we have general commitments based on our roles and responsibilities within our organizations. In addition, we may have committed ourselves to other activities, such as being a mentor, advising a cross-functional team, writing an article or giving a speech for a trade organization, serving on an outside board, or even playing first base on the company softball team. In our personal lives, there may be essential relational commitments to spouses, children, siblings, parents, and friends. In conjunction, the possibilities for commitment are almost endless—volunteering at schools, religious organizations, political parties, nonprofit organizations, and so on. We may also have committed ourselves to making improvements to our house or garden or to ourselves (learning a language, engaging in spiritual practices, etc.).

In my experience, people rarely take stock of all they are already committed to, making this is an important and sobering exercise for many. In completing this exercise, I want you to become aware of three key tendencies that can often undermine your best intentions.

- *Underestimating the actual number of people and activities you are already committed to.* Write them down and see if I'm not right about this.

- *Underestimating the time that each commitment requires.* Don't get me wrong: I'm not saying that mentoring a business colleague, being a Big Brother or Big Sister, leading the United Way campaign, joining the softball team, or remodeling your house are not worthwhile activities. What I am saying is that when people say yes to things, they usually miscalculate the time commitment they just made. Consider the softball team: Did you factor in the practices, sharing pizza after games, and—if you should be so lucky—the playoff season? Now add this miscalculation to the one about how many commitments you have and you may see yourself rapidly approaching the point of diminishing returns. At this point you may start to feel that you are not doing justice to many, or any, of your commitments.
- *Making inappropriate commitments.* I want to be clear about my use of the word "inappropriate" here. While many of the commitments you have made are admirable or worthwhile, and even enjoyable, making another one is inappropriate if it does not make sense given your current workload, existing commitments, and the impact it will have on your life.

Trust me, I have observed these three tendencies often in myself and many others, which is why I am asking you to take this first, very important step: identify your current commitments, using the commitments worksheet supplied here.

COMMITMENTS WORKSHEET

Commitment	Time Required
Business	_____
Key Relationships	_____
Community (educational, nonprofit, religious, political, sports)	_____
Self-Improvement	_____

Reflect on the key areas of your life where you are most likely to have made time commitments. Write down all the commitments that you have made or feel that you are responsible for (e.g., to care for a parent or a sibling with medical problems). Provide a rough estimate of the time required for each commitment; don't forget to include travel time, thought time, and so on.

At the end of this activity, take some time to reflect on your list. Did you find any surprises or gain any key insights from looking at what is already on your plate?

Setting Priorities

In the Introduction, I mentioned that a key success factor for executives is the ability to correctly prioritize and, when indicated, be able to reprioritize, quickly, if necessary. In order to do this, you must be able to focus on the biggest challenges to, or biggest payoffs from, your career and/or organization.

Although it sounds straightforward and logical, several skills are required to prioritize well. Thus, the priorities exercise in this exercise is designed to first heighten your awareness about what is currently very important to you.

NOTE

In Chapter 3, you will learn about the Shifts and Drifts tracking system, which can help you reprioritize more effectively. In Chapter 5 you will learn how to optimize your time by working on the highest payoff activities. The Laws of Diminishing Returns and Gradual Change have at some point negatively impacted all executives, including myself. Pushing past the point of diminishing returns has undermined their own efforts, and/or they have gradually drifted away from core values and commitments by failing to focus appropriately on top priorities and long-term goals. The most effective way I've found to help them, and myself, is to start with some clarifying exercises that bring these areas to light. My purpose is not to provide answers or solutions; rather, it is to help you get a clear, accurate view of your current situation. I'll provide the appropriate technique to counteract these laws in later chapters.

Commitments versus Current Priorities

Just as there is a strong correlation between our values and our commitments, there is a link between the commitments and current priorities we choose to make.

For the purpose of this activity, I want you consider commitments as longer term. For example, you may be committed to your business role and responsibilities, key relationships (spouse, parent, child), and community or religious organizations. Your current priorities flow from your commitments and values but they are more immediate and urgent. So, though your general responsibility may be as your company's CEO, based on your assessment of the challenges and opportunities facing your organization, your current priorities could be:

- Analyzing current changes and trends in your industry
- Making some key hires
- Setting up "top to top" meetings with your key customers
- Accelerating innovation in your organization

Two key words from the previous paragraph are *challenges* and *opportunities*. It is useful to remember that your current priorities are fluid, and the demands are often variable. If difficulties arise in your business or personal life, it is appropriate that your priorities shift to respond to those challenges. Examples could range from your competitors hiring away some of your top talent to discovering that your child has a learning disability or emotional problems to learning you or someone close to you is facing a serious medical problem.

Current priorities should also shift to take advantage of an open window of opportunity. In business, this could include pursuing a crucial joint venture or acquisition, accelerating development of a new technology, or taking the opportunity to work on a project that will have life-long meaning to you and others. In your personal life, it might be taking a much-needed getaway with a romantic partner, sharing a meaningful experience with a child, or taking on a project that will have a major impact on a cause to which you are devoted.

While thinking about your current commitments and the particular challenges and opportunities in each of these areas, use the worksheet provided here to determine your current priorities.

CURRENT PRIORITIES WORKSHEET

Business Role

Key Relationships

Community

Self-Improvement

Long-Term Goals

Long-Term Goals

Filling out this worksheet will give you a sharper sense of your current key priorities. This is important since, obviously, your time and energy and the number of things you can focus at any one time are finite. This means that you will designate certain activities as low priority and relegate them to the "nice to do" category. If this is a conscious choice based on an accurate assessment of what really matters to you and your time constraints, this is probably a wise decision. Assigning some things a low priority is smart and necessary. Unfortunately, many of us have a tendency to, unwittingly, put very important activities on the "back burner," activities that would actually help us achieve our long-term goals.

If you have read books or taken classes in time management, you are probably familiar with this phenomenon. The concept is referred to as "important versus urgent" or sometimes as the "tyranny of the urgent." Basically, it is a useful reminder that long-term goals, goals that we have decided are meaningful to us, often do not seem urgent unless there is a crisis. Because other things in our life may have greater immediacy and, therefore, draw our attention, it is possible, sometimes likely, to have long-term goals but not be doing much to advance them. Remember, no bell will ring to remind you that you are neglecting this stated goal. In fact, as I explore in more depth in the discussion on overcoming procrastination, some goals look so large or overwhelming that we avoid getting started. The cost of neglecting these goals is to our self-interests or even self-image. Here are some examples of common long-term goals that are too often left unattended:

- *Health:* Ideally, everyone has a long-term goal to maintain his or her health. As many people have wisely remarked, it is our only true wealth—all the things we want to achieve are based on it, in fact. Sadly, for too many of us, we state maintaining our health as a goal but then act as if we take it for granted. In Part II, we will look at the behaviors such as exercise, nutrition, medical check-ups, and so on that can increase your chances of achieving this goal.
- *Financial goals:* Most of us have some goals in this area, typically expressed in terms such as financial independence, secure retirement, college tuition planning, or a cruder variation, accumulating "take this job and shove it" resources. Many people are diligent in working toward these goals; just as many others, however, may neglect the record-keeping, investment analysis, and advice or systematic saving necessary to achieve them.
- *Spiritual/religious goals:* I have met many who state that their goals in this area are more important than any other they have. Of course, each individual defines this aspect of life differently. For some, the emphasis is on personal faith and piety; for others, the spiritual path must also include service to others and society. Some want to take positions of responsibility in their religious organization. This important area for individuals and families is still vulnerable to the Law of Gradual Change, and we may drift from our practices without realizing it until a spiritual crisis develops.
- *Business/career goals:* This category can include specific long-term goals for your organization, such as delivering world-class customer service or becoming the employer of choice in your industry. It can also include personal career goals you have, such as being promoted to general manager or starting your own business. In future chapters,

we will focus on what you are doing this week or this month to advance these goals.

- *Community/society:* If your values lead you to want to "make a difference" or "give something back to society," you may have a wide variety of goals in this category. Some people may want to get in a position to change things by running for political office. Others may want to do hands-on work like improving sanitation and housing in Mozambique, or help a nonprofit organization that is doing this type of work closer to home.

- *Self-improvement and personal goals:* In addition to all these other areas, it is useful to think about our individual goals. Some might be shared by a majority of people, such as having a long-term romantic relationship or being a parent, but others may be specific to you. Perhaps you've always wanted to write a novel or book of poetry, paint, learn to dance, or learn a new language. Maybe you've always dreamed of traveling, or walking the Appalachian Trail. Sometimes these goals fall more in the "nice to do" category, but there are some that, if we get to a certain age and realize that we haven't moved toward them, will cause strong regret.

As long as we're talking about goals, let me say that mine here, in this discussion, is to trigger thoughts in you that will help you determine what your long-term goals are. If you need additional help, try these two techniques to stimulate your reflection.

- *The Tombstone effect:* Or "What would I want people to say at my funeral?" Think about the end of your life. What would you want to have achieved or emulated?

- *Future perfect:* For those of you who are uncomfortable thinking about your own death, or just have a more optimistic nature, consider this exercise: Imagine your future 5, 10, and 20 years from now. Everything has gone perfectly in your life. What does your life look like?

Summary

I conclude this first chapter by asking you to list your long-term goals.

Long-Term Goals

_____

_____

_____

_____

_____

2 | Is Your Schedule Aligned with Your Priorities?

For a moment, imagine a friend of yours has told you that, for her, maintaining her health is a very high priority because she is the main wage earner in her family. You want to believe her but you notice that she doesn't exercise, skips breakfast in favor of a quick donut at 11:00 A.M., and says she is too busy to go to the doctor for regular check-ups. Because you care about her and have an honest relationship, you point out the inconsistencies between her words and her actions. She agrees with you and then reiterates that her health is indeed a priority for her, and promises to devote more time and attention to it from now on. Again, you want to believe her—for sure, you believe *she* believes she will change her behavior—but you realize that, down the road, you might have to have another "tough love" conversation with her, saying: "Being healthy is *not* a top priority for you, judging by how you spend your time. Your actions tell me other things are more important to you."

A Friend in Deed

In my view, if you had such a difficult conversation with someone you care about, you would be acting like a true friend, willing to hold that person accountable for his or her own best interests. We should consider ourselves very fortunate if we have friends, family members, business colleagues, or members of our religious organization who would do as much for us. This is *not* to say that any of us should impose our values on others; rather, that we should help one another to be accountable to the values and priorities that we espouse. Sadly, too few people have the right combination of insight, skill, and courage to have this kind of chat with others.

I have had that kind of good fortune. I can think of three conversations similar to the one I just described in which friends held up a mirror to me. These were crucial at specific junctures in my life, and I am grateful for each one. Of course, I can't know if you have someone in your life who is doing this for you on a regular basis, so I want to show you how to do this for yourself, to hold yourself accountable. More, I want to guide you in ways that enable you to eventually align your time, energy, and focus with what is most important for you to maintain or achieve in your life.

It's a three-step process that I ask you to follow:

1. Revisit your answers to the questions in Chapter 1. In a new set of activities you will identify where the current gaps are between your values, commitments, current priorities, long-term goals, and the actual time you devote to them.
2. If you see a lack of alignment, identify the reasons the gap has persisted. In my experience, gaps are usually a result of one of four reasons:

   - It may be that your stated value or priority really is not a deeply embedded value or priority. For example, community service or saving for retirement may not, ultimately, be that important to you.
   - You may have a problem with procrastination. For example, executives may know that strategic thinking is vital for the success of their organization, or that becoming better at public speaking is very important for their careers, yet they still procrastinate about

doing these activities. In Chapter 12, we will discuss how to overcome procrastination, which I have seen even at the CEO level.

- You are overcommitted. This is very common, and can be a result of having a very demanding role at work, combined with frequent travel, a long daily commute, and expectations of 24/7 availability. Added to this may be many other personal and familial commitments, coupled with an underestimation of their impact. If being overcommitted is the reason why your schedule is not aligned with your priorities, then the systems you will learn in Chapter 3, "The Minimums and Shifts/Drifts Systems," will help you make useful corrections and good decisions about what to say yes to.
- Unintentionally, and often without awareness, you may be spending too much time on low-payoff, low-priority activities. There can be many reasons for this, ranging from not controlling your schedule, having a difficult time saying no, doing something you like to do versus something you need to do, or even developing time-wasting addictions. I will discuss each of these patterns, and others, starting in Chapter 11, and I will provide many useful, practical tips.

3. After identifying the gaps and analyzing the reason(s) they exist, the final step in the process is to learn the skills and adopt the systems that will bring you into alignment. The methods you will learn have the additional advantage of letting you know, early on, when you are drifting in key areas.

Most Common Gaps

The answers to the alignment exercises in this section will, of course, be unique to you. Furthermore, they will be unique to you at this specific point in your life. Nevertheless, to help you get started it may be useful to you to hear about the most common areas where wide gaps begin to surface for most people.

Health and Wellness

Any of us can drift away from good practices in this area of life. Chris Carmichael, coach to professional athletes (including Lance Armstrong) and executives, and a former top competitor himself, tells his own story in his new book *5 Essentials for a Winning Life* (Rodale Press, 2007): "In fact, as I approached 40, I was unhealthy in a lot of ways. I was fat, out of shape, and dealing with the stress of starting my own business. Somewhere, I had lost contact with the high-performance aspects of life and replaced them with mediocre stand-ins. Instead of taking stairs two at a time, I took the elevator. Instead of relishing stimulating conversation over nutritious meals, I gobbled takeout on the drive home. The scariest part was that I didn't even know I had changed, because it occurred gradually."

Financial Planning

I've coached many executives who were at a crossroads in their careers, but their choices were restricted because they did not have sufficient financial resources. Often, it was creative, entrepreneurial individuals who, feeling stifled in their current role, wanted to start their own business or make a career change. They felt stuck because they hadn't saved enough or, worse, were in debt. The two main tendencies to be concerned about in this area are:

- Procrastination about doing the record-keeping, investment analysis, or financial planning required.
- Blurring the line between a "luxury" and a "necessity" and allowing expenditures to rise in tandem with income. Savings may not accrue, delaying financial independence.

Business Priorities

At the highest levels of business, competition is fierce, both internally and externally. In the first half of 2006, there was a record number of CEO changes. It's possible to lose focus and not devote sufficient time to any number of business priorities. Too many executives neglect one of the most important—monitoring change and understanding the implications of change. This happens both inside the organization and to customers and competition. In terms of our responsibility to our organizations and management of our careers, this must be a constant priority. But because the impact may be longer term and the changes gradual, we may not spend as much time as we need to in this area.

Religious/Spiritual Practices

If all those who either practice a formal religion, conduct their own spiritual practice, or feel it is important to serve humanity were grouped together, we would have an overwhelming majority of the U.S. population. Common activities in these areas include regular attendance and volunteering at religious institutions, prayer, reading from holy books, meditation and reflection, family rituals, and community service. Many people report that there were periods in their life when they did these consistently, and found them rewarding, and yet gradually stopped doing them.

Relationships

I have a vivid memory from coaching an executive who called home during one of our breaks: the look on his face after he talked to his six-year-old daughter, who had been crying, asking him when he was coming home. Maintaining our personal relationships is probably the most important and most difficult challenge in today's competitive business environment. The two key questions I often hear are:

1. How can I maintain the romance in a relationship? Or how can I find the time and energy to find a romantic partner?
2. How can I maintain strong bonds and lines of communication with my children?

Core Values

No doubt you've read or heard about the individuals involved in the notorious corporate scandals of recent years. Probably you also noticed the disconnect between what some of these people said about having high values and living up to them. Eventually, the difference between what they said and what they did led to their downfall. What happened to them? And if it happened to them, could it happen to you?

With regard to compromising your business values, it is vital to be on guard for the following:

- *Conflicts of interest*: There are many opportunities to develop conflicts of interest in business—with vendors, our own clients and consumers, or even shareholders. It requires rigorous self-discipline to refuse to act in our self-interest when it comes at a cost to others. The smartest thing to do personally and organizationally is to remove temptation.
- *Increase in power*: One result of acquiring power is that you may begin to believe you've somehow become smarter, funnier, and more attractive (after all, don't the people around you tell you that?). Another is that you may begin to think you can "get away with things." For some people, this process of breaking rules with no consequences, or having other people (lawyers, accountants, publicists, etc.) who will fix subsequent problems, opens a gap between their values and their behavior, which, over time, tends to widen.

Coming into Alignment

In the '60s and '70s research on body language and body-centered therapies (bioenergetics, Rolfing, etc.) led to a popular expression, "The body doesn't lie," meaning that we may say things that are deceptive but that our nonverbal expressions and/or the condition of our body tell the truth. I will extrapolate from that and say, "The calendar doesn't lie"; that is, we can tell ourselves, and others, that A, B, or C is very important to us, but the truth is in how we actually spend our time. That gives us a more accurate snapshot of our current priorities.

To get a realistic picture of yourself, look at the choices you make. How do you spend your time? Your money? Whom do you associate with? The choices we make are usually obvious to the people around us, but not always to ourselves. So as you engage in the next exercise I'd like you to try to make the starting point your *current reality*. Based on your actual schedule, I want you to find the gaps between your stated priorities, values, and goals, and the time you are devoting to them.

This exercise will help you in several ways:

- You may realize that you are overcommitted and be motivated to reconsider some of those commitments, or reprioritize them.
- You may become more determined to close the gap(s) and apply the Executive Stamina techniques that you are about to learn.
- Given the details of your actual schedule, you may admit to yourself that, at this point in your life, some of the things you identified as priorities really are not.

Alignment Exercises

Before you begin these exercises, take the time to review your notes from the reflective exercises in Chapter 1. To complete the charts here, first list your core values, commitments, priorities, and goals, then place a checkmark in the columns that most accurately reflect your current attitude toward the correlating value, commitment, priority, or goal; add any helpful notes or examples.

CORE VALUES

Value	Living consistently with this value	Drifting away from this value
1. _____	_____	_____
2. _____	_____	_____
3. _____	_____	_____

4. _____   _____   _____
5. _____   _____   _____
6. _____   _____   _____
7. _____   _____   _____
8. _____   _____   _____

COMMITMENTS

Commitment	Meeting This Commitment	Not Doing Enough
1. _____	_____	_____
2. _____	_____	_____
3. _____	_____	_____
4. _____	_____	_____
5. _____	_____	_____
6. _____	_____	_____
7. _____	_____	_____
8. _____	_____	_____

CURRENT PRIORITIES

Current Priority	Allotting the Right Amount of Time	Not Scheduling Enough Time
1. _____	_____	_____
2. _____	_____	_____
3. _____	_____	_____
4. _____	_____	_____
5. _____	_____	_____
6. _____	_____	_____
7. _____	_____	_____
8. _____	_____	_____

LONG-TERM GOALS

Long-Term Goal	Doing What's Necessary to Help Me Reach This Goal	Not Doing Enough to Reach This Goal
1._____	_____	_____
2._____	_____	_____
3._____	_____	_____
4._____	_____	_____
5._____	_____	_____
6._____	_____	_____
7._____	_____	_____

Summary

To conclude these exercises, and this chapter, ask yourself what the most important things are that you have learned about yourself and your current situation. Where are you living your priorities? Where are the gaps between your stated objectives and actual behavior? Make a list of these revelations.

3 | The Minimums and Shifts/Drifts Systems

The previous two chapters were designed to help you establish what is of primary importance to you, and to make you aware of, or remind you about, risks you face in these areas.

This chapter explains how to implement two very important systems—Minimums and Shifts/Drifts. These systems will help you create a plan for living in alignment with your priorities. You will design and customize this plan to meet your specific circumstances and goals. Later, as changes occur in your career or personal life, the plan will shift to reflect those changes. This will allow you to regularly reprioritize and make appropriate and targeted choices about future commitments. Used in tandem, these systems have proven to be very effective in helping people make sustained changes in their behavior, because they are grounded in what is realistic and practical for each person, at this moment in time.

Often, when we finally become aware of or alarmed about a gap in our lives, our tendency is to commit to drastic change.

"I'm going to start running four miles a day."
"No more sweets or soda for me."
"I need to adopt a very different leadership style."

"I'm going to start coming home for dinner every night that I am in town."
"This organization needs to break down the silos and embrace
    collaboration."

Most of us have made these types of resolutions in an effort to change
behaviors, but then found ourselves gravitating back to established, familiar
patterns. Sure, we embark on a new program or regime, but over time, and
often without realizing it, abandon it. And if we factor in that many of us are
already quite committed or overcommitted, it's understandable why it is so
hard to implement change. As a result, many people react with despair or frustration. In my practice, I hear such statements of frustration as, "You've shown
me how little uncommitted time I actually have, and now you've convinced
me I need to spend more time in certain areas. How can I bridge these gaps?"

It's true, too often, we dig ourselves into a hole. Most of us have heard
the folk wisdom that if you've dug a hole for yourself, the smartest thing to
do is to stop digging. We are going to look at how to stop digging and
slowly climb out of the hole.

The Minimums System

In my doctoral studies in clinical psychology at Temple University, I attended
many lectures on behavior change. One concept that stuck with me was the
idea of focusing on the *smallest, meaningful unit* of change. The idea is that to
get the change process started, and to improve the chances that change will be
sustained, start small. The proposed change needs to be small enough that it is
well within our abilities and resources to accomplish yet meaningful enough
to represent visible progress. It was this concept that led me to create my Minimums system when I began my coaching practice 15 years later.

What Is a Minimum?

A *minimum* in this context is an activity that you commit to doing in any of
the key areas (core value, commitment, current priority, long-tem goal)

where you perceive gap or a risk. It is a small step in the right direction that demonstrates to you and those around you that your priorities and actions are coming into alignment. It is *not* what you wish you could do if there were more hours in the day; it represents forward motion and demonstrates your commitment. Here are some examples:

- I don't like talking to the media, but it is now a bigger part of my job and I can see I am avoiding it. My minimum is that within the next two weeks I am going to talk with a CEO in my network who is effective at interacting with the media. I am going to ask her for some tips or find out about the training she received.
- Maintaining my health is one of my top priorities but I've essentially stopped exercising. My minimum is to walk at least 30 minutes, four days a week. I'm going to accomplish this by walking to and from the train. I'm also going to use the stairs (two flights) instead of the elevator at the office.
- I really care about environmental issues but I haven't made any changes in my lifestyle. My minimum is to use the carpool option in my community twice a week and sign up for a newsletter on environmental action steps.
- It's important to me to maintain the romantic part of the relationship with my wife. My minimum is to keep at least one night a week for ourselves when we are not exhausted and not just trading to-do lists, when we can have fun, have sex, or talk about what's important to us.
- I want to maintain the bonds with my children, especially as they become teenagers. Right now, between my unpredictable schedule, my travel, and their activities, we are ships passing in the night. My minimum is to talk with each of my children 10 minutes a day, be home for a family dinner at least one night a week, and spend one hour alone with each child on the weekends.

The key to minimums is they must be reasonable to you based on your schedule. You are going to set them (sometimes based on discussions with the other people involved) and commit to them.

Another powerful way to look at minimums is to consider the consequences of not meeting those you have designated. By setting a minimum, you are saying this is a very important area of your life. You are saying this is the minimum you need to do to support it. You are saying this is a small-enough commitment that you can definitely do it. So, if you don't achieve your minimum, what does it mean? You might have to admit:

- It is not really a priority.
- You are willing to conduct your life in a way that puts this area at risk.
- You are overcommitted and need to make some changes.

By now you should be able to see both the more obvious and the more subtle benefits of setting and scheduling minimums.

- *Progress not perfection:* A very high percentage of people follow through on their minimums when they focus on a small-enough step, which they have designated and committed to, and for which they have allotted a place in their schedule. This leads to further steps in a positive direction, and an increase in self-esteem. It also means they are keeping promises and are predictable in a positive way.
- *A warning system:* A minimum is an obvious marker. If you start missing your minimums, it will quickly be apparent to you and the people around you. This will help you get back on track rapidly. Without this warning system you are vulnerable to the Law of Gradual Change, and your alignment gap may grow wider. The Minimums system is your "canary in the coal mine," signaling to you that you are neglecting an important area in your life.
- *Self-knowledge and self-awareness:* Consistently missing your minimums is not a good sign, but it usually leads to deeper reflection on root causes of failure, which is a good thing. Ask yourself:
  - Did I neglect to schedule my minimums on my calendar?
  - Was I overly optimistic about what I committed to?

- Am I diverting time to lower-priority activities?
- Am I overcommitted and do I need to revisit some of my current obligations?
- Is this something I think *should* be important but in fact it isn't?
- Are my demanding job and my inability to set limits and boundaries combining to thwart my best intentions?

The point in creating minimums in key areas is that you gain no matter what the outcome. Either you set yourself on a positive trajectory, or you identify the significant behaviors you need to change, the skills you need to acquire, or the decisions you need to make.

Setting Minimum "Size"

Some of you looking at the examples just given of possible minimums might think they too small or too easy. I want to address this concern before I ask you to set some minimums for yourself.

Consider the woman who pledges to walk 30 minutes and use the stairs. True, this won't get her to very high levels of fitness quickly, but right now she is doing nothing. This low-level amount of activity will help build her capacity, self-esteem, and, hopefully (in conjunction with Joshua's tips in Part II), motivate her to increase her fitness.

What about the father who is committing to 10 minutes a day of conversation and an hour on the weekend alone with each of his children? His minimum may seem like not much, but recent studies show that the average executive father spends less than this amount of time with their children.

And, remember, we can always expand on any minimums we set, based on perceived need or increased desire. For example, learning more about media training might motivate an executive to acquire new skills. Spending uninterrupted time with a child might lead to deeper and lengthier conversations, a clearer understanding of the child's struggles and needs.

Here's my five-step process for setting minimums successfully:

1. Work alone to create the minimums that make sense to you.
2. Ask for feedback from a trusted advisor who knows you and is willing to be straightforward with you.
3. Discuss your initial thoughts with the people involved (family, co-workers, direct reports, etc.) and calibrate your plans based on their input. They will have important insights into what will make the minimum both realistic and impactful.
4. Schedule your minimum. This is probably the most important step, as doing so increases the chance you will follow through, that you will protect the time against other requests and demands.
5. Align with an accountability partner, someone who will "inspect what you expect" to ensure you are following through.

Getting Started

Think about some minimums you wish to achieve and put your initial thoughts in the minimums chart provided here. In later chapters, I will describe many techniques for achieving your minimums in the areas of job performance, career management, health, and relationships. After reading those, it will be useful to come back to this chart and refine your thinking.

MINIMUMS CHART

Core Values	Gap	Minimum
1. _____	_____	_____
2. _____	_____	_____
3. _____	_____	_____
Commitments		
1. _____	_____	_____
2. _____	_____	_____
3. _____	_____	_____

Current Priorities

1. _____ _____ _____
2. _____ _____ _____
3. _____ _____ _____

Long-Term Goals

1. _____ _____ _____
2. _____ _____ _____
3. _____ _____ _____

The Shifts/Drifts Tracking System

The Shifts/Drifts Tracking system is designed to make you aware of change, and the implications of change, in your career and personal life, and then to help you use this awareness as a springboard to take timely action—to re-prioritize your time and shift your focus to maximize opportunities and deal effectively with threats. It also is a simple, yet very effective mechanism for overcoming the Law of Gradual Change. I recommend you use the system at least once a month, and more often if necessary. But before I explain the system and how you can begin to use it, I want to highlight hazards and difficulties regarding change.

Facing Change

Everyone is familiar with the buzzwords widely used to describe a trend in their professions, catchy words or phrases that spread quickly. Though they may tend to become overused, they do, nevertheless, usu-ally point to something that is important (e.g., brand promise, an icon, etc.). A recent one I have heard is, "He/She is good at looking around corners," used to describe a highly valued executive in an organization. "Looking around corners" refers to the person's ability to spot mean-ingful trends or changes early, thereby giving the company the oppor-tunity to be proactive or preventative versus reactive or defensive. This has always been an important trait to ensure viability in the marketplace; but, more recently, corporations regard this ability as a key competitive advantage necessary to ensure success. Thus, people who demonstrate a track record in this competency often rise to the top at their companies.

Behind the urgency in this area is the rapid increase in the amount and pace of change in the marketplace, no matter what the industry. Let's look at some common areas of change in the business world:

- External changes (outside your organization) and internal changes (within your organization)
- Technology
- Competitive intent and practices
- Media; information delivery
- Macroeconomics (interest rates, growth rates, exchange rates)
- Global shifts in economic power
- Supply of labor; "war" for talent
- Consumer tastes and expectations
- Innovations (products, marketing)
- Supply chain, sourcing
- Mergers and acquisitions (your competitors, your clients)
- Mergers and acquisitions (your company)
- Senior management or corporate board
- Your manager
- Restructuring
- New role/responsibilities
- Key new hire(s)
- Internal priorities, strategies (based on external changes)
- Performance and profits

In addition to these changes that might impact your job performance and/or your career, you must also face regular change in your personal life and circumstances, making it another vital area to monitor.

Shifts

Some business changes are discrete, visible, and easy to recognize—if we are looking for them. I refer to them as *shifts*. There are two kinds of shifts: positive and negative.

Positive Shifts

Positive shifts are opportunities that open up and should be capitalized on quickly. They are usually straightforward and welcome, but still require new commitments of time, energy, and focus. Thus, it is useful to pause before making the decision to take one on, to ascertain how doing so might impact how you deal with what is already on your plate. Examples of positive shifts include:

- A joint venture opportunity in China
- A chance to acquire a competitor that possesses an important patent
- An invitation to speak at a key conference or be featured in a trade journal
- An opportunity to do a market tour with the CEO of your largest customer
- Better than expected performance that gives you the credibility to present new ideas
- Information that senior management is starting to focus on an issue about which you are very knowledgeable
- The chance to go to a retreat where you will meet other singles who have interests similar to yours
- A volunteer opportunity at your church where you can work on a very meaningful project with a partner you respect
- The offer to become general manager of a start-up division

Negative Shifts

Negative shifts are changes outside or inside our organizations or in our personal lives that pose immediate or potential threats. We may notice the shift but do not always think about the implications. What actions do I need to take? What skills do I need to acquire? How do I need to shift my priorities? Here are just a few of many examples of negative shifts:

- You are faced with an impending merger or acquisition at work. I worked closely with employees impacted by the Citibank Travelers merger and the AOL–TimeWarner and PepsiCo–Quaker acquisitions. In each situation I saw very intelligent people who neglected to analyze and respond to the changes that occurred in power structure, values, and core networks. They wound up either leaving the company or getting demoted.
- You are asked to take a new role that will involve more travel. What are the implications regarding other areas of your life? How will these new demands on your time affect your:
  - Fitness and nutrition practices
  - Family and relationships
  - Existing commitments
  - Ability to maintain your network at headquarters
  - Ability to manage your team

    Many people either don't think through these scenarios or underestimate the impact in these areas.
- Your mother, who lives alone, is no longer able to take care of herself. If you take more responsibility for her care, what will you have to let go of? What will be the new demands on your time and financial resources? How will it affect your other family relationships or your job obligations?
- You learn that one of your children is being bullied at school, a serious, complex issue. If you seek counseling or advice from professionals or educators, you may receive mixed messages. It may require a considerable amount of time to gather and sort out the information, align with your spouse, and support your child. How you handle it is likely to become an embedded memory for your child (and siblings).

As you can see, there are many possibilities, some of which can be handled with a generalized, appropriate response; but most of the solutions will depend on your specific values and priorities.

To summarize, even though shifts are visible, and so people may notice them, many of us do not reflect adequately on the implications and, therefore, don't take the necessary and appropriate actions to deal with the change. By systematically focusing on shifts and their impact, you put yourself in a position to make better personal and professional decisions.

Drifts

In contrast to shifts, which are immediate and easy to recognize, *drifts* are gradual changes that often go unnoticed. Recall from Chapter 1 that the Law of Gradual Change tells us that it is very likely that we will not notice small changes and trends in our life. For example, we don't acknowledge how much we need a vacation until we go on one, even though it is obvious to others in our lives. Like the executive who bragged to his friend, "I haven't had a vacation for three years." To which his friend replied, "I could tell."

The purpose of including drifts in my tracking system is to improve the chances that if you do begin to drift in an important area of your life, you won't do so for more than a short period of time. For the purpose of this discussion, I will use a month as the period of time after which I recommend you check in on drifts that may have taken place in your life. A month is long enough to enable you to recognize the change that is taking place but short enough so that you can prevent the drift from causing large alignment gaps from developing.

Filling Out a Shifts/Drifts Chart

Using a fictional character, Lawrence, I will show you a what a sample shifts/drifts chart would look like for January 2008. After we review it, I will explain how you can create your own customized chart.

Lawrence completes his shifts/drifts chart at the end of every month. In addition, he checks it weekly to remind himself of his priorities before scheduling his calendar. He pays attention to important shifts as they happen, but also gets a big-picture view of what has changed in his life on a monthly basis.

SHIFTS/DRIFTS TRACKING CHART

Core Value	Shifts (Yes or No)	Drifts (Yes or No)
Integrity	N	N
Give back to society	Y	N
Spiritual practice	N	N
Commitments		
Romantic partner	N	N
Son	Y	N
Daughter	N	N
Best friend	N	N
Religious organization	N	N
Current Priorities		
Create network in new organization	Y	N
Improve customer service	N	Y
Fitness program	N	N
Long-Term Goals		
Run for public office	N	N
Financial planning	N	Y

MONTHLY SHIFTS AND DRIFTS

Shift	Implications	Action Steps
Opportunity to work on literacy project at church		
Joining a new division of your corporation		
Son has been invited to join traveling soccer team		

Drift	Implications	Action Steps
Did not have enough alone time with romantic partner		
Did not review customer service proposal		
Have not been tracking monthly expenditures		

Let's look at Lawrence's January 2008 chart. There are three shifts, each of which could be seen as positive but which also, in different ways, may require a change in focus and priorities.

1. The literacy project at church is very meaningful to Lawrence. What is the time commitment required? Can he commit that much time? Is there something else he will need to let go of if he takes on this responsibility?
2. The traveling soccer team is an honor and an opportunity for his son. How will it affect Lawrence's other activities? How will it affect his weekends and other children?
3. Joining a new division may mean Lawrence will need to spend more time building a network and studying the culture's norms, values, and taboos.

Lawrence also noted three drifts:

1. The one-on-one time he committed to sharing with his wife did not occur often enough in January. He slipped under the minimum that they agreed to. His analysis was that they became too lax on their scheduling process and then allowed other activities to intrude on their time together. Therefore, his action step is to use Sunday evening to schedule time for them for each week in February.
2. Improving customer service is one of Lawrence's top business agendas. However, he realizes that he has not taken a key first step: to

review the customer service training proposal. Upon reflection, he realizes he has been procrastinating because he is not that knowledgeable about training design. His action step is to schedule a meeting with a person on his team who is competent in this area, to help him review the proposal. He feels this will get his questions answered quickly and help him to move forward.

3. Last year Lawrence met with an accountant and realized that he was not saving money commensurate with his level of compensation. A further insight was that he both underestimated how much his family spent, and was not fully aware of what they were spending money on. He saw that he could gain more control over his finances and increase his chances of reaching his long-term goals in this area if he started tracking his monthly expenses. In January, however, he did not do this. He commits to figuring out why not, and to making the necessary changes to ensure he follows through in February.

Now it's time to fill out your shifts/drifts tracking chart. You can use the blank chart provided here.

YOUR SHIFTS/DRIFTS TRACKING CHART

Month Core Values	Shifts (Yes or No)	Drifts (Yes or No)
1. _____	_____	_____
2. _____	_____	_____
3. _____	_____	_____
4. _____	_____	_____
5. _____	_____	_____
Commitments		
1. _____	_____	_____
2. _____	_____	_____
3. _____	_____	_____
4. _____	_____	_____
5. _____	_____	_____

Current Priorities

1. _____ _____ _____
2. _____ _____ _____
3. _____ _____ _____
4. _____ _____ _____
5. _____ _____ _____

Long-Term Objectives

1. _____ _____ _____
2. _____ _____ _____
3. _____ _____ _____
4. _____ _____ _____
5. _____ _____ _____

MONTHLY SHIFTS

Shift	Implications	Action Steps
1. _____	_____	_____
2. _____	_____	_____
3. _____	_____	_____
4. _____	_____	_____
5. _____	_____	_____

MONTHLY DRIFTS

Drift	Implications	Action Steps
1. _____	_____	_____
2. _____	_____	_____
3. _____	_____	_____
4. _____	_____	_____
5. _____	_____	_____

Summary

If, in Chapter 2, you identified important gaps between your values/
priorities and your schedule, use the Minimum system to achieve better
alignment. It can help you even when you don't follow through by making
it easier for you to see the gap and diagnose why it exists.

The Shifts/Drifts Tracking system will prevent gradual change from
sneaking up on you and serve to alert you to the implications of change in
your life.

4 | Finding Your Career Sweet Spot

I had the experience of finding a "sweet spot" before I had ever heard the term. It was 50 years ago, in Marine Park, Brooklyn, when I was 13 and playing baseball with a hard ball for the first time. I had swung at a low pitch and thought I hit the ball, but then hesitated before running because I hadn't actually felt the contact. Then I heard my dad screaming for me to run. I looked up and saw the second-most beautiful sight of my life to that point: the ball soaring into the distance, way past the right fielder. (The most beautiful sight was Bobby Thompson's home run in 1951 to win the pennant for the New York Giants.) In spite of the fact that there were no fences, and the ball rolled and rolled, my late start and lack of speed prevented me from getting all the way home. But all these years later, I still clearly remember that moment and how it felt.

Perhaps you can relate to the experience I'm describing when swinging at a golf ball or tennis ball. A physicist could probably explain why a certain motion at a precise moment will lead to a maximum transfer of energy and power. But all that's necessary to understand in the context of Executive Stamina is that finding the sweet spot yields an optimal result, with minimal stress or wasted energy—and it feels great! That's why the focus of this chapter is on finding your career sweet spot.

Defining Your Career Sweet Spot

In baseball, the sweet spot experience results from having the right combination of equipment, swing, timing, and the ball itself; similarly, in your career, finding the sweet spot requires a coming together of the right elements:

- *Competence:* What you are good at
- *Enjoyment:* What you like to do
- *Interest:* What you are deeply and sincerely curious about
- *Meaning:* What fits with your values and can serve a higher purpose

We can see all these elements reflected in, for example, Gandhi's "higher calling"; he was buoyed by unity in a cause with hundreds of millions of people. There are many, many executives who also have found their right combination of these four factors, including the world's most successful investor, Warren Buffett. Modestly and wisely, he has remarked, "If there is any difference between you and me, it may simply be that I get up every day and have a chance to do what I love to do, every day. If you want to learn anything from me, this is the best advice I can give you." Recently, he gave the largest gift in the history of philanthropy: over \$30 billion to the Gates Foundation.

A Worthwhile Search: To Find Your Sweet Spot

Before I lay out for you the ways to increase your self-awareness and guide you to your sweet spot, I want to explain why it is so important. Remember from the discussion on the Law of Diminishing Returns that if we go past a certain point in our efforts, we increase the risk of specific derailment factors. In addition, we are likely to experience more symptoms of burnout, including:

- Chronic fatigue
- Increased irritability
- Cynical thinking

- Sadness and depression
- Neglect of routine, maintenance activities
- Reduced immune system
- Increase in physical complaints
- Indulgence in daydreams of escape and radical change
- More addictive behavior
- Infrequent feelings of joy

Sometimes burnout is due to overcommitting ourselves, neglecting our own needs, or being too focused on perfectionism. These are causes that I will address in greater detail in later chapters. It is another contributor to burnout that I want to focus on now; that is, being in a career or role that is not right for you in some fundamental ways.

There are many reasons why we don't always make the best decisions about our career path:

- In our late teens or into our twenties, we may have had limited awareness of important insights about ourselves.
- We may have had a narrow view of the career options and choices that are available in the marketplace.
- We may have allowed external forces—society, media, parents, or peers—to influence our decisions. Doing what others think is right for us often causes misalignment with our deeper motivations, values, or interests.
- Financial considerations may loom large in our decisions. People on Wall Street will tell you that the two things that move markets are fear and greed. Fear (e.g., caused by debt) or greed (e.g., chance to make a high starting salary in a "hot" profession) can often influence career choices, too.

If we look at these factors together, we can see that there is a fairly high probability that our early decisions may not have been fully aligned with the factors that contribute to finding our sweet spot (competence, enjoyment, deep interest, meaning).

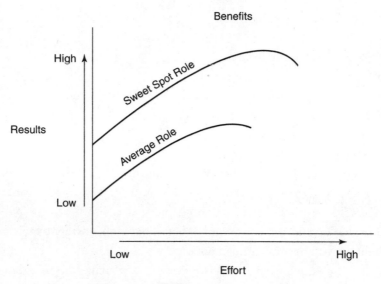

Figure 4.1   Sweet Spot Benefits

Whatever your age or circumstance, it can be very useful to improve your self-awareness in these areas. In my own case, it was thinking about my potential contribution or legacy that has led me to want to achieve a better balance between executive coaching and writing, along with mentoring two people to take over my business.

Look at Figure 4.1, which illustrates, in general terms, the benefits of being in a sweet spot career or role. Let me quickly point out that being in a sweet spot does not safeguard you against the laws of nature; you will still be prone to the same pitfalls and obstacles as your peers, and you will also have to face your point of diminishing returns. However, as the figure depicts, your effectiveness will be greater at all points; your optimum results level will be higher; and it will take you much longer to reach your inflection point.

What this means is that people who are a great fit for their role are likely to:

- *Demonstrate high levels of energy and enthusiasm for their work.* This quality is obvious to everyone around them. It draws others to them and gives them greater influence.

- *Sustain a long-term interest in and curiosity about their career focus.* This leads to continual improvement and life-long learning. Successful professionals are not just good at what they do; they know why they are good. This places them in an excellent position to mentor or educate others.
- *Experience less stress and greater job satisfaction, and therefore lower the risk of burnout.* Think of burnout as a semistarvation diet: lots of pangs and pains, very little nourishment. Those in their sweet spot careers may work extremely hard but they experience sustaining quantities of satisfaction and/or meaning. This emanates from being able to use their skills and strengths, harmonize with their values, and to become absorbed in enjoyable work.

Guidelines to Locating Your Sweet Spot Career

As a starting point here, I'd like to quote a bit of Hebrew wisdom, which comes in the form of questions:

If I am not for myself, who will be?
If I am only for myself, what am I?
If not now, when?

Similarly, George Ivanovich Gurdjieff (1866–1949), an Armenian-Greek mystic, advised that you should find something that is good for you and good for others. This description of a balanced self-interest is a useful guideline to making the right choices. And no doubt you've heard mythology professor and writer/speaker Joseph Campbell advise, "Follow your bliss." This, too, is useful in reminding yourself to pay attention to what draws your interest and nourishes you.

Psychology professor and writer Mihaly Csikszentmihalyi, in his best-selling book, *Flow: The Psychology of Optimal Experience* (Harper & Row, 1990), explained that when we are in "flow," we are fully absorbed in an activity. The task may be challenging, but we feel that we have the skills and resources to meet the challenge. And we are so focused that we lose track of time, and are often performing at peak levels ("in the zone").

With these insights in mind, I want to introduce you to other signs and signals that you can use to confirm you are on a positive path to finding your sweet spot.

Recognize Key Signs and Signals

To find your sweet spot, it is essential to pay attention to the following four aspects of your experience:

1. *Energy level:* When engaged in activities, notice your energy and enthusiasm, or lack thereof. How long are they sustained? Get feedback from those who work with you or know you. They are privy to the verbal and nonverbal cues you send out, and so may have valuable insights into when you are engaged, or not.
2. *Interest level:* A strong interest level is demonstrated by a high degree of curiosity. What are the areas in which you have sustained your curiosity (e.g., you ask questions, learn from others, read a lot)? These are also activities in which you experience "flow" because you become absorbed and give them your full attention.
3. *Enjoyment:* Have you ever worked long hours, fully concentrating on a task, and when you finished said to yourself, "I should be tired but I'm not"? Or a coworker may remark after you've finished an arduous assignment, "It was challenging but I had a lot of fun"? These experiences can yield useful insights into what constitutes enjoyable work for you.
4. *Daydreaming and mindshare:* Our thoughts often drift in the direction of our needs. If we are feeling a lot of stress and pressure, and few rewards, we may start daydreaming about what would make us feel better. Pay attention to the direction of such thoughts, and how much time you are devoting to them; doing so will give you insights into your deeper needs.

Find Satisfaction and Meaning

Herb Otto, a pioneer in research on strengths and potential, believed that useful insights into what is most important to us could be derived from examining our peak experiences. A peak experience is an event that causes powerful, memorable emotions, and is a high point or turning point in our lives. In our personal lives this could include the birth of a child, falling in love, a religious conversion or epiphany, being in harmony with nature or a group of people, an outstanding achievement, or an act of dedication or integrity that enhanced your self-esteem. Of course, what constitutes a peak experience is unique to each of us, which is why being aware of these experiences can reveal your deepest feelings and needs. Ask yourself:

- What do you regard as career peak experiences?
- What are some of the high points in your life overall that you treasure?
- What are the elements that gave these experiences so much meaning and significance for you?

The answers to these questions may point you toward key aspects of your sweet spot.

Identify Fit Factors

Other characteristics that help to determine whether you are in your sweet spot I refer to as "fit factors," those things that let you know you are a good fit for your role. By now you're aware that I'm a big believer in improving self-awareness. I regard it as a crucial leadership skill, as well as life skill, that helps us make better choices.

I list here six fit factor questions I'd like you to read and answer for yourself. Your answers can point you to the fit factors that will make a role ideal for you.

1. *Are you independent and self-reliant or interdependent and team-oriented?* Not everyone likes working in teams and/or relying on others. If this is true for you, it could be very stressful for you to work in a heavily matrixed organization.

2. *Do you prefer to exert power over others or share it?* Some of us have a high need to control (to have power over). Others of us have an easier time sharing power and making decisions collaboratively. If you have a high need for control, certain collaborative roles or organizational structures will only serve to amplify your frustrations. Or you may enjoy working with teams as long as you are the clear leader and have established decision-making authority.

3. *Do you have a high or low need for creativity?* For some of us, having the opportunity to be creative is a "nice to do." If we don't get many of these opportunities, it doesn't bother us. If headquarters tells us, "Just run the play," we are fine executing someone else's strategy. But to others with strong need to be creative, they want regularly to be innovative, to break new ground, and put their unique handprint on a project. For these executives, executing someone else's plans, or doing work that has become routine and repetitive, can be an excruciating experience.

4. *Do you have a high tolerance for risk or a high need for security?* Executives with a higher risk profile may do well in a start-up or working on a turnaround assignment; they may prefer to be an entrepreneur or start a consulting business; and they do not mind not having a guaranteed income. Other people with similar skills, competencies, and work ethic would not do well in these careers because their high level of anxiety caused by job uncertainty would hurt their effectiveness. You need to determine your risk tolerance versus your need for security.

5. *Are you extremely ambitious or only mildly driven?* I've coached executives who have achieved financial independence, high rank in their organizations, and the respect of their peers. But they are never satisfied, always aspiring to do more, be more. They may feel in competition with their MBA classmates who have "gone further"; or

compare their net worth with hedge fund managers they read about; or they may want to play on a bigger playing field and have greater impact. Whatever the reason, if this describes you, it merits consideration in choosing your career alternatives.

6. *What's more important to you, to be good for society or good for you?* There are executives whose overriding career goal is compensation. It doesn't matter much to them what products their companies manufacture or the services they provide. Executives in this category, obviously, have the widest range of choices in the marketplace; they will work almost anywhere if the money is right. Conversely, there are executives to whom the integrity of a company, and the product or service it provides, matter a very great deal. These execs take their time to find the right industry and the right company within that industry. Especially important in the wake of the corporate scandals is a company's integrity. They want to be associated with a company that is helping consumers and is, in general, a good "corporate citizen."

If, after considering these questions, you feel you are at neither extreme in any of them, you probably don't need to factor them into your decisions. If, on the other hand, you conclude you are at one of the extremes, and that fact is not reflected in your current role, this information should become something that influences future career decisions you make.

Focus on Strengths

Earlier, I mentioned Herb Otto. I had the good fortune to start my career working for him in 1971, in San Diego. His research on families in the 1960s convinced him that most people were only dimly aware of their strengths and, as a result, were unable to see their true potential. He found that not only did people spend little time thinking about their strengths, they often didn't know what qualified as a strength. For example, is it a strength if you are not perfect and sometimes make mistakes? Can you claim to have a strength if others are better than you in the same competence? Is it a strength if you have a natural talent that you didn't work hard to develop?

To Herb, the answer to all these questions was an unqualified yes, yet his research indicated that many people were confused about or discounted their strengths. Consequently, he went on to develop the Strength Acknowledgement activity and other methods to help people clearly identify their strengths and what their potential would be if they used all their strengths.

In 2001, Marcus Buckingham and Donald Clifton of the Gallup organization refined this process of identifying human strengths. In their best-selling book, *Now, Discover Your Strengths* (Free Press, 2001), they introduce the Strengths Finder profile, a tool based on a Gallup study of 2 million people. This tool has been enhanced recently and an updated version is described in Tom Rath's *Strength Finders 2.0* (Gallup Press, 2007).

I recommend these worthwhile instruments to aid in understanding what you are good at, and learning to "play to your strengths," both cores components of finding your sweet spot.

Unearth Deeply Embedded Life Interests

The term "deeply embedded life interests" was coined by Timothy Butler and James Waldroop, authors of *Discovering Your Career in Business* (Addison-Wesley, 1997) and the creators of an excellent online tool, Career Leader (www.careerdiscovery.com). They define deeply embedded life interests as "long-held, emotionally driven passions that are intricately entwined with personality." Their research indicates that finding a role that coincides with these interests greatly increases your changes of being happy in your career. The Career Leader tool has been very useful to many of my clients and can complement what you learn about your strengths.

Real-Life Examples

Finding executives who love what they do, and have found a way to combine their passion and values with their career success, is not difficult. If you are not yet in this category, I hope this chapter helps you become one of them soon. As further inspiration, here are examples of some of the people I've worked with who have found their sweet spot.

- A financial services executive who meticulously researched companies in her industry in order to find one that was dedicated to the interests of its customers. She was passionate about helping people plan wisely for their retirements, and this became the focus of her work at her new firm.
- A seemingly tireless, globe-trotting executive for a medical devices company who works closely with NGOs, UNICEF, and his internal R&D team to help fight the spread of AIDS and to increase the availability of vaccinations around the world.
- A number of food products executives whose concern for their own children's nutrition has led them to become pioneers in improving the quality of their company's offerings to its consumers. These execs haven't changed companies, their roles, or industries; rather, impelled by their personal values, they have drawn their jobs closer to their sweet spot.
- Then there's me. When I was 19 years old, I became fascinated with the realization that people can change, grow, and develop their potential. I was very fortunate to find work about which, 44 years later, I am still enthusiastic and curious.

Summary

In this chapter, we looked at the key components of a career sweet spot (competence, enjoyment, interest, meaning) and the benefits of finding yours. Additionally, I provided guidelines and tools to illuminate the elements you might combine to create this kind of role for yourself.

While these reflections are still fresh in your mind, I recommend you write down your thoughts in the spaces below or in a personal journal. What did you learn about yourself or your career in these categories?

Energy level _____

Interest level _____

Enjoyment _____

Mindshare _____

Satisfaction and meaning—career peak
    experiences _____

Fit factors _____

Strengths _____

Deeply embedded life interests _____

You may not want to, or be able to change you industry, company, or current role. However, you can use this self knowledge to shape the components of your job through:

- what you say yes or no to
- hiring and delegation decisions
- proactive, creative proposals to your boss to restructure aspects of what you do.

PART II

BUILDING YOUR STAMINA

5

The Impact
of Stress

You've no doubt heard Frederich Nietzsche's famous saying, "That which doesn't kill me makes me stronger." Certainly, it can be applied to business executives, who daily face intense competition, internally from colleagues, and externally, from national and, more often today, international competitors. Economic, technological, or regulatory changes can disrupt operating plans and change the playing field overnight for a company or an industry (e.g., Mayor Michael Bloomberg's announcement to prohibit the use of all trans fats in New York City's restaurants, and to require posting of the nutritional content of all meals). Add to their everyday responsibilities, execs typically work late nights, must travel to branch offices or vendors, and are virtually tethered to their personal communication devices. It is not surprising that, in 2001, *Jobs Rated Almanac* rated senior corporate executive as the third most stressful career (behind president of the United States and firefighter).

But, in the case of stress, as Nietzsche wisely pointed out, it can make you stronger and better—if you learn how to manage it. For example, when you lift weights or chop wood, you are physically stressing your muscles, and they may incur small tears. But if you are adequately nourished, and give them enough recovery time, your muscles have the capacity to repair themselves and become bigger and stronger. Similarly, the demands and stresses of corporate life can psychologically and intellectually stretch you, which can help you develop your strengths and expand your potential. Recall from the Introduction the article I mentioned on extreme jobs. In addition to citing the negative effects of these roles, many people also report finding them exhilarating, rewarding, and a contributing factor in accelerating their professional growth.

My point is that it is neither possible nor necessarily desirable to eliminate all stress. In fact, there is a positive kind of stress; it even has a name: *eustress*. Eustress is different for each individual but it is usually characterized by balance—that is, the demands and pressures that tax us are matched by the resources, competence, and confidence that we marshal to meet them. Eustress fosters growth and the realization of our potential.

So maybe it's more accurate to label the type of stress that can hurt our health and productivity as *distress*, for that is what most of us mean when we refer to stress. Our experiences of stress usually result in a combination of unpleasant emotions (worry, anxiety, irritability, frustration, anger), physiological reactions (rising levels of epinephrine, norepinephrine, cortisol), and physical responses (neckache, shoulder strain, headaches, etc).

External causes of stress are easy to identify—heavy workload, a noisy environment, crowding, long lines, travel delays, disruptions, difficult people, and so on; few of us think about a very important internal factor: how we perceive stressful events and how we choose to react to them. This often is the major determinant of how much stress we actually experience. What this also means is that we can control stress more effectively if we *choose* to do so.

John Galleteria, head of sales for the Retirement Plan Services division of T. Rowe Price, is an example of someone who made this choice during a recent family vacation, and successfully converted a potentially stressful situation into a positive one. He and his family were returning from a wonderful vacation in the Cayman Islands. The airport was bursting with people, and his flight was delayed four hours. In addition, it was difficult to get information updates, and he was surrounded by upset, complaining passengers. John recognized that getting angry was not going to help his situation, so he redirected his focus so that he could remain calm. Here is a sampling of his inner dialogue: "Getting angry is not going to get me home any sooner. I'll just upset myself and the family. I just had a wonderful vacation with my family; why ruin it because of something I can't control." Two recent events had influenced his new approach to stress. He had read a book on leadership that described the importance of modeling behavior. A phrase from the book came back to him: "the shadow of a leader," and he decided he wanted to take the opportunity to be a role model to his 11-year-old son on how to manage anger. Second, and more important, he had recently learned of the serious illness of a sibling. Reflecting on that helped put the current situation in its proper perspective—it was an inconvenience, nothing more.

As a result, for John and his family, the four-hour delay yielded many positive outcomes. The family alternated between talking about the high points of the vacation, playing games, and marveling at John's new composure. And when John finally reached the head of the long line of passengers, he shocked the beaten-down service representative by displaying humor and empathy, which was much appreciated.

Later, in the discussion on self-talk, you will learn the technique John used. For now, I just want to establish the idea that you have the potential to influence three aspects of stress:

1. *Frequency:* How often you experience stress. This is a key factor because repeated secretions of stress hormones will have a "wear and tear" effect on your nervous systems and mood.
2. *Duration:* How long you stay upset. Does it ruin your day? Your vacation? Or do you recognize stress signals early and use effective stress management skills to minimize the time you are upset?
3. *Intensity.* How upset you get. Are you disappointed, mildly frustrated, somewhat anxious, or do you tend to have a full-blown meltdown?

It's imperative that you recognize that your perceptions and the way you frame events drive your stress, making you a key contributor to your own pain. Furthermore, in your own mind, you may have all kinds of unrealistic expectations that add to your stress levels. For example:

- Expecting perfection from yourself and others.
- Overreacting to mistakes and failures.

- Being extremely competitive and status conscious.
- Trying too hard to meet other people's expectations.
- Blurring the lines between luxuries and necessities.
- Experiencing inconvenience and frustration as catastrophic.

I think you can see that if we add the considerable external causes of stress to the potential internal causes that high-achieving, hard-charging executives often experience, it becomes vital to take a multifaceted, holistic approach to dealing with executive stress. This is the main focus of the chapters in Part II. In Chapters 6 through 8, you will learn how improving your fitness levels and eating right will both reduce your stress and increase your capacity to handle it. Chapters 9 and 10 will detail how you can develop your own stress management program, including ways to monitor and minimize stress before and after work, at the office and on the road.

And keep in mind you've already learned one excellent stress management strategy, in Chapter 4—how to find your career sweet spot. This will help you experience less stress while finding greater satisfaction and meaning in your professional life.

Stress Fallout

My goal in this chapter is to motivate you to acquire stress management skills and techniques, and then integrate them into your workday. I intend to convince you (in case you aren't already) that developing your own effective system for dealing with internal and external pressures is essential to your future success and well-being. To begin, let me point out the detrimental "fallout" of high levels of stress in five important categories:

- Health and energy
- Sleep
- Development of addictions
- Relationships
- Career

Health and Energy

Our brain and nervous system have a highly developed capacity for dealing with stressful events and perceived stressors. We've all experienced one of the most basic human reactions to stress: the "fight or flight" response. When we go into this mode, our system begins to secrete stress hormones—epinephrine (adrenaline), norepinephrine (nor-adrenaline) and cortisol (a steroid hormone that helps us get through stressful situations). These hormones are effective and potent. They increase our heart and breathing rates and divert blood to our muscles, preparing the body for action. They can deliver a quick burst of energy and temporarily lower our sensitivity to pain. It's an effective and vital system, to be sure, as long as we don't activate it too often and unnecessarily.

Problems emerge when we activate our stress response system inappropriately and with not enough recovery time in between. Instead of using this system to address true threats to our survival, we begin to invoke it to deal with stressful situations of everyday life, initiating this response so frequently that it begins to cause serious wear and tear on our bodies, impacting us physically and mentally, and eventually depleting our energy levels and stamina. Some of the conditions linked to living with chronic stress and our overreactions to it include:

- Increased aging
- Susceptibility to infection
- Diabetes
- High blood pressure
- Heart disease
- Headaches, migraines
- Dental problems
- Bone, muscle loss
- Burnout, depression

Sleep

"O, sleep! O, gentle sleep! Nature's soft nurse . . ."

—Shakespeare, *Henry IV*

One of the clearest indications of an increased pace of life and overall stress level is the reduction in the amount of restful sleep we get. Consider these recent findings:

- The National Commission on Sleep Disorders Research estimates that 40 million Americans suffer from chronic sleep problems, and as many as 30 million more have occasional difficulty sleeping.
- As the stressors in our lives increase, the amount of time we spend recuperating seems to be decreasing. According to the National Sleep Foundation, Washington, DC, in 2006, only 26 percent of adults got eight hours of sleep a night, compared with 38 percent in 2001.
- Rather than take preventative measures for sleep disorders, most Americans seek a "quick fix," which led to a record 43 million sleeping pill prescriptions written and filled in the United States in 2005, at a cost of more that $2 billion.
- Francesco Cappucio, a professor at the University of Warwick Medical School in the United Kingdom, recently completed a 17-year study of 10,000 government workers in that country. People who got by on five hours or less a night (one-third of the group) had twice the risk of cardiovascular death, compared to those who slept seven hours or more.
- The U.S. Surgeon General estimates that sleep deprivation and related disorders cost the nation $16 billion in annual health care expenses, and about $50 billion in lost productivity each year.
- Vivian Abad, medical director of the Clinical Monitoring Sleep Disorders Center in Cupertino, California, says, "There are just too many demands on people in terms of what they need to accomplish. People end up going to bed later and getting up earlier. People treat sleep as a luxury. It's not a luxury. It's essential."

The last point is my central starting point here. Certainly, individuals may vary in the amount of sleep they need to function optimally, but all of us do require a certain amount of restful sleep to maintain a basic level of health and well-being. It is the hours we sleep when we restore, recuperate, and prepare to respond to the next-day's challenges. The irony is that our opportunity to recover from stress can be undermined by stress itself. There are myriad ways that our busy, stressful lives contribute to our sleep deprivation:

- *Too many demands on our time:* This is a pure numbers calculation. If you have more commitments and obligations than there are hours in the day to meet them, you may try to accomplish them by going to bed later and waking up earlier.
- *Not taking time to wind down:* If you gradually taper off your activities and start to relax, it will usually be easier to drift off to sleep at bedtime. These days, too many of us work frantically at tasks or go online right before going to bed. This has the effect of stimulating our thought processes, making it difficult to fall asleep or have a restful sleep.
- *Unfinished business:* I hear executives use the phrase "what keeps me up at night" a lot. Sometimes it comes as a statement: "What keeps me up at night about the project . . ." or as a question, "What's the one thing that keeps you up at night about our competition?" The phrase says a lot about sleep. If we have a worry, concern, or unresolved issue, it probably will interfere with our sleep in a variety of ways, making it harder to fall asleep and causing disturbed sleep patterns (restlessness, muscle or jaw tension) and nightmares.
- *Use of stimulants and depressants:* One common negative pattern induced by stress and relating to sleep is that people begin to use stimulants to overcome tiredness and boost energy and then counter those with depressants (sleeping pills) to help them get to sleep. The most popular stimulant worldwide is caffeine, consumed in coffee, tea, and soft drinks. Caffeine has been shown to improve short-tem performance in both athletic and conceptual tasks. However, it is all too easy to get into a stimulation-fatigue-stimulation cycle. Caffeine also triggers doses of stress hormones, causing your body to experience a mild, usually pleasant form of stress and heightened alertness, but

typically followed after a few hours by a "crash," when you feel drowsy and fatigued. This usually leads to ingesting more caffeine. Then, at night, the presence of these hormones may inhibit adenosine absorption, which calms the body for sleep. Thus, unable to sleep naturally, many come to rely on Ambien or Lunesta, two popular sleepingpills.

Effects of Sleep Deprivation
- Fatigue and low energy levels
- Increase in mistakes
- Faulty decision making
- Irritability and poor emotional self-control
- Lowered immune system

Development of Addictions

Human beings are creatures of habit, prone to developing persistent patterns of behavior. We become easily attached to activities and substances, which provide enjoyment, excitement, or relief from boredom, stress, and/ or pain. These activities, and practices, become so integral to our lives that we feel "off" or "not right" somehow in their absence. It would be difficult to find someone who isn't addicted or at least very strongly attached to something. When addictions are formed, the brain has been altered, or "rewired," so that certain activities or substances become a top priority, in spite of their consequences to health, reputation, or relationships.

If we have a healthy sense of ourselves, we can make good choices about our patterns, creating positive attachments and patterns. Among healthy and beneficial activities and behaviors are exercise, prayer, meditation, and productive work; these may all be categorized as "positive addictions." Typically, though, the term *addiction* is used to describe negative attachments.

In the past, the concept of addiction was associated primarily with substance abuse, to alcohol, heroin, cocaine, amphetamines, tobacco, pain killers, and sleeping pills, for example. It is now recognized that activity or stimulation addictions (e.g., to gambling, eating disorders, surfing the Net, shopping, video games, sex, Internet pornography, PCDs, etc.) can be just as powerful and dangerous.

Executive Stress as a Cause of Addiction

The potential damage of some of these addictions to one's career is obvious; others are more subtle. In Part IV, when I discuss how important it is to executives to use their time wisely, you will see that even a mild addiction can divert your focus and chew up your time in ways that can be detrimental to your effectiveness and work and personal relationships. In this chapter, however, my specific focus is on stress and addiction.

There are many causes of addictions, including genetic predisposition, but excessive stress can also be a prime contributor. When stress levels get too high, we experience it as some form of pain, and, naturally, we want it to disappear. If we have developed good habits, like being in touch with nature, having an exercise routine, talking with friends, or engaging in relaxing hobbies, prayer, meditation, or yoga, we can rely on these positive ways to help us cope. Unfortunately, too many people look for the easy and quick way to take away the pain, by using alcohol, drugs, or tobacco to numb the discomfort; or by finding something that distracts and excites us, such as gambling, shopping, sex, video games, the Internet, and many others. And before we know it, we have become dependent upon and comfortable with these behaviors or products. In fact, when deprived of them, we may become agitated, moody, depressed, or worse.

My goal in this discussion is not to moralize; it is to introduce a practical approach to addressing this very serious problem. To begin, I ask you to examine honestly your habits and patterns by asking yourself these questions:

- Does this behavior pose a risk to my reputation?
- Is this activity diverting too much time away from my personal relationships?

- Are there health risks associated with this activity?
- Am I wasting time on this activity that I need for my business or career priorities?
- Am I losing respect for myself or lowering my self-image?

Answering these questions can be difficult to do if you are highly attached or addicted to something, for your strong tendency will be to deny or rationalize your behavior. If in doubt whether you can answer the questions objectively, I strongly recommend you talk with someone you trust and ask for his or her help and feedback.

Once you have determined that you have an attachment or pattern that is negatively impacting your life, the next step is to develop a positive stress management program to aid in alleviating the deleterious effects of stress. Chapters 6 through 9 will help you do that.

Relationships

Stress can also have a negative impact on the interpersonal skills central to creating and maintaining strong, healthy relationships. Part V of this book is devoted to the goal of maintaining positive relationships with the key people in your life; here, I want only to briefly address four vital aspects of managing relationships successfully:

- Listening skills
- "Reading" other people
- Two-way discussions
- Noninflammatory language

Executive Profile

Sam Su, President, YUM! Brands, China

I predict that someday books will be written about Sam Su, and what he and his team have accomplished at the China division of YUM!

Brands. In particular, KFC is one of the most successful businesses in China. It has increased its dominance over McDonald's (in 2007, there were 2,000 KFC stores versus 800 McDonald's) and is adding 400 restaurants a year.

Sam assembled and, even more remarkably, retained a strong management team, despite the intense competition for competent leaders in China. He is also respected throughout Asia; in China, he has achieved almost legendary status. YUM! China's sustained growth is even more amazing when you consider that in recent years it has been buffeted by three formidable food safety crises: SARS, avian flu, and Sudan red (food dye). In each instance, KFC suffered several drops in business but recovered and went on to gain an even stronger position in the marketplace.

I interviewed Sam to understand how he dealt with the stress of these and other challenges. He articulated a very clear leadership approach, which he says helps him personally at the same time it provides a model for his team. His goal is to devote all of his time, energy, and focus to finding effective options while maintaining peace of mind. These are his keys to success in handling stressful situations:

- *Face reality.* Sam says he tries to learn as much as he can about the reality of any circumstance as soon as possible. Many times he has seen leaders in denial, wishing things would go away, or procrastinating. To help him do this, he consults with experts and leaders with relevant experience. He seeks advice so that he clearly understands his options in each situation.
- *Leave your ego at the door.* Sam believes the main source of stress for leaders under crisis is worrying about themselves, their reputations, careers, salaries, stock options, or promotions. Instead, Sam stays totally focused on the desired outcome. He has trained himself to strive to do his absolute best. When he

(*Continued*)

Sam Su, President, YUM! Brands, China (Continued)

does, he retains his peace of mind and so is able to accept whatever the outcome is, and is able to acknowledge there are many factors he cannot control.

■ *Remember the long term.* Crises by definition require short-term tactical decisions. Sam believes that what has helped the KFC brand during difficult times is that he has always stayed conscious of longer-term aspirations. He was able to balance immediate concerns by reminding himself of the big picture: What kind of company do we want to be? What are the core values of our culture? What do we want our brand to stand for? What type of person do I want to be?

■ *Learn and improve.* Sam is not a perfectionist. Rather, he wants only to continue to improve and to stay one step ahead of his competitors. For example, when Sudan red food dye, a component of KFC seasonings, was found to be a threat to consumers, the supplier to KFC was identified. KFC took responsibility for the problems and demonstrated concern for consumer safety. Sam responded by instituting many measures to demonstrate this priority: a food safety office, labs, testing facilities, random testing, food safety panels, and revamping the supply chain system. He used the crisis as an opportunity to learn more about food safety, upgrade KFC's systems, and demonstrate the company's concern for consumer safety to Chinese society.

Listening Skills

One of the first signs of stress is that your ability and willingness to listen to others will fall off. To be an effective listener, you must first give the speaker your full attention. Then, it helps to show you are tracking what the person is saying, that you are with him or her in the conversation. It is important to make eye contact with the person speaking, exhibit curiosity about what he or she is trying to convey, and allow the person to complete his or her thoughts—that is, don't interrupt. Finally, you can demonstrate or test your comprehension by summarizing for the person what you understood to be his or her message.

Under stress, each of the listening "steps" becomes more difficult to execute. Stress tends to narrow our focus to the cause of our more immediate concern, whatever that might be. In short, we become more self-focused and less other-focused. The simple task of giving someone else our complete attention becomes difficult because we are preoccupied with our thoughts and issues. We aren't very curious about what the other person is saying, and this usually shows in our body language and absence of interest.

Finally, stressed people are rarely patient. They often interrupt others before they have finished speaking and, sometimes, take conversations in a different direction. We all exhibit poor listening behaviors from time to time, but as stress accumulates, lack of patience and poor listening skills can create additional difficulties.

"Reading" Other People

Daniel Goleman, in his best-selling book, *Emotional Intelligence* (Bantam, 1997), noted a variety of competencies that contribute to success and well-being. One of them is the ability to "read" other people. This includes noticing their body language, facial expressions, and choice of words. When we do this well, we not only become aware of what someone else is feeling and what is important to them, we get data on the impact we are having on them. Knowing how they are feeling about us, and our message, is vital information. This wisdom is echoed in the famous dictum among those in the sales profession, "People will tell you how to sell them."

So, if being able to read people is a crucial navigational skill for persuasion, team alignment, or positive relationships, how is this ability affected by stress? As I mentioned in the last section, stress tends to make people more "me" focused. Our peripheral vision diminishes as we narrow our attention scope. The odds go down that we will pick up key signals from others, and that we will notice the effect our behavior is having on those around us.

Two-Way Discussions

Constructive two-way discussions are crucial for exchanging information and viewpoints, resolving problems and conflicts, and sustaining balanced relationships. Communication experts postulate that using the 40/60 rule provides a good framework to use to have an even exchange where all parties involved will feel positive about the conversation. The 40/60 rule suggests that participants in a two-way discussion each speak more than 40 percent but less than 60 percent of the time.

If, say, you and I have a different point of view or are even in conflict, yet are both relatively calm and in a problem-solving mode, we will probably work it out. One of us will persuade the other; we will come up with a win-win solution or a compromise; or we may even agree to disagree. But if I am stressed or angry, a different scenario will unfold, because when my "caveman" brain takes over, I won't be interested in a two-way exchange or finding a win-win conclusion. I will want to win! I will want to be right, to get in the last word. If I am listening to you at all, it will be to find the holes in your argument or figure out a way I can use your words against you. Of course, interruptions are a given. And this is how excess stress jeopardizes two-way discussions, which are an essential part of teamwork and positive personal relationships.

Noninflammatory Language

In all aspects of life, it is easier to resolve conflicts and solve problems if we use noninflammatory language, language that conveys information, needs, goals, or perspective but that doesn't accuse, criticize, demand, or threaten. Examples are:

> Would it be *possible* to . . . ?
> I'd like your thoughts on an *alternative* . . .
> One *option* I see . . .
> We're *considering* . . .
> My *point of view* is . . .
> A *suggestion* that I think has potential is . . .
> This is your decision but *if it were my call,* I would . . .
> If we go in that direction, an *issue* that may surface is . . .
> I understand the potential of this project. My *concern* is . . .
> Based on our experience with these kinds of launches, we feel the
> biggest *challenge* is going to be . . .
> As we go forward it will be useful to *pay attention to* . . .
> Let's stay *focused on* . . .
> I am *not as confident* as you are. Here's why . . .

These words and phrases won't always lead to alignment or agreement, but they give all parties an opportunity to air their views and exchange information that is helpful. The most important benefit is what *doesn't* happen: that conflict does not escalate.

This method of communicating is effective "executive vocabulary." When we are stressed or angry, patterns of communication take a different turn:

> We talk louder and faster.
> We many start to exaggerate.
> We use more names and labels.
> We criticize or put down.
> We threaten more

And this is the kind of language we use:

> You *never* deliver . . .
> This *always* happens . . .

Every time I ask you . . .

This is the *worst* example . . .

This is a *disaster.*

It's *irresponsible.*

That lacks *integrity.*

I've forgotten more about this subject that you currently know.

I can't believe after three months you come up with this.

They'll never go for it. You wasted a lot of our time.

It's not going to work the way you think. You are being naïve.

Over my dead body.

You don't know who you are dealing with.

We'll see who gives in first.

If you want to play hardball . . .

Needless to say, conflicts and different points of view are inevitable in business and in our personal lives, but if we are able to listen well, read people, and conduct polite two-way discussions using noninflammatory language, most times, we can resolve issues and improve relationships. If we are overly stressed or the caveman brain takes over, chances are we will add the burden of "relationship stress" to what we are already struggling with.

Career

Having a successful career, one that takes you where you want to go professionally without sacrificing your health, values, or relationships is the central theme of this book. We put our careers in peril when we fail to manage stress, bringing about:

- Potential health issues, which could keep you away from work or diminish your energy and vitality when you are there.
- Sleep deprivation, which affects alertness and acuity, causing mistakes.

- Poor decision making, because we become impulsive, or the opposite: paralyzed and afraid to act.
- Caveman communication skills, including poor listening and extreme language, damages relationships and escalates conflict.
- An overall image of being overwhelmed causes others to question whether we are up to the task and to hesitate about giving us more responsibility.

Are you wondering at this point if I am trying to scare you? No, but I am trying to get your attention, and motivate you to want to acquire and integrate the skills and strategies that I unveil in the next chapters. For those of you who have already developed effective ways of reducing stress and recovering from it, I hope to add to your repertoire of techniques so you can design an even more effective and sustainable plan that you can use at home, at the office and on the road.

6 | Increasing Your Fitness

> *If you are too busy to exercise, you are too busy.*
>
> —Anonymous

> *You are too busy not to exercise.*
>
> —The authors

In this chapter, I call on Joshua's expertise to help me introduce you to the essential training principles and practices that for years he has used to:

- Develop professional athletes, including both national and world champions.
- Help executives reach fitness levels that range from basic to world-class and attain their peak performance state

Our goal in this chapter is to demonstrate that contrary to popular belief, staying fit does not *cost* you time, it *gives* you time. We recognize that your schedule is already tightly packed, so we offer many tips for dealing with that reality. Our starting premise, however, is that it is precisely because you face so many demands and challenges that the energy-yielding, stress-fighting benefits of exercising are essential. We will show that it is in fact being fit that will enable you to reach your ideal performance level. You will be more efficient, have the ability to think clearly and concentrate, coupled with the energy you need to execute. You will save hours and hours that you would otherwise spend on coping with mistakes that you could have avoided making. Internally, you will enjoy the physical sensation of having a fit body; externally, you will exude enthusiasm and confidence.

As you will see in the sections to come, increasing your fitness is no longer reserved for a few dedicated individuals, but is now a necessity to maintain career longevity and perform at the level you desire. It is your gift to use to achieve the results you want in career, life, and relationships. This chapter is about getting you to move, to counteract the many so-called improvements in our lives that have contributed to us all becoming more and more sedentary—you know, computers, fax machines, printers, cell phones, videoconferencing. Most of us do most of our work in a chair. And even when we do get up, escalators, elevators, and executive parking spaces mean we hardly even have to walk from one place to another.

Your body is designed for movement and effort. In the absence of action it slowly starts to deteriorate. Bone density, muscle strength, and aerobic capacity decline, and your basic metabolism slow. Even if your weight stays the same, your body is replacing muscle with fat, lowering you calorie burn rate even more.

Our approach to fitness starts with you as a unique individual. We will describe a variety of fitness levels, activities, and workout plans to increase your options. But we want you to design a plan that reflects your specific reasons for wanting to be fit along with the particular circumstances of your life and career at this point in time. For example, you may want to be fit so that you can perform better at work; enjoy competitive sports; for health and longevity; to reduce stress; to increase energy and stamina; to participate in more activities with friends and family; or all of these. From our point of view, any reason to want to get fit is a good reason. The time and effort you decide to devote to it will be influenced by issues such as child care or elder care responsibilities, commuting/travel demands, physical challenges, or even by what you enjoy doing.

Getting on the Road to Fitness

Here are the topics we'll cover in this chapter to help you customize a practical, sustainable, and effective plan that puts you on a permanent path to fitness:

- Definition of fitness
- Multiple benefits
- Training principles

Definition of Fitness

Increasing your endurance builds your capacity to maintain a high level of energy and sustained effort. This enhanced work capacity allows you to meet more readily both expected challenges and surprise stressors. Overall fitness includes: aerobic conditioning maintaining flexibility, and building strength.

Aerobics

Let's start with aerobics. The term means "'with oxygen." If you have ever been to high-altitude locales like Mexico City or Aspen, Colorado, you no doubt experienced the fatigue that occurs when there is less oxygen in the air. Simply put, when your body does not get the oxygen it needs, your energy and work capacity diminish. When your fitness increases, your entire system (red blood cells, blood vessels, heart) becomes more efficient in delivering oxygen to tissues and muscles, enabling you to have more energy, endurance, and work capacity. In addition, more oxygen to your brain enables clear thinking and concentration.

Flexibility

Flexibility is another essential component of overall fitness. Stretching and flexing our muscles and joints reduces stiffness and tension. Without flexibility activities our agility, coordination, and balances become impaired, and our risk of injury increases. And if you are injured, your aerobic fitness program may get derailed. Moreover, being flexible simply feels good, through physiological sensations, increased circulation, and in the ability to enjoy a wider range of movement. In addition, as you will learn in Chapter 10, stretching helps to relax you and reduce stress.

Building Strength

The third part of fitness involves building the strength of your muscles, joints, and bones. This is achieved through some form of resistance training activity or weight lifting that taxes your muscles. Strong bones and muscles help us do work and avoid injury. Particularly important as we age, these activities maintain our bone mineral density (BMD), which wards of fractures. Extra muscle mass also can improve how you look and feel; and muscles burn more calories than fat. Overall strength and flexibility help you achieve your aerobic goals by allowing you to participate in a wider range of activities at a higher work rate.

Executive Profile

Eric Foss, CEO, Pepsi Bottling Group (PBG)

PBG was spun off from PepsiCo in March 1999. Since then it has achieved solid success and expansion, growing to a $13 billion business. Eric Foss has been there from day one and has been and continues to be an important contributor to PBG's achievements. He was named CEO in 2006.

I've known Eric for 18 years and he looks about the same as when I first met him. One reason is that he makes fitness a high priority—he misses his one-hour run (on the street or on a treadmill) only five or six days in a year. Eric decided early in his career that being physically fit was necessary if he was to be able to meet ongoing time and travel demands and mental challenges. Each year, he sets his spiritual, family (his wife and three daughters), and fitness goals and priorities to make sure they do not get crowded out by business objectives.

A very high priority for Eric is to maintain a close connection with his daughters. They are all athletes, so in addition to attending their track events and lacrosse matches as often as possible, he has made the time to coach their basketball teams. According to Eric, this has yielded multiple benefits consistent with the Executive Stamina strategy of *combining,* as follows:

- His relationship with his daughters is enhanced through the time he spends with them and the interest they share in basketball.
- His daughters are aware how demanding his job is, including international travel, and so they appreciate his commitment to them and know they can trust him to do what he says he is going to do where they are concerned.
- The coaching skills and flexibility he has gained from working with his daughters' teams has expanded his leadership skills as CEO.
- He receives positive feedback from PBG executives for modeling work/life balance behaviors. They often tell him that his actions inspire them to make similar choices, and have greater impact than speeches on achieving a work/life balance.

Eric's emphasis on health and fitness has been carried forward by David Kasiarz, a human resources vice president at PBG. His three-year program focused on health improvement was one of only two initiatives awarded the C. Everett Koop National Health Award for 2007. This honor is given to programs that demonstrate health improvements and cost savings (healthproject.Stanford.edu).

Multiple Benefits

Although you are no doubt already familiar with many of the benefits of getting fit, we would like to present a comprehensive list here. There may be some you were not aware of and; later on, we will show you how to use this list to motivate yourself to expand your fitness activities.

Increased Energy and Stamina

When you activate your entire circulation system, it increases your oxygen efficiency. Just like a car that will go further on high-octane fuel, your body will have more energy, a greater work capacity, and be less likely to experience fatigue. A NASA study demonstrated that people who exercise regularly can work at full efficiency the entire day, in comparison to those who don't, but lose 50 percent efficiency in the final two hours.

Better Health

In addition to boosting your overall immune system, regular exercise is credited with reducing the risk of high blood pressure, heart disease, obesity, diabetes, stroke, and some cancers. Even consistent, mild exercise, like walking 30 minutes several days a week, can reduce your chances of cardiovascular disease by 40 percent.

Stress Management

The American Council on Exercise reports that exercise breaks down cortisol (which promotes the storage of belly fat) and other hormones that build up during periods of stress. Research has shown that muscle tension also decreases after exercise. A recent British study found that chronically stressed female workers were 73 percent more likely to be obese than their more relaxed coworkers, despite similar exercise patterns. When we exercise, we are also giving ourselves a mental break from our worries, thereby increasing our sense of control and a reduction in stress.

Mood Elation

If you exercise for long enough periods, your body releases more endorphins, which elevate serotonin, the "happiness hormone," which wards off depression, and dopamine, which stimulate our motivation. That is why aerobic exercise programs have proven effective in helping people who are moderately depressed improve their state of mind.

Improved Relationships

Many fitness activities are easily infused with a social component that can help create or maintain relationships. To name a few: walking, hiking, jogging, cycling, rollerblading, cross-country skiing, tennis, racketball, basketball, soccer, dancing, and yoga.

Additionally, the more fit, flexible, and agile you are, the more you will be able and willing to participate in a wide range of activities with business associates, friends, and family.

Better-Quality Sleep

If you exercise during the day, your body will experience a natural tiredness at night. It will seek rest and recovery, and you will be more likely to experience deep, restful sleep, with less tossing and turning. This will increase your chances of waking up feeling refreshed and invigorated, and means you will be more alert and active in meetings.

Improved Decision-Making Capabilities

Oxygen efficiency helps more than our muscles. Increased oxygen to our brain cells also aids our capacity for clear thinking. We can maintain our concentration and focus for longer periods. Many people who push themselves to do more and more difficult workouts also report that the discipline and persistence required to meet physical challenges adds to their mental toughness.

Besides leading to higher mental acuity, being fit helps us to make better decisions. Think of some of the impulsive, faulty decisions you have made when you were feeling tired, stressed, or "burned out."

Image and Impact

Let's face it, though we may not like it, in the business world, executives are often judged on the impression they make physically. When you are fit, you present an image of discipline, self-confidence, and energy. Conversely, if you exhibit low energy or fatigue, people may question your capacity to meet the challenges you are facing. Research using the Campbell Leadership Index confirms that regular exercisers are perceived to have many leadership qualities. When observers rated exercising executives versus nonexercisers, the fit executives were rated as

- Having more energy
- Being better organized
- Being more productive
- Being more optimistic
- Being more reliable
- Having a higher level of trustworthiness
- Being more flexible
- Being more resilient

Corporate Benefits

Fit executives as a group provide more benefits to their companies, as well as to their families. Corporate fitness programs at Steelcase Corporation,

Union Pacific Railroad, DuPont, Canadian Life Assurance Company, and Blue Cross/Blue Shield of Indiana have been shown to:

- Reduce health care costs.
- Increase productivity.
- Lower the incidence of absenteeism.
- Reduce turnover.
- Provide positive return on investment.

Training Principles

In Chapter 7, we will delve into the three levels of fitness to which you may aspire—basic, advanced, and world-class. For each of these levels, we will provide a series of workout plans that will enable you to steadily progress toward your fitness goals. But first we want to introduce you to the proven training principles we used to design those workout sequences, so that you will better understand how the workouts will build your capacity.

To give you encouragement, consider Joshua's own story. He had no experience in endurance racing until his early twenties. His background was in team sports, like soccer and baseball. To catch up with his peers, he focused solely on building his capacity using the principles we offer here. Within two years, he was winning ultra endurance races involving 24 hours of continuous riding, on his way to a professional career and competing in the world championships. In 2004, he was invited to coach five participants in the Lance Armstrong/Bristol Myers Squibb Tour of Hope. The majority of the riders in this cross-country, eight-day journey from Los Angeles to Washington, DC were cancer survivors. Some of them were recreational cyclists who were riding only an hour or two a week, so to get them ready for the event, Joshua had to train them to be able to ride in six-hour blocks for eight days. In the six-month preparatory period, he had to ensure that they maximized their effort while their body capacity progressed at a sustainable pace. All the riders were able to dramatically increase their capacity and complete the event in style, to be welcomed by thousands of people waiting near the nation's capitol. The principles that follow are what allowed all of this success to occur.

- Ease into Your Program
- Do Systematic, Progressive Workouts
- Make Fitness Permanent

Ease into Your New Program

If you attempt a workout that is too far above your current capacity, you risk aches and pains, injury, and/or discouragement. We always recommend checking with your physician first; find out what he or she thinks is a reasonable beginning point given your current physical condition. In addition, to ensure a clearer understanding where to start and how you are progressing, we recommend the following approach:

Conduct Fitness Testing

A number of gyms have facilities for testing your overall fitness, through treadmill tests, flexibility measurements, and strength exercises. Executive health centers, like the Cooper Clinic in Dallas, provide state-of-the-art testing in these areas, in addition to conducting extensive medical check-ups. If you don't have the time, money, or access to those options, there are several ways to gauge your fitness on your own. Although there are a few options, for simplicity we recommend the following test.

Your fitness level is a measure of your body's capacity to work. If you are more fit than your peers, you can perform at higher levels with a similar expenditure of effort. In this test, a quicker time at a lower heart rate signals higher fitness. Gauging your current level will help you select which one of Joshua's workout plans (basic, advanced, world-class) to start with. You can also retake the test every three months to monitor your

---

Rockport Fitness Walking Test (RFWT)

This is a simple test, ideal for people who may have difficulty running but can walk briskly. The test involves walking as quickly as you can, without running, for one mile. At the end of the mile, take your pulse by placing a finger on your wrist for 10 seconds. Multiply the number of beats you feel by 6 to obtain your heart rate. Then go to www .rockportfitnesswalkingtest.com and type in your sex, age, weight, distance, and heart rate, and you will obtain a score measuring your aerobic capacity (VO_2-max) and be able to compare yourself with your peers.

---

progress. The following tables list sample scores and relative levels of fitness.

MALE: 50 YEARS, 180 POUNDS

Time	Heart Rate	Result
14 minutes	85	>93% Excellent (higher than 93% of peers)
14 minutes	115	>77% Good
14 minutes	135	>66% Basic
18 minutes	60	>50% (average of peers)

FEMALE: 40 YEARS, 130 POUNDS

Time	Heart Rate	Result
16 minutes	90	>94% Excellent
16 minutes	135	>62% Basic
17 minutes	100	>77% Good
18 minutes	90	>66% Basic

Do Systemic, Progressive Workouts

In Chapter 7, we will be presenting a series of workout plans, specific to your current level and your fitness goals. Embedded in these schemes are the following principles that allow you to optimize the effectiveness of each workout and derive the most benefit from the time you can devote to building your capacity.

Progression

A good workout will put the right amount of stress on your body. Too little, and there will be few gains; too much, and you risk setting back your entire program. Your plan will gradually progress in challenging you, helping you maintain the right amount of motivation and the effort your body needs to develop.

The workouts allow progression in two ways. First, your system will increase its ability to work harder, and the workout plan allows your body to get used to this higher level. Second, your increased strength and endurance then enable you to do the harder workouts that take you even further.

Interval Training

If you incorporate short bursts of high-intensity exercise into some of your workouts, you can turbo-charge your fitness gains. Interval training, which involves injecting alternating peaks and valleys into your routine, has been shown to produce more improvement than steady efforts alone. A study published in *The Journal of Applied Physiology* (2005) found that 75 percent of the college-age men and women tested doubled their endurance after just two weeks of interval training. Jason Talaman, an exercise scientist at the University of Guelph in Ontario, has also found that interval training improves the body's ability to burn fat even during moderate exercise. Note, however, in keeping with our principle of safety and easing into an exercise program, interval training will only be part of those workouts we provide for regular exercisers.

This increase of intensity, pushing the lungs, heart, and muscles to work harder, is what led to Joshua's development and the Tour of Hope participants' success. In the plans you will read about, from which you'll select for your own program, you will be guided to use one of five intensity levels at different points in your workout. We will show you how to determine intensity levels using measures such as perceived effort, heart rate, breathing patterns, and ease of communicating.

Adaptation, Overload, and Recovery

Adaptation is the process by which we increase our fitness and strength. If a new demand is placed on our body (without overwhelming us), over time it adapts to handle the experience in the future. Signals are sent to your muscles and circulatory system to grow stronger to meet increased demand. But this wonderful process occurs *only* if we allow for the right amount of rest and recovery. This is why our workout plans balance intense effort with recovery. We want you to be able to move forward feeling fresh and energized. If you keep pushing your body to work harder without giving it a change to repair and recover, your fitness will plateau, and eventually take a downturn. That is why it is so important that your workout plans alternate between easy and more challenging activities.

Make Fitness Permanent

By now you should be convinced that making fitness an integral part of your life is not a "nice to do" but a "need to do." The time you devote to it is not a luxury; it is a personal and business *necessity* you need to plan for. Yet we remind you, we are creatures of habit, and unless we already have some form of vigorous activity in our lives, it can be difficult to accommodate this critical activity in our daily schedules. That is why we offer the following techniques to stack the odds in favor of establishing a long-term fitness pattern in your life.

Self-Motivation

Some people prefer to work with a personal trainer or fitness coach, or even a friend or family member, to encourage you to exercise. But the simple fact is, eventually the success of your fitness plan will depend on your ability to motivate yourself. You will need this to get started and to lean on along the way when you encounter obstacles. We offer these two important guidelines to self-motivate:

- *Focus on the benefits.* Earlier in this chapter, you read about the different ways you can benefit from being fit. Review those now and identify the ones that are most important to you; make a list and keep it handy to remind you. Before you work out think about how doing so is going to help you take another step towards your fitness goals. Do not—we repeat, do not—think about what you don't like to do or how difficult it will be.
- *Shape your destiny.* Every day your body replaces about 1 percent of its cells. That means that in three to four months you have an opportunity to regenerate most of your body's building blocks. Are you going to strengthen them or allow them to get weaker? You have a chance to shape your destiny. Research shows that the aging process can actually be very slow and gradual. You have the opportunity to create a healthy strong body that will sustain you for a long time. Take it!

Combining and Enjoying

Two key principles of our fitness approach are *combining* and *enjoying*. Combining simply means to meld as many other goals, priorities, or activities with your fitness practice as you can. At a minimum, this saves you time and, potentially, makes the process itself *enjoyable*, something to which you actually look forward.

Examples of combining fitness with other activities to make your workouts more enjoyable, or at least save you time, include:

- Commuting, through walking, cycling, or running all or part of the distance.
- Learning, by reading or watching videos while on a stationary bike or treadmill, or listening to podcasts or books on tape.
- Watching your favorite TV shows, movies, or sporting events; listening to your favorite music; or reading newspapers and magazines (again, while on a stationary bike, treadmill, or Stairmaster).
- Doing work like reading important papers on stationary equipment or thinking about key issues when walking or running.
- Communing with nature while hiking, walking, or mountain-biking.
- Forming new, or solidifying current, relationships by engaging in fitness activities with friends, family, or business associates.
- Contributing to charitable causes by signing up for fund-raising races/walks or "sweat equity" projects that align with your societal priorities.
- Engaging in a sport or event that meets your need to compete.
- Experiencing "flow" by finding activities that are challenging enough to command your full attention.

You'll also find it worthwhile to experiment with different activities or sports, because if you find one you truly love to do, you'll find you won't need any help getting motivated. Here are some that work for a number of people:

- Cross-country skiing
- Rollerblading
- Dancing (ballroom, salsa, hip-hop, Bollywood, aerobic, flamenco etc.)

- Soccer, basketball, tennis, swimming, racquetball, squash
- Yoga (power yoga, bikram yoga, etc.)
- Rowing, kayaking

It is more difficult to become fit with certain, less-active sports, such as golf, but if you find one you love, aim to participate at a higher level. The point is, there are countless options available to make fitness fun, or at least not a chore, so be creative and willing to try many things until you find what works for you.

Executive Profiles

Daniel Naor, Senior Vice President, Frito-Lay, and Ty Mitchell, Economist, U.S. General Accountability Office (GAO)

Daniel Naor

Daniel Naor, senior vice president of Transformation and Strategy for Frito-Lay, has a crucial and complex role in leading major business innovations and change programs across his company. His background in management consulting (he was a partner at McKinsey), along with his advanced degrees, mean Daniel could choose from a wide variety of executive positions. But as a single parent (he shares joint custody of his daughter, Nathalie), he has made career choices that enable him to balance his roles as father and executive. To accomplish this balancing act, Daniel fully leverages communications technology (phone and videoconferencing, remote computer access, PDAs, etc.). He also credits his current CEO, Al Carey, with being an excellent model of someone who achieves work/life balance.

Daniel has also become something of an expert at incorporating the combining and enjoying principles to his personal fitness program. His passion is ballroom and Latin dancing, and he has won many competitions, including first place in the Super-Rama Pro-Am Scholarship event in New York City. He also works out with a personal trainer several times a week. One night a week and twice on the weekends he does cardio, stretching and weight training at his fully equipped personal gym, which he built in his home with the help of his trainer. His fitness program is much enhanced by the presence of his daughter, who, since the tender age of 7, has demonstrated an interest in and talent for dancing. She has even been his partner in competitions and performances. Recently, she started participating in his workouts with Daniel's trainer.

Ty Mitchell

Twelve years ago, after his son was born, Ty Mitchell, an economist with the U.S. General Accountability Office in Washington, DC, bought a house in Arlington, Virginia, about 10 miles from his office. Every workday since then he has been commuting to work by bicycle. It takes him about 35 minutes each way. This activity, combined with some stretching exercises and pushups after his rides, comprises his entire fitness program. Ty has found his daily bike ride to serve many purposes.

- It helps him live in alignment with his values regarding the environment.
- He cuts down on his commuting time, and by combining commuting with fitness, eliminates "gym time."
- It makes him happy to make it home in time to have dinner with his children.

Customize and Commit

When you learn to combine and enjoy fitness activities, you will find yourself several steps closer to customizing your fitness plan. We encourage you to design a program that will work for you *now*, that you will be motivated to implement and be able to sustain. Here are some additional factors to consider when designing your fitness schedule.

- *Personal commitments:* Where are you in your career and personal life? Are you are a parent? If so, what are the ages of your children? Are you involved in a new romantic relationship? Are you responsible for care of an elder? Do you hold an important position at a place of worship or school board? All these and many others relevant to your life need to be factored in to your program.
- *Job scope:* What are the current demands of your role? Are you in a turnaround situation? Launching a new product? Is your company under attack from a competitor?
- *Travel demands:* How long is your daily commute? How many days a month are you "on the road," out of town?
- *Optimum time:* Based on your commitments and schedule, when is the best time to work in your fitness activities: before work, at lunchtime, after work, on weekends?

Take the time to answer these questions so you can more effectively design and commit to a fitness plan. Staying fit requires planning. Demonstrate your commitment by blocking out time on your calendar. If you don't know in advance when you plan to work out, and set aside time, it is highly likely something or someone will get in the way. Don't forget to let the key people in your world know about you workout schedule—including your administrative assistant, your business associates (boss, direct reports, peers), and your family and friends. Begin to treating this time as sacred, or at least special. This means that you or someone else will need a powerful reason for you to be willing to sacrifice your workout for another priority.

Be Consistent

In the sixties a physician, William Glazer, coined the term, *positive addiction,* to describe those activities for which we can develop the good kind of addictive "cravings." Clearly, some fitness activities meet this definition. If you consistently follow your workout plans, you will get to a point where the good feelings in your body, endorphins in your system, and comfort in your routine combine to create a positive addiction. If you miss one of your normal workouts, not only will you mind, but your consistency up to this point will allow you the confidence to get right back on track the next day. Without this consistency, missing a workout easily turns into missing a few more and eventually you can lose momentum. Staying consistent reduces this possibility.

Get Support

In addition to self-motivating, combining and enjoying, customizing and committing, and being consistent, we also recommend that you build a support network. Consider for inclusion in your network the following:

Trainer/coach: If you can afford it, work with a trainer or fitness coach, an expert and motivator who can monitor your technique and progress. In terms of commitment, it helps to make an agreement with this person that you will pay for sessions you cancel on short notice.

Workout partner: When a friend or colleague shows up at your door ready to run or go to the gym or a yoga class, it is more difficult to renege on your commitment. If it fits your schedule and circumstances, we highly recommend that you team up with someone who will, by his or her presence, keep you aligned with your fitness priority.

Summary

The techniques presented in this chapter are not foolproof—all of us can rationalize and make excuses for not exercising. Our goal was to give you the tools to overcome the most common obstacles preventing you from initiating and then persevering with your program. The workout plans you will read about in the next chapter are designed to progressively prepare you to take the next steps on your path. But before you go there, be aware of common excuses you are likely to make, so you can be prepared to deal with them:

- *I'm too tired.* If you are too tired from lack of sleep or illness, this is valid; but more often than not, we become energized if we just start moving.
- *I don't have control of my time.* Chapter 12 addresses how to take control of your schedule.
- *Working out is not fun.* Reread the principle of combining and enjoying in this chapter to remind yourself how to make exercising more pleasurable.
- *I don't have the time.* Remember, when you say you don't have time for fitness, you are really saying it is not a priority for you.

Now you are ready to enhance your plans. In Chapter 7, we describe in detail specific programs for basic, advanced, and world-class fitness levels.

7 | Your Lifelong Fitness Plan

Now that you are aware of the multiple benefits of increasing your fitness, as well as the necessary principles to follow, in this chapter Joshua and I will go into specifics regarding defining and developing your own customized fitness plan, categorized by basic, advanced, world-class fitness levels.

To customize your plan, first use the factors in the section "Finding Your Fitness Level" to identify at which of these three levels will be best to begin. Then, using the Combining and Enjoying section in the Chapter 6, select your specific activities, such as reading while on the stationary bike, to plug into the weekly plans. Remember these activities can change as needed to meet your demands for ease, spontaneity, and enjoyment. The next step is to solidify your plan by blocking out the time in your schedule and entering in your new workouts immediately. Please reference the Customize and Commit section in Chapter 6 for the ways to do this most effectively.

Finding Your Fitness Level

You will determine your fitness level by how often, how long, and how intensely you work out, as well as your goals for the future. If you answer yes to any of the following statements, we suggest that you begin at the basic level of fitness activity. For everyone else, please use the three factors that follow to determine at which level to begin.

- You don't exercise at all or are a sporadic exerciser.
- You received a 50 percent or lower score on the Rockport mile walking tests, or didn't think you were ready to take it.
- You feel that you are at basic level of fitness and want to maintain it.
- You want to gradually build your exercise capability to the advanced level.

Here are three factors to consider before you start in order determine which level is best.

1. *Fitness test results:* If you were in the 60 to 66 percent range on the one-mile walking test, you are at the basic level. These plans will help you maintain that. If you want to experience more of the benefits of fitness, choose the higher volume (time spent exercising) and the higher intensity (time spent in high exertion activities) plan. If you were at 50 percent or below, your initial goal is to get to the basic level scores. Start with the easier set of workouts.

2. *Current activity level:* Over the past six months, how often have you engaged in aerobic, flexibility, or resistance training? How long were your workouts? How difficult? These are important questions, whose answers should guide you to your starting point. If you achieved a basic score (less than 65 percent) on the fitness test but haven't been exercising much lately, start slow and build from there. Implementing a plan also means altering your schedule, which may require some time to put into practice. If the workouts are too easy, you can always increase the length and intensity.

3. *Goals:* We are only looking at two levels of goals: *maintenance* and *progression*. If your goal is maintenance, you can strive for workout levels that deliver an aerobic benefit and stay within a desired range, (see below for details on intensity levels). If your goal is to increase your capacity and/or reach the advanced or world class level, then you will need to pay attention to the hard/easy portions of your workouts and spend more time at the higher intensity levels.

For each of the three fitness levels you will find aerobic, flexibility and strength workouts unique to that plan.

Basic Fitness

People define basic fitness in a variety of ways. For us, each way of defining basic fitness is useful if it helps you determine where to start and how to customize your workout plan. The next section defines three approaches: Guidelines from Leading Institutions, 10,000 Step Approach, and Joshua's Fitness Plans. Based on your needs you will select one of these approaches as the best one for you to reach and sustain your basic level of fitness.

Guidelines from Leading Institutions

Experts in the field of health and exercise vary somewhat in what they believe constitutes the minimum amount of activity each of us should be doing. In reviewing the advice presented by the Cooper Clinic, the American College of Sports Medicine, the American Heart Association, and the Surgeon General's Office we arrived at a range of recommendations. Our motto, by the way, is "Improvement, Not Perfection," and we suggest that you set a goal and a plan that makes sense for you based on that advice.

Aerobic Activity

Most of the organizations we consulted suggest that you do at least 30 minutes of moderate aerobic activity several days a week. For example, if that is walking at a moderate pace, you would expend about 1,000 calories per week during your walks, bringing you to the Surgeon General's minimum. The Cooper Clinic sets the minimum at 1,500 calories per week, burned off in aerobic activity. To meet this standard, you would have to walk longer (40–45 minutes); or, if you keep to 30 minutes, walk quicker or run to cover a greater distance (walking or running a mile burns 100 calories).

You can build on your minutes during the day in 10-minute increments. If you prefer this approach, the 10-minute activity should be more intense than a normal walking pace (e.g., climbing stairs, running, brisk walking, hiking uphill, fast cycling, aerobic dancing, and so on).

Moderate-intensity exercise increases your heart rate and, if sustained, allows you to gain an aerobic benefit. Ranges vary but generally these organizations recommend that you get your heart rate up to 50 to 70 percent of maximum capacity. Maximum heart rate (MHR) can be calculated using different formulas but the one we recommend is:

$$MHR = 206 - (\text{your age} \times .685)$$

A 60-year-old, then, would have an MHR of 165, and a 45-year-old an MHR of 175.

Flexibility

Flexibility exercises such as stretching, yoga or Pilates are included in a fitness program to maintain a range of motion, and prevent muscular tension or injury. Whichever approach you choose, you should stretch the major muscle groups twice a week (see more on the uses of yoga in Chapter 9).

Strength

Yoga and Pilates can add to your core strength, but leading experts also recommend some form of resistance training. The goal of resistance training or weight lifting is to enhance strength, muscle endurance, and bone health as well as maintain your level of fat free mass.

The exercise should be progressive, so that your muscles work hard, without injury, and then recover. The major muscle groups (arms, chest, back, shoulders, legs, midsection) should be stimulated twice a week. Usually, this can be done in a series of 8 to 10 exercises. Each exercise is done in a set of 8 to 12 repetitions. If you are older, or concerned about injury, you can safely derive equal benefit by using less weight but doing each repetition more slowly and carefully (10 seconds to lift and 5 seconds to return to position).

The 10,000-Step Approach to Basic Fitness

Building on the research about activity and health, some fitness experts came to the conclusion it would be more motivational for people, and easier for them to measure their efforts, if the basic fitness goal was set at 10,000 steps a day. Think about it: most of us take about 2,400 steps a mile, which works out to about 4 miles a day. To track the number of actual steps/day you take, however, you need to wear a *pedometer*, a popular device that records each step and offers instant feedback. When Chevron introduced its "10K a day" program, 40 percent of its 22,000 U.S. employees signed up for pedometers. (As of the summer of 2007, the participants had taken a total of 814 million steps and lost an average of 4 pounds.)

In the course of a normal day, most people will walk about 5,000 steps just going about their daily chores and work responsibilities, so finding other ways to incorporate walking is necessary to get to 10,000. Here are some suggestions: Use the stairs instead of the elevator, park farther away from the office or in shopping centers, speak to someone in person instead of using e-mail or the phone, stroll with a friend while you are brainstorming about a project.

If you like this idea, get yourself a pedometer and increase your daily step total gradually. To get started, contact the Health Enhancement Services at www.10Kaday.com. They can provide you with pedometers and walking programs.

Joshua's Fitness Plans

These four-week sequences of workouts (which can be reset each month at higher levels) are designed to get people moving and to help them experience an increase in energy and reduction in stress brought about by regular exercise. The key to a progressive plan is the inclusion of varying levels of intensity to maximize the time spent training, so please use the information below to begin to understand how to use intensity levels to get the most out of your training. If you are already exercising, you can take advantage of the progressive nature of the workouts and start at higher intensity levels.

Intensity Levels

To maximize your training benefit, these plans direct you to work out at a specific intensity, or effort, level for each workout. Many people are confused about how hard and how long to push themselves. These plans remove the guesswork, so you know what you should be doing at each stage of your workout. Starting with whatever your fitness level is now, varying intensities will allow you to realize gains from interval training, which allows your body to fully recover. The following is a guide to intensity levels, which range from 1 to 5. (Note: For the basic plan, you will be at the lower intensities; but we describe all five levels here, for convenience).

First, however, because increased effort will be apparent to you in different ways, we introduce you to four important indicators to help you develop a keen awareness of how hard you are working. This will help you smoothly transition between the stages of your workout.

- *Perceived effort:* This is the most basic indicator. How taxing does the workout feel? This will range from the mild effort of a normal walking pace to maximum exertion that you can sustain for only a minute or two. As you learn to pay attention to your muscles, amount of perspiration, and other personal indicators, you will develop a clear sense of how hard an activity is for you.
- *Breathing rate:* More effort requires more oxygen, and so your pace of breathing increases. At lower levels, the increase will be so slight that you may not notice it. At the higher levels, your breaths will become short and rapid.
- *Ability to talk:* Our capacity to converse parallels our breathing rate, so we include it as indicator because it provides a quick test of intensity. You can continue a normal conversation at level 1, but as you increase effort, it will be more and more difficult to talk.

- *Heart rate:* From a medical perspective, this is the most accurate sign of the effort your body is making. You can measure this by wearing a heart rate monitor, using the heart rate sensors on a treadmill or stationary bike, or taking your pulse for 10 seconds and multiplying by 6. Each intensity level will match with a certain heart rate range based on your maximum heart rate (MHR), as defined previously in this chapter.

Now, here are the definitions of the five levels: Refer to these once you take a look at your plan so you have an idea of how hard each workout will be. Then you will reference them as you begin to understand more and more how hard you are pushing yourself and how hard you need to be going. They will eventually become second hand to you where you can easily know whether you are at a level 5 or 3.

Level 1: Perceived effort is light to very light. You will know you are working but your muscles will feel slight to no strain, and you will maintain an almost normal, easy walking pace. Your breathing rate will increase slightly but not be significantly noticeable. Your ability to talk will be about the same or almost the same as when you are not exercising, meaning you can carry on a conversation as normal. Heart rate = 55–65 percent maximum

Level 2: Perceived effort is easy to moderate. You will feel the effort in your muscles but not feel a significant strain. You will also feel as if you can maintain this pace for a while. Your breathing rate will not be rhythmic but very controlled, and you will not feel out of breath. You will be able to talk in long sentences but notice how doing so stresses your breathing. Heart rate = 70–75 percent maximum

Level 3: Perceived effort is more difficult. Your muscles will now feel consistent strain. Your breathing rate will be rhythmic but also deeper and more labored. You will still feel in control of your breath, and be able to talk in short sentences, but holding a long conversation would be difficult. Heart rate = 80–85 percent maximum

Level 4: Perceived effort is very difficult. Your muscles will feel extremely strained. This pace is a very high level of intensity, which can only be reached by individuals in the advanced or world-class plans and held at most for 8 to 20 minutes before needing to stop. Your breathing rate will be rapid and deep but still rhythmic and in control. You will be able to speak only three to four words at a time, and be unable to express a full sentence without losing your breath. Heart rate = 85–90 percent maximum

Level 5: Perceived effort is the most difficult. Your muscles will feel intense strain, and you will be able to maintain the effort for only 30 seconds to 3 minutes. Your breathing will no longer be rhythmic or controlled, rather short and rapid. You will not be able to talk at this pace, as you will be using all your effort to breathe.

Our primary goal in describing these difficulty ranges is to optimize your workout time; our secondary goal, which is as important, is to increase your body/mind awareness. Paying attention to your breathing, heart rate, muscle strain, and so on will, over time, evolve into a keener sense of what is happening to you during the workday. In Chapters 9 and 10 you will learn a variety of techniques for making important adjustments during the workday to reduce stress and recover balance. Your deployment of each of these skills will be enhanced by your awareness of when you need them most.

Four-Week Progression Plans

The four-week progression plans detailed in the table in this section will enable you to exercise longer at higher levels. You will eventually be able to do three level 2 workouts of 20 minutes or more a week. By gradually adding level 3 minutes, you are preparing yourself for the next increase in your capacity.

For each aerobic workout, to determine the intensity level and time spent at each level you will refer to the second column in the table. For example, in Week 2 Day 3 of the Basic Fitness Sequence, the overall aerobic time of 30 minutes is accomplished by following the levels in the second column listed as level 1: 10 min, level 2: 10 min, level 1: 10 min.

To continue advancing you can repeat this four-week sequence again and again, increasing either the workout length or the workout intensity each week. We suggest that you alternate between increasing the time spent working out one week and the time spent at higher intensity the next week, just as shown in this four-week plan (See pages 122–123). You will make the most consistent sustained progress by maintaining your increase rate at the 10 to 15 percent range from week to week. To clearly understand how to increase from one week to the next, please note the *sections after each week to determine how each week increased from the next.

As you can see, by not increasing too rapidly, this system gives your body an opportunity to rest, recover, and adapt during the week and over the month. In general, you can increase your level of intensity by picking up the pace (walking to jogging), or introducing climbs, or by increasing the difficulty level if you use gym equipment such as a treadmill, stationary bike, or Stairmaster. The details on the next two key components of your fitness sequence, flexibility and strength workouts, are below.

Flexibility Workouts

Stretching activities are part of all the weekly plans. These exercises can be used effectively in the morning to jump-start your day, after workouts to reduce stiffness, and, as you will read in Chapter 10 on yoga, at the office at key points in the workday.

The following is a complete workout for full-body flexibility. Once you learn each stretch and increase your body awareness, you can pinpoint specific exercises as needed.

Guidelines for Stretching

Even though stretching requires no formal training, there are a few ground rules you should follow to maximize both your results and enjoyment of

WEEK 1

Day 1	Day 2	Day 3	Day 4	Day 5	Day 6	Day 7
Aerobic: 25 min	Strength training: 35 min, whole body	Aerobic: 30 min	Strength training: 35 min, whole body	Aerobic: 25 min	Aerobic: 40 min	Day of rest
Level 2: 25 min		Level 1: 30 min		Level 2: 25 min	Level 1: 20 min 2: 20 min	
Flexibility activity: 20 min		Flexibility activity: 20 min		Flexibility activity 20 min		

WEEK 2*

Day 1	Day 2	Day 3	Day 4	Day 5	Day 6	Day 7
Aerobic: 25 min	Strength training: 35 min, whole body	Aerobic: 30 min	Strength training: 35 min, whole body	Aerobic: 25 min	Aerobic: 40 min	Day of rest
Level 2: 25 min		Level 1: 10 min 2: 10 min 1: 10 min		Level 2: 25 min	Level 1: 20 min 2: 20 min	
Flexibility activity: 20 min		Flexibility activity: 20 min		Flexibility activity: 20 min		

*Increase **Intensity** by adding 10 minutes of level 2 to day 3's workout.

WEEK 3*

Day 1	Day 2	Day 3	Day 4	Day 5	Day 6	Day 7
Aerobic: 35 min	Strength training: 35 min, whole body	Aerobic: 30 min	Strength training: 35 min, whole body	Aerobic: 35 min	Aerobic: 40 min	Day of rest
Level 2: 35 min		Level: 1: 10 min 2: 10 min 1: 10 min		Level 2: 35 min	Level: 1: 20 min 2: 20 min	
Flexibility activity: 20 min		Flexibility activity: 20 min		Flexibility activity 20 min		

*Increase **length of aerobic activity** by adding 10 minutes to day 1 and day 5's workouts.

WEEK 4*

Day 1	Day 2	Day 3	Day 4	Day 5	Day 6	Day 7
Aerobic: 35 min	Strength training: 35 min, whole body	Aerobic: 30 min	Strength training: 35 min, whole body	Aerobic: 35 min	Aerobic: 40 min	Day of rest
Level: [2: 12 min 3: 3 min] repeat 2 × 2: 5 min		Level: 1: 20 min 2: 10 min 1: 10 min		Level: [2: 12 min 3: 3 min] repeat 2 × 2: 5 min	Level: 1: 20 min 2: 20 min	
Flexibility activity: 20 min		Flexibility activity: 20 min		Flexibility activity: 20 min		

*Increase **Intensity** by adding 6 minutes of level 3 to day 1 and day 5's workouts.

your routine. To begin, you should be relaxed and engage in a sustained stretch with your attention focused on the muscles you are targeting.

Basic Stretching Guidelines

1. Do not bounce up and down, and you should never stretch to the point of pain. If you stretch correctly and regularly, you will find that every movement you make becomes easier. Keep in mind; it will take time to loosen up tight muscles or muscle groups, however the time is quickly forgotten as you start to feel good.

2. When you begin, spend 10 to 15 seconds in each stretch. Stretch to the point at which you feel mild tension, and relax as you hold the stretch. The tension should subside as you hold the position. If it does not, ease up slightly and find the degree of tension that is comfortable. You should be able to say, "I feel the stretch, but it is not painful." The easy stretch reduces muscular tightness and tension, and readies the tissues for the developmental stretch.

3. After the easy stretch, slowly move a fraction of an inch further until you again feel a mild tension; hold for 10 to 15 seconds. Be in control. Again, the tension should diminish; if not, ease off slightly. The developmental stretch is designed to increase your flexibility as you continue your routine.

4. During a stretch session, keep your breathing slow, deep, and under control. Never hold your breath while stretching. Breathing helps you to relax, which will in turn relax the muscles you are stretching.

Increased Flexibility Routine

1. *Torso and arm stretch:* Stand with feet hip-width apart. Inhale; reach arms out to the side, interlacing hands together above head. Exhale; turn palms up toward the ceiling, stretching the arms up. Stretch rib cage toward the ceiling without jutting chest forward. Keeping feet firmly planted on floor, stretch interlaced fingers to

the right. Keep body squared to wall and in alignment. Come to center. Stretch to left. Bring arms down. Repeat 3 to 5 times.

2. *Toe touch—hamstring and spine stretch:* Stand with feet hip-width apart. Exhale; bend at the waist, reaching fingers toward the toes/floor. Do not lock the knees but work to keep them straight. You can do this by lifting the flesh above the knees. (If back thigh muscles are extremely tight, or you have a lower-back problem, bend the knees slightly.) Stay for 3 to 5 cycles of breath. Repeat 3 to 5 times.

3. *Split-leg toe touch:* Stand with feet 3.5 feet apart. Stretch arms out to side, parallel to floor. Exhale; reach right hand across body and down, touching left toes, if possible. Inhale; come up. Repeat opposite side. Do 10 repetitions.

4. *Chest stretch:* Stand in the center of a doorjamb. With left and right hands, hold sides of doorjamb, at wrist level. Step forward, moving hands up doorway, lean pelvis forward, keeping legs straight. Lift chest up toward the ceiling; stay for 3 to 5 cycles of breath. Step back or release jamb to come out. Repeat 3 to 5 times.

5. *Shoulder/upper back stretch:* Stand with feet hip-width apart. Reach arms up, parallel to floor. Hold left wrist with right hand, and pull left arm across centerline of body to the right, as far as your body will allow. Keep your feet firmly planted on the floor, continuing to stretch left arm to right. Stay 3 for to 5 cycles of breath. Repeat other side.

6. *Forward lunge—hip and groin stretch:* Stand with feet hip-width apart. Bend at the hip crease, fingertips coming toward the floor. Step right foot back 4 to 5 feet. Bring hands firmly on floor, on either side of left foot (if necessary, place hands on chair or bench). Sink into lunge; square hips. Stay for 3 to 5 cycles of breath. Step right foot forward. Repeat left side.

7. *Sitting—hamstring and spine stretch:* Sit with legs straight and parallel to the floor. Inhale; lengthen spine up toward ceiling. Exhale; reach arms toward feet. Keep reaching thighs into floor (it releases the spine). Stay for 3 to 5 cycles of breath. Come up; repeat 3–5 times.

(Continued)

Increased Flexibility Routine (Continued)

8. *Knees to chest:* Lie on floor. Bring knees to chest, holding just be-low the knees (you may need a strap or towel to reach). On exhale, draw knees closer to chest as you stretch your tailbone away from your head. Stay for 3 to 5 breaths. Repeat one more time.
9. *Sitting twist:* Sit with both legs straight and parallel to the floor. Keeping the left leg straight, cross the right leg across body; place foot near outside of left knee, right hand on floor near right buttock. Wrap left arm and hand around right bent knee. Lift spine up toward ceiling. Exhale; deepen twist to right. (Instead of looking over right shoulder, keep eye on left big toe to bring twist higher into upper spine and out of neck). Repeat opposite side.
10. *Reclining spinal twist:* Lie on your back on the floor/carpet. Bend knees, feet flat on floor. Exhale; let both knees tip over to right side; left buttock comes off the floor. Try to keep both shoulder blades on floor. Stay for 3 to 5 cycles of breath. Inhale; come back to center. Repeat opposite side.

Strength Training Workouts

Getting started with strength training can be confusing—which exercises should you do? How many repetitions and sets of repetitions? How much weight?

The routine you choose will be based on your fitness goals as well as the equipment you have available and the time you allow for workouts. All three plans include two of these workouts per week.

Types of Strength Training Workouts

■ There are four basic types of exercises: machine, free weight, com-pound movement, and bands. Please read the descriptions to deter-mine which type is best suited for your needs. Machine exercises are done on devices that have adjustable seats, with handles attached to the weight, which is also adjustable. Machine exercises help prevent injury by guiding your movement and helping ensure proper form. For this reason, beginners and those with limited strength will find machines very helpful, comforting, and beneficial, while also producing great gains in strength.

- If and when you are comfortable handling free weights, you will move on to these exercises because they ensure other muscles in your body are working as you exercise in order to stabilize and control the weight. This is an advantage over machines and helps produce a balanced body that can stabilize itself, which reduces the risk of injury in your life. For this reason, free weights and the following compound movements are part of the advanced and world class plans.

- Compound movement exercises involve more than one joint at a time. For example, a bicep curl moves just your elbow, whereas a bench press uses your wrists, elbows, and shoulder joints. For this reason, these exercises work a number of muscle groups at a time, as well as strengthen the stabilizer muscles that you rely on throughout your day. Compound movements are used to achieve maximum strength gains that apply to your real-world activities and health, as well when you are short on time because they work so many muscle groups with each movement. These are the ideal exercise to include in your fitness plan.

- Resistance band exercises are popular and recommended because they can be used at home or on the road with relative ease. You can modify all of the strength workouts in this program for use with resistance bands.

Guidelines

1. Always warm up before you start lifting weights. This helps get your muscles ready and prevents injury. You can warm up with light cardio or by doing a light set of each exercise before going to heavier weights.

2. Lift and lower your weights at a moderate, controlled pace. Don't use momentum to lift the weight. If you have to swing to get the weight up, chances are you are using too much weight for your current level of fitness.

3. Breathe. Don't hold your breath, and make sure you are using full range of motion throughout the movement.

4. Stand up straight. Pay attention to your posture, and engage your abdominals in every movement you're doing to keep your balance and protect your spine.

5. To determine how much weight you should use, start with a light weight and perform one set. Continue adding weight until you can do *only* the desired number of repetitions. The last rep should be difficult, but not impossible, and you should be able to maintain good form.

6. Do large muscle group exercises before small muscle group exercises.

7. Do multiple-joint exercises before single-joint exercises.

WARNING

If you are unsure of the proper technique for an exercise, please seek the guidance of a personal trainer.

Basic Strength Training Plan

Initially in this plan you will choose one exercise per body part (see the following list). If you are a beginner at strength training or haven't been doing this type of exercise recently, we recommend that you start with only one set for each exercise you choose. A set can be a series of 8 to 12 repetitions of an exercise.

The plans call for you to do two full-body workouts, twice a week, separated by at least 48 hours.

Full Body Workout Using Machines

    Chest: Chest press, fly machine

    Upper back: Pull down, seated row machine

    Shoulders: Overhead press machine

    Legs: Leg press, leg extension machine

    Biceps: Curl machine

    Triceps: Triceps extension machine

    Lower back: Extension machine

    Core/abdominal: Crunch machine

When you are able to complete a set of 12 repetitions without excessive strain, you can progress in three ways:

- Start doing two sets, 10 repetitions each
- Increase weight lifted by 5 to 10 percent
- Move to free weight exercises detailed in the advanced fitness strength training section of this chapter.

Advanced Fitness

These workout plans are for people who are already regular exercisers and want to leverage interval training and progression to attain the additional benefits of fitness. Fitter is better: more energy, more stamina for sustained effort, more positive sensations in every step, and more confidence in your ability to meet challenges.

Please refer to the section Joshua's Workout Plans in the Basic Fitness section for the details on how these four-week plans progress as well as how to determine your desired intensity levels for each workout. In these plans you will be increasing the frequency, duration, and intensity of workouts as per the guidelines detailed in the "Four-Week Progression Plans" section of the Basic Fitness section. As you will see in the *sections after each week of the plan to follow, you will still increase at most 10–15

WEEK 1

	Day 1	Day 2	Day 3	Day 4	Day 5	Day 6	Day 7
	Aerobic: 35 min	Aerobic: 30 min	Aerobic: 35 min	Aerobic: 30 min	Aerobic: 35 min	Aerobic: 60 min	Day of rest
	Level:	Level: 2: 30 min	Level:	Level: 2: 30 min	Level:	Level: 2: 60 min	
	[2: 8 min		[2: 11 min		[2: 8 min		
	3: 2 min]		3: 4 min]		3: 2 min]		
	repeat 3 ×		repeat 2 ×		repeat 3 ×		
	2: 5 min		2: 5 min		2: 5 min		
	Flexibility: 20 min	Strength, whole body: 35 min	Flexibility: 20 min	Strength, whole body: 35 min	Flexibility: 20 min		

WEEK 2*

	Day 1	Day 2	Day 3	Day 4	Day 5	Day 6	Day 7
	Aerobic: 35 min	Aerobic: 30 min	Aerobic: 35 min	Aerobic: 30 min	Aerobic: 35 min	Aerobic: 60 min	Day of rest
	Level: [2: 7 min	Level: 2: 30 min	Level:	Level: 2: 30 min	Level:	Level: 2: 60 min	
	3: 3 min]		[2: 11 min		[2: 7 min		
	repeat 3 ×		3: 4 min]		3: 3 min]		
	2: 5 min		repeat 2 ×		repeat 3 ×		
			2: 5 min		2: 5 min		
	Flexibility: 20 min	Strength, whole body: 35 min	Flexibility: 20 min	Strength, whole body: 35 min	Flexibility: 20 min		

*Increase **Intensity** by adding 3 minutes of level 3 to day 1 and day 5's workouts.

WEEK 3*

Day 1	Day 2	Day 3	Day 4	Day 5	Day 6	Day 7
Aerobic: 35 min Level: [2: 7 min 3: 3 min] repeat 3 × 2: 5 min	Aerobic: 40 min Level 2: 40 min	Aerobic: 35 min Level: [2: 11 min 3: 4 min] repeat 2 × 2: 5 min	Aerobic: 40 min Level 2: 40 min	Aerobic: 35 min Level: [2: 7 min 3: 3 min] repeat 3 × 2: 5 min	Aerobic: 60 min Level 2: 60 min	Day of rest
Flexibility: 20 min	Strength, whole body: 35 min	Flexibility: 20 min	Strength, whole body: 35 min	Flexibility: 20 min		

*Increase **length of aerobic activity** by adding 10 minutes on day 2 and day 4's workouts.

WEEK 4*

Day 1	Day 2	Day 3	Day 4	Day 5	Day 6	Day 7
Aerobic: 35 min Level: [2: 7 min 3: 3 min] repeat 3 × 2: 5 min	Aerobic: 40 min Level: 2: 40 min	Aerobic: 35 min Level: [2: 10 min 3: 5 min] repeat 2 × 2: 5 min	Aerobic: 40 min Level 2 2: 40 min	Aerobic: 35 min Level: [2: 7 min 3: 3 min] repeat 3×	Aerobic: 60 min Intensity Level 2: 60 min	Day of rest
Flexibility: 20 min	Strength, whole body: 35 min	Flexibility: 20 min	Strength, whole body: 35 min	Flexibility: 20 min		

*Increase **Intensity** by adding 2 minutes at level 3 on day 3, and 3 minutes on day 5's workouts.

percent each week in order to allow for maximum progress while ensuring adequate recovery. For flexibility workouts you will also refer to the details in the Basic Fitness section.

As you can see, this four-week plan extends your capacity to train at level 3. Eventually, your ratio of level 2/level 3 interval time will be 2:1, which is a very high sign of fitness. As with the basic plans, this four-week sequence can be repeated, alternating small increases in time and intensity. If you follow this plan, be sure to "listen" to your body. Fatigue and lower motivation may be signs that you need an easy week. In this case, revert to a previous weekly plan that has shorter, less intense workouts, typically half of the week you just completed. This will not slow down your progress, and may actually prevent a plateau or injury.

Advanced Strength Training Plan

In the advanced plan, you will be doing at least two sets of each exercise, at increased weight. At this point you also are strong enough to realize the benefits of using free weights and compound movement exercises. Begin by again selecting one exercise for each body part and completing 10 repetitions of the exercise per set.

Full Body Workout Using Free Weights
> Chest: Pushups, dumbbell press, bench press
> Upper back: Pull down, seated row
> Shoulders: Overhead press, lateral raise
> Legs: Squats, lunges, dead lifts
> Biceps: Barbell curls, dumbbell curls
> Triceps: Overhead extensions
> Lower back: Bent-over row, back extension
> Core/abdominal: Abdominal crunches

When you are able to complete both sets of 10 repetitions without excessive strain, you can progress in two ways:

- Increase weight lifted by 5 to 10 percent.
- Move to more compound movement exercises detailed in the advanced fitness strength training section of this chapter.

World-Class Fitness

Do you need to be at world-class level to be healthy and achieve career success? Not necessarily. As we've said, many of the benefits of fitness can be realized at moderate ranges. However, you may notice that many of the executives profiled in *Executive Stamina* are extremely fit, and they make a direct connection between their effectiveness at work and the consistency and duration of their fitness training.

Do you remember when you were in the best shape of your life? What did it feel like, just walking around each day? What were your energy and confidence levels? How optimistic were you? The answers to these questions are the best reasons we can give you for following the world-class plan sequence.

For complete details on how to follow these plans, including how you progress from week to week and how to determine your intensity level, simply refer to the information included in Joshua's Workout Plans in the Basic Fitness section. The full information on the flexibility workouts that will be included in this plan are also found in that section.

If you are using the world-class plans (see pages 134–135), you are already experienced and knowledgeable about fitness. We hope that these specific guidelines about how much and when to work harder, and when to rest, will enhance your stamina in a safe, sure way.

World Class Strength Training Plan

At the world-class level you will do three sets of each exercise, at increased weight. At this point, assuming your strength training experience matches your level of fitness, you also are strong enough to realize the benefits of using predominantly compound movement exercises. Begin by selecting one exercise for each body part and completing 8-10 repetitions of the exercise per set.

WEEK 1

Day 1	Day 2	Day 3	Day 4	Day 5	Day 6	Day 7
Aerobic: 45 min Level: [2: 5 min 3: 6 min 2: 4 min] repeat 3×	Aerobic: 30 min Level 2: 30 min	Aerobic: 50 min Level: [2: 5 min 3: 15 min 2: 5 min] repeat 2×	Strength: 45 min Whole body: 45 min	Aerobic: 50 min Level: [2: 15 min 3: 5 min 2: 5 min] repeat 2×	Aerobic: 2 hr Level: [2: 20 min 3: 10 min] repeat 4×	Day of rest
Flexibility: 30 min	Strength, whole body: 45 min	Flexibility: 30 min		Flexibility: 30 min		

WEEK 2*

Day 1	Day 2	Day 3	Day 4	Day 5	Day 6	Day 7
Aerobic: 45 min Level: [2: 5 min 3: 8 min 2: 2 min] repeat 3×	Aerobic: 30 min Level 2: 30 min	Aerobic: 50 min Level: 2: 5 min 3: 20 min [2: 5 min 3: 5 min] repeat 2× 2: 5 min	Strength: 45 min Whole body: 45 min	Aerobic: 50 min Level: [2: 15 min 3: 5 min 2: 5 min] repeat 2×	Aerobic: 2 hr Level: [2: 20 min 3: 10 min] repeat 4×	Day of rest
Flexibility: 30 min	Strength, whole body: 45 min	Flexibility: 30 min		Flexibility: 30 min		

*Increase **Intensity** by adding 6 min of level 3 on day 1 and 5 min on day 3.

WEEK 3*

Day 1	Day 2	Day 3	Day 4	Day 5	Day 6	Day 7
Aerobic: 45 min Level: [2: 10 min 4: 3 min 1: 7 min]; repeat 2× 2: 5 min	Aerobic: 30 min Level 2: 30	Aerobic: 50 min Level: 2: 5 min 3: 20 min [2: 5 min 3: 5 min] repeat 2× 2: 5 min	Strength: 45 min Whole body: 45 min	Aerobic: 50 min Level: [2: 15 min 3: 5 min 2: 5 min] repeat 2×	Aerobic: 2 hr Level: [2: 20 min 3: 10 min] repeat 4×	Day of rest
Flexibility: 30 min	Strength, whole body: 45 min	Flexibility: 30 min		Flexibility: 30 min		

*Increase **Intensity** by introducing 9 minutes of level 4 on day 1.

WEEK 4*

Day 1	Day 2	Day 3	Day 4	Day 5	Day 6	Day 7
Aerobic: 45 min Level: [2: 10 min 4: 3 min 1: 7 min] repeat 2× 2: 5 min	Aerobic: 30 min Level 2: 30 min	Aerobic: 50 min Level: 2: 5 min 3: 20 min [2: 5 min 3: 5 min] repeat 2× 2: 5 min	Strength: 45 min Whole body: 45 min	Aerobic: 50 min Level: [2: 12 min 3: 8 min 2: 5 min] repeat 2×	Aerobic: 2 hr Level: [2: 20 min 3: 10 min] repeat 4×	Day of rest
Flexibility: 30 min	Strength, whole body: 45 min	Flexibility: 30 min		Flexibility: 30 min		

*Increase **Intensity** by **adding 6 minutes** of level 3 on day 5.

Full Body Workout Using Compound Movements
Chest: Pushups, dumbbell press, bench press
Upper back: Seated row
Shoulders: Overhead press, Upright row
Legs: Squats, lunges, dead lifts
Biceps: Barbell curls, dumbbell curls
Triceps: Overhead extensions
Lower back: Bent-over row, back extension
Core/abdominal: Abdominal crunches, leg raises

When you are able to complete three sets of 8–10 repetitions without excessive strain, you can progress in two ways:

- Increase weight lifted by 5 to 10 percent
- Alternate exercises to target different muscle groups

Summary

Higher levels of fitness enhance our ability to respond to, and recover from, challenges. However, to make the plan complete we need the right fuel to power these activities, enable our bodies to reap the full benefits, and provide us with a consistent source of energy through out the day. Chapter 8 focuses on the instrumental role of Nutrition in your *Executive Stamina* plan.

8 | Nutrition

In the mid-nineteenth century, Henry David Thoreau told us, "Every man is the builder of a temple, called his body . . . " In the mid-twentieth century, we were advised, "You are what you eat." Now, well into the first decade of the twenty-first century, what are we to derive from these two pieces of wisdom? Simply this: that the personal choices we make regarding our bodies shape our health and energy.

The connection between nutrition and stamina is straightforward: food is fuel. Along with oxygen it is our primary source of energy. Just as we will become fatigued, and perform at a lower level, when deprived of enough oxygen, our energy will drop off when given inadequate nourishment. That is why in this chapter we are going to focus on how the choices we make regarding what we eat and drink can either support—or undermine—our objectives in key areas of stamina:

- Keeping our energy level high, without drop-offs
- Strengthening our immune system and increasing longevity
- Maximizing the fitness gains from our workouts
- Helping our bodies recover from stress, and experience deep sleep
- Providing good nutritional options while traveling

In the previous chapters on fitness we explained that you need to transition slowly from your current level of activity to the eventual workout plan you aspire to. Doing so takes into account your current habits and how slowly the body adapts to change. Nutritional habits tend to be even more ingrained, reinforced by family traditions, culture, advertising—even our taste buds. So when it comes to improving your nutrition, we recommend gradual change, and stress improvement not perfection. To that end, we will guide to you transition to different patterns gradually.

Nutritional Overview

Fortunately these days, it is easier than ever to make healthy food choices. Public concerns, consumer demands, and, in some cases, regulatory changes, are pushing food manufacturers, restaurants, and even the media to focus on a "better for you" approach. Of course, easier doesn't mean easy. That is why our goal in this chapter is to offer you key concepts to serve as a guide to your day-to-day decision-making process where food is concerned, and to provide you with many simple, convenient choices that can help you move in the direction of high-stamina eating. We divide these concepts into three categories:

- Nutrient-rich foods
- Glycemic Index
- Nutritional alerts

Nutrient-Rich Foods

To look and feel our best, and to be able to perform effectively, we need an array of vital nutrients. Besides the right amounts of carbohydrates, proteins, and fats, we need minimum quantities of minerals, vitamins, and micronutrients (antioxidants and phytonutrients). The challenge is to ingest these nutrients at the right times and, in many cases, in the right combinations, and absent excess and unnecessary calories.

The place to start is with *nutrient-rich* foods. What does that mean? When a food yields a rich supply of essential nutrients without excess calories, scientists refer to it as "nutrient dense." George Mateljan, in his book,

The World's Healthiest Foods (George Mateljan Foundation, 2007), has compiled a list of the top 100 foods that meet this criterion, which he calls "nutrient rich." Not only do they provide maximal nutritional value per calorie, they are all *whole foods* that contain combinations of vitamins, minerals, fiber, and micronutrients, which enable full absorption by our bodies. Whole foods are important because research indicates that many nutrients are lost in processing or in overcooking, and so we also lose the essential nutritional combination that nature has provided.

Science is still in the early stages of figuring out the role of various nutrients in ensuring our health and vitality. This is understandable, given that food scientists estimate there are more than 40,000 phytonutrients (micronutrients found in plants) in our food. Here's just a small sampling of recent discoveries in this field of study:

- A team of researchers at the University of California–Berkeley and Michigan State, led by food science professor Leonard Bjeldanes, found that the diindolylmethane compound can aid in the prevention of cancer and activate the immune system to prevent viruses. This compound is found in *brassica* vegetables such as broccoli and cabbage.

- Cornell scientist Rui Hai Liu's research on nutrient combinations indicates that although an apple may only contain 6 mg of vitamin C, it has enough additional antioxidants to produce as much antioxidant activity as 1,500 mg of vitamin C taken alone. Tomatoes contain a phytonutrient called lycopene that correlates with a lower risk of prostate cancer.

So what we already know and what we are discovering every day points toward the benefits of including more whole foods in our diet. A partial listing of the foods that make Mateljan's top 100 are:

Vegetables: broccoli, spinach, carrots
Fruits: strawberries, cantaloupe, oranges, grapes, tomatoes
Fish: tuna, salmon, shrimp

Nuts and seeds: sunflower seeds, flax seeds, almonds
Meat: calf's liver, beef (grass-fed), lamb, chicken
Beans/legumes: lentils, lima beans, tofu
Dairy/eggs: eggs, yogurt, low-fat milk
Grains: oats, brown rice
Herbs: parsley, mustard

Matjelan recommends, and we concur, lightly steaming or "healthy sautéing" more of these foods using chicken or vegetable broth. Remember, highly processed or overcooked foods lose much of their nutrients and thus have less value for us. In the next section, you will learn that some processed foods can even work directly against us, based on the Glycemic Index.

Glycemic Index

The Glycemic Index (GI) is a measure of how quickly blood glucose rises after we eat carbohydrates. Carbohydrates are converted to glucose, which powers our muscles and our brains. Some simple carbohydrates like sugar are absorbed quickly into our bloodstream, causing glucose levels to shoot up. Other complex carbohydrates, like whole grains, are absorbed more slowly and evenly. To calculate the GI of a food, blood glucose levels are measured at 30-minute intervals for two hours after the ingestion of 50 grams of a particular carbohydrate. Scores range up to 100, which is pure sugar. Here are the GI scores of common foods:

High-GI Foods
- White bread, bagels (nonwheat)
- Doughnuts, cookies
- Candy
- Sugar, honey, fructose, corn syrup
- White rice

Medium-GI Foods
- Brown and long-grain rice
- Whole-grain bread and cereal, pasta
- Baked potato
- Many fruits

Low-GI Foods
- Lentils, most beans
- Apples
- Bran
- Millet
- Peanuts
- Barley

GI and Energy

When you provide your muscles and brain with a steady, even supply of energy (about 2 calories per minute), you are able to exercise longer, work more efficiently, and stay alert. This is what medium-GI foods deliver to your system. Because the flow of converted glucose is a consistent stream, you won't experience a dramatic dip in your energy or ability to concentrate. High-GI foods, in contrast, give you a dramatic boost as large amounts of glucose enter your bloodstream more quickly. However, high amounts of blood glucose also trigger a reaction from our pancreas: the production of insulin. Short term, the effect of insulin is to *remove* glucose from our blood, which is why a "sugar high" may last only 20 or 30 minutes. That is why when you opt for a high-GI snack, you get a temporary boost but also set yourself up for a "crash."

Consuming more medium-GI foods instead of high-GI foods can mean the difference between staying alert and engaged versus feeling fatigued and withdrawn at a meeting or conference. The steady energy delivered by the right foods can, for example, help you skillfully guide a difficult conversation to a positive resolution. But if your energy is depleted, the same conversation might spiral downward. And, of course, most of us can remember (and regret) decisions that we made when we were overtired.

A more long-term, and damaging, consequence of relying on too many high-GI foods is that your insulin production mechanism may become impaired. Initially, this can result in more of your food being deposited as fat; over time, however, it is a leading cause of obesity and diabetes.

Don't misunderstand; it is not practical or necessary to eliminate all high-GI foods, but it is important to understand their impact. Clearly, for our Executive Stamina goals of maintaining energy and mental alertness, a mixture of low- and medium-GI foods will deliver the steady flow (2 calories/ minute) that we need. Later, we will discuss how this concept can be applied to breakfast (including when to have it) and midmorning/midafternoon snacks.

Executive Profile

Tamar Elkeles, Chief Learning Officer, Qualcomm

If you ask Tamar Elkeles' associates to describe her, you will inevitably hear the words "energy" and "enthusiasm" in the first sentence. I asked how she always has such a high level of energy, and learned she incorporates a number positive practices into her daily life.

She also credits her company, Qualcomm, with helping its employees to achieve a work/life balance, by offering flex-time options, providing access to gyms and personal trainers, and helping to solve child and elder care dilemmas. Tamar, herself, is conscientious and consistent in her efforts to balance her priorities, which, along with a demanding job, include a husband, five-year-old daughter, and a dog. Here's how she does it:

Nutrition: Tamar is a vegetarian, drinks a lot of water during the day, and limits her intake of caffeine to a small amount early in the day.

Fitness: Tamar continued her early-morning runs up until the last two weeks of her pregnancy. In addition to the obvious fitness benefits, she treasures it as her time for herself. She also practices yoga and Pilates, and does other "little" things that add to her fitness level, such as always climbing the stairs instead of using the elevator.

Work/family balance: While at work, she gives everything to her job and company, but she is very clear about where and when her work role ends. For example, when she comes home, she immediately changes clothes to send a signal to herself and her family that work is over; and she limits her use of the phone, computer, and her BlackBerry. She is also rigorous about attending her daughter's school functions and events. When possible, Tamar takes her family with her on business travel.

Career management: While acknowledging that every job includes some activities that are not exciting or interesting, she strives to spend most of her time on what she is passionate about. In Tamar's case, that often revolves around learning. She considers herself a life-long learner and devotes her energy to finding creative ways to enhance the learning of others. She feels this will be her legacy to Qualcomm and its employees.

Nutritional Alerts

So far, we have reiterated much of what you probably already know, from your parents, teachers, nutritionists, even government agencies about the importance of eating more whole grains, fruits, and vegetables. We also summarized the concepts of nutrient-rich foods and the Glycemic Index. Now let's look at some foods and beverages that we should use in moderation or, in some cases, eliminate altogether:

- Sugar
- Caffeine
- Alcohol
- Trans fats

Sugar

Over the past 120 years, sugar has gone from being regarded as a luxury that only the rich could afford to a ubiquitous substance found in more food products than we imagine. Refined sweeteners and processed sugars like sucrose (table sugar), maltodextrin, fructose, lactose, and high-fructose corn syrup are in so many products that the *Encyclopedia of Natural Medicine* estimates that more that half of the carbohydrates consumed in the United States derive from these added sweetening agents. Clearly, sugars of all kinds are being overused. Consuming too much and at the wrong times will work against our fitness and stamina goals. Fortunately, there are several alternatives:

- *Stevia:* If you seek sweetness but without the empty calories, and are concerned about artificial sweeteners, a natural alternative is stevia. This herb, from the chrysanthemum/aster family, is native to Peru. It is sweeter than sugar but with 0 calories, and a 0 Glycemic Index. Millions of consumers in China, Japan, and Europe use it, and its popularity in this country is increasing, where it is sold in many health food stores. You can find out more about it at www.stevia.net.
- *Agave nectar:* This is another natural sweetener, made from the juice of the agave plant. It has a consistency like syrup and pours easily. Its main advantage over honey or sugar is that is has a low Glycemic Index. This allows you to sweeten your foods and drinks while maintaining a steady release of calories.

Our most important recommendation, however, is to *use sugar wisely*. It is very difficult to totally eliminate sugar from you diet because it is virtually everywhere. Gradually cutting back on its use, and choosing naturally sweet foods like fruit, will help. In particular, avoid using it in isolation as your "pick me up" energy source; instead, consume it only at mealtimes, with other foods.

Caffeine

Caffeine is without question the most popular, habit-forming stimulant on the planet. If used judiciously, it can help our effectiveness by increasing our alertness and energy level. But, as with sugar, there are a number of serious downsides to using too much caffeine, and/or at the wrong time:

- Absorbing too much can cause jitters and nervousness.
- Getting too "speedy" can impact your interpersonal skills, in particular listening and collaborative problem solving.
- There is usually a drop-off, in this case, drowsiness, which occurs when caffeine wears off. Caffeine keeps you stimulated by blocking the effects of adenosine, a sleep-inducing brain chemical that accumulates as your day unfolds. When the caffeine leaves your system, you may get sleepy.
- If you restimulate with more caffeine, it may eventually interfere with deep, restful sleep.

Here are our suggestions for the safe use of caffeine:

- *Gradually use less and less.* Our bodies adapt to caffeine; as this process occurs, we begin to consume more and more to get the same "buzz." Reverse this process by tapering off your intake gradually. Then you will be in a position to use it selectively, such as when you need extra energy to perform at a high level—for example, if you have an important meeting after a sleepless night spent traveling.

- *Consider other options.* When you are experiencing a drop-off in energy, revive yourself in other ways—get some fresh air, take a short walks, so some yoga stretches, drink water or eat a healthy snack.
- *Observe your sleep patterns.* Identify the point in your day when you need to cut off caffeine, so that it doesn't disturb your sleep.

Alcohol

Our objective in discussing this topic is to serve as the voice of moderation. The damage of alcohol abuse have been well documented, so we will only briefly review them here:

- Alcohol is highly addictive; alcoholism has been shown to have a genetic component, making it difficult for those predisposed to the disease to manage it in even small quantities.
- Alcohol inhibits fat metabolism; it is also high in calories and so may contribute to abdominal obesity.
- Taken before you go to bed, alcohol can interfere with rapid eye movement (REM)—that is, deep—sleep.
- Alcohol inhibits your ability to made good judgments and decisions. That is why casinos offer free drinks to active gamblers. It also tends to loosen our tongues, leading us to say things we will regret. When we drink too much, we also tend to, eat too much as well.
- Drinking even small amounts of alcohol impairs our ability to drive, thereby endangering our own and the lives of others.

Given these risks, paying attention to your alcohol consumption—amount, timing, and setting—is *critical*. Know your limit, and don't go past it. And when you do drink, always, drink lots of water so that you remain hydrated.

Trans Fats

For years we were warned about saturated fats, which is why many people began choosing lean meats, chicken, and fish. Now it appears that there is something worse for us: hydrogenated or partially hydrogenated oils, or trans fats (TFA, trans-fatty acids), another ingredient found in many food products. Fortunately, today, the Food and Drug Administration (FDA) requires food manufacturers to list the trans fat content on their ingredient labels.

Trans fats have been shown to increase LDL (bad) cholesterol levels, reduce levels of HDL (good) cholesterol, and lead to hardening of the arteries. These concerns have led many restaurants and food manufacturers to use healthier oils (e.g., sunflower oil) in their food processing and cooking practices. In New York City, trans fat have been banned entirely from use in city restaurants.

Our advice here is twofold:

- *Read labels.* There are many new products that no longer use trans fats.
- *Use healthier oils.* Cook with sunflower, safflower, canola, and olive oils.

Achieving Stamina through Smart Eating

With the preceding general guidelines and alerts in mind, here are specific, targeted suggestions to help you achieve your persona stamina goals in five areas:

1. Sustained energy
2. Health maintenance
3. Workout benefits
4. Restful sleep and recovery
5. Smart traveling

Sustained Energy

You know now the value of eating low- to medium-GI carbohydrates, to allow for the steady release of calories. They also increase the production of serotonin, which has a calming effect.

Other nutritional aspects to pay attention to include:

- *Digestion*. When your food is digested properly, energy production is maximized. Eating slowly improves digestion and helps you become aware when you have eaten enough. By eating lighter meals, which end when you are satiated, you will enhance your energy. Include some fat with each meal, but avoid too many fats, as they can reduce the oxygen available to your cells.
- *Breakfast*. To get a fast start at work and have the energy for a full workout, eat something within an hour of waking up. When you do this, you trigger an increase in leptin. Dr. Michael Cowley, a neuroscientist at the Oregon National Primate Research Center says, "When leptin goes up, you feel less hungry, and you increase energy expenditure." People who eat breakfast rev up their metabolism and start supplying fuel to their brain. That is why people who eat breakfast regularly score higher on mental, verbal, and concentration tests than those who don't.

    If you exercise early, you may want to divide your breakfast into preworkout and postworkout portions. Combinations of protein and fiber-rich carbs are ideal. Consider these options:

- Cottage cheese topped with berries
- Two scrambled eggs in whole wheat pita
- Peanut butter on a whole wheat bagel
- Oatmeal topped with chopped bananas and ground flax seeds
- A bowl of whole-grain cereal with chopped dried fruit and milk
- Whole wheat toast with low-fat cream cheese and pineapple slices
- Granola or muesli; fruit salad and yogurt
- Omelet with spinach and whole-grain toast

- *Snacks.* If you exercise early in the day and you are eating lighter meals, you may get hungry late morning or midafternoon. At such times, it is tempting to reach for sweets or caffeine (or both) to give yourself a boost. Give yourself better options, such as:

  - 100-calorie snacks:

    - Instant oatmeal with stevia sweetener
    - Three thin peanut butter sandwiches made with multigrain crackers
    - Raw vegetables (broccoli, carrots, etc.) in a low-fat dip
    - Half a baked potato topped with salsa
    - Half cup of edamame

  - 200- to 300-calorie snacks:

    - Apples with peanut butter or cubed cheese
    - Whole-grains cereal
    - Grapes or watermelon
    - Whole-grain pretzel
    - Vegetable juice
    - Cottage cheese and raisins or dried dates
    - Raisins or berries
    - Peaches, plums, oranges, or pineapple
    - Brazil nuts, almonds, sunflower or pumpkin seeds
    - Dry-popped popcorn with a little olive oil and white cheddar sprinkle, mixed in a bag

      The key is to have the snacks you need and enjoy readily available. This will prevent you from grabbing something that is not part of your overall plan.

- *Hydration.* Lack of energy can be caused by dehydration, resulting from hard workouts; consumption of beverages containing caffeine (coffee, tea, colas); overheated, dry offices; or simply not drinking enough water. Make sure that you drink water regularly. When you do, you may not even need snacks to boost your energy. Each of us has different needs for water, based on factors such as amount of exercise, climate, environment, and so on, but as a general guideline, drink eight 8-ounce glasses a day.

- *Iron.* Iron is vital to our health and energy generation. Linked with protein, it forms oxygen-carrying hemoglobin in our cells. Iron deficiency can lead to fatigue, immune system weakness, and loss of concentration. Iron-rich foods include spinach, shiitake mushrooms, green beans, raisins, sesame seeds, black beans, and red meat (particularly calf's liver). And note that eating iron-rich foods with those that contain vitamin C increases iron absorption.

Health Maintenance

Our health maintenance recommendations may seem like common wisdom, but, unfortunately, they are not common practice. In spite of researchers showing the cardiovascular benefits of eating a few servings of whole grains, fruits, and vegetables each day, studies indicate only a small fraction of us are doing it—4 out of 10 people in the this country eat no whole grains, and fewer than 1 in 10 eat the recommended three servings. A study by the U.S. Centers for Disease Control (CDC) of 305,000 adults found that fewer than one-third ate the minimum recommended amount of fruits and vegetables.

Workout Benefits

Many of us are not in a position to dramatically increase the time we can devote to exercising, so it makes sense that we get as much benefit as possible out of our workouts. The workout plans in the previous chapter are designed to help you do that, but you need to supply the fuel, in the form of proper and adequate nutrition. Although some people prefer to work out on an empty stomach, you will have more energy if you eat at least a small amount (200 calories) of carbs and protein a half to one hour before you begin. After a workout, eating right is essential, to restock the glycogen used during exercise and provide protein to jump-start the process of muscle repair, thus solidifying your fitness gains.

Monique Ryan, author of *Sports Nutrition for Endurance Athletes* (VeloPress, 2007), recommends a postworkout snack or meal containing a mix of 75 to 80 grams of carbohydrates and 15 to 20 grams of protein (based on body weight of 150 pounds). Examples are:

- Egg salad on a whole wheat bagel with cranberry juice
- Spaghetti with meat sauce; grapes
- A smoothie with yogurt or milk and fruit
- Whole wheat waffles, yogurt, and blackberries
- Kashi Go-Lean crunch (1 cup), bananas, and skim milk; orange juice

Lunch and dinner should be combinations of carbs, protein, and healthy fats that contribute to your feeling of satisfaction, such as:

- Baked fish with baked sweet potato
- Black bean burrito (whole wheat tortilla) with rice and salsa
- Whole wheat lasagna with cheese and vegetables
- Green salad with tuna
- Grilled chicken with baked potato and green beans

Restful Sleep and Recovery

The importance of sleep cannot be overstated, and too many business executives these days are sleep-deprived, due to the 24/7 nature of many jobs, communications technology, and the globalization of business. The right amount, and the right kind, of sleep, delivers benefits such as mental alertness, improved concentration, and mood elevation. Sleep is also the key to allowing our muscles to undergo the adaptation process for fitness gains, and to enable our immune system to recover from stress.

Why do we include sleep in this chapter on nutrition? Because sleep deprivation decreases the production of two important hormones that regulate appetite: ghrelin and leptin. Ghrelin, produced in the stomach, signals the brain when it is time to eat; leptin tells your brain you are full. The net result is that we eat more when we don't need it. Here are some tips for regular, restful sleep:

- Make sleep a priority; stick to a consistent sleep schedule.
- Avoid big meals, caffeine, excess alcohol, and intense exercise just before bedtime.
- If you do work at night, try to pick tasks that you can complete before bedtime; and leave time to transition from work to bed (light reading, TV, conversation).
- Keep your bedroom dark.
- Eat chopped walnuts before retiring. They contain melatonin, the hormone that sends your body the signal to sleep.
- Exercise regularly so that your body will be tired enough to experience deep sleep.

Smart Travel

Even in our daily routine, it is difficult to maintain a healthy eating program. It's even more difficult to stay on track when we travel, when we have less control over the kinds of food available to us. The result for many executives is undereating or overeating or making suboptimal choices. To ensure that your smart eating plan doesn't unravel on the road, follow these guidelines:

- *Carry healthy snacks and small meals.* Travel these days is unpredictable to say the least, and the odds are you will be delayed and get hungry at some point along the way. While choices are improving at airports, restaurants, and hotels, we recommend you bring along some of the snacks we've mentioned earlier. Additionally, carry trail mix (raisins, nuts, dried fruit, whole wheat pretzels) or energy bars.
- Airplane food, when available, may not often meet the criteria itemized in this chapter. Ask ahead of time for the vegetarian option, and you will usually get a healthier meal.

- If you are going to a set of meetings, seminars, or a conference, contact the meeting planner about providing good food at meals and breaks.
- Get information in advance about restaurants near where you are going. SparkPeople (www.Spark.People.com) provides 24-hour access to nutritional guidance for travelers.

Additional Advice for Eating Smarter

- *Consult a nutritionist.* He or she can guide you as to what to buy, how to prepare it, how to organize your kitchen, and how to set up meal plans.
- *Treat yourself to a spa vacation.* In addition to helping you with fitness and stress reduction, spas give you a chance to change your tastes and eating habits, while experiencing new foods, food preparation techniques, and taste combinations.
- *Measure and record.* Designate a week during which you will keep track of what you eat and how much. This dose of reality will yield key insights into what parts of your eating regimen to focus on.
- *Choose organic food.* Organic food is now widely available. When possible, choose it (especially locally grown) over food cultivated with pesticides and preservatives.

Summary

Good fitness and nutritional habits are the foundation of our stamina. In the next two chapters we are going to add to this foundation building blocks of how to manage, and recover from, stress.

9

Stress Management: Your Individual Plan

It's important as I begin this chapter to emphasize the importance of individuality in all of the discussions throughout this book. Yes, many executives face similar challenges and have personal and professional dilemmas in common. But your individual commitments, priorities, values, long-term objectives, extended family constellations, and set of circumstances are specific to you. So, to develop a stress management program that will be effective for you, you will have to use self-knowledge to design the plan that specifically addresses where you, and only you, are at in this stage of your life.

Let me raise again the importance of distinguishing between "nice-to-have" and "need-to-have" objectives. The chapters on fitness and nutrition should have convinced you that an exercise program and healthy diet fall into the need-to-have category, and are integral to succeeding at your job. Stress management techniques likewise fall into the need-to-have category. Your ability to reduce stress and recover from it will help you avoid the negative impacts of burnout discussed in Chapter 5.

General Concepts and Guidelines

To begin, we are going to review some general stress management concepts and guidelines, in four categories: simplicity, enjoyment, control, and self-awareness. Then, we'll move on to specific practices that will enhance your well-being on a long-term basis and that you can use throughout your day: self-talk, prayer, meditation, breathing, the relaxation response, and yoga.

Simplicity

Henry David Thoreau, in *Walden*, advised, "Simplify, simplify, simplify." This is an excellent starting place for reducing stress. The executive business world is incredibly complex, and getting more so every day, so looking for areas to simplify is a worthwhile endeavor. A couple of areas where it can be beneficial to keep in mind the value of simplicity is in

- Organizational design
- Acquisition of possessions

Many organizations are designed with matrices and layers that seem to make sense but, sometimes, ignore some realities of communication. Every additional complexity adds to the need for many more conversations, which usually also increases conflict and misunderstanding. People often find themselves confused about proper channels of communication and decision making. To move something forward there need to be many conversations, often across several time zones and cultures. This is not a book on organizational design but, wherever possible, making simplicity at work a priority can be beneficial on many levels. I am not suggesting that you eliminate all matrices. I am inviting you to factor the "cost of complexities" into some of your organizational design decisions.

When it comes to possessions, it is also useful to look at the complexity factor. Of course, many people get tremendous pleasure from vacation homes, extra cars, boats, big estates, and the like. However, if you feel like your pace is frenetic and you are overcommitted it may be worthwhile to examine the additional maintenance and time that possessions demand. For example, the second or third home may seem enticing but have you factored in the travel time, upkeep, expenses, and so forth?

Enjoyment

While some people may thrive on "all work and no play," most of us are more effective long term when we make sure to allow time for activities and people we enjoy. Here, naturally, what you like to do is all that matters. Warren Buffett and Bill Gates like to play bridge in their leisure time. Bobby Baldwin, CEO of MGM-Mirage, uses some of his vacation time to enter the World Series of Poker. Gretchen Park, chief personnel officer of T. Rowe Price Associates likes to take her boat onto Chesapeake Bay.

The key is to make sure to set limits at work so that you can create the space to do what you enjoy when you're not being a business executive. You may like to garden, cook, dance, read, commune with nature, spend more time with friends. . . . The list is endless.

Control

Often, the most extreme levels of stress are experienced by people who feel they have little control over their circumstances. In the case of the executive's life, feeling trapped by the job, for whatever reason, is a primary cause of stress. Some may feel that for financial or family reasons, they can't leave their jobs, even though they are working for someone who is abusing or taking advantage of them. Others may endure racism or sexism or questionable ethics in their organization, but fear that speaking out will jeopardize their job security. If you have ever been in such a situation, or know someone who has, you know the damage it can cause.

None of these situations is easy to deal with, but I can offer suggestions for learning how to avoid them, and to increase the probability that you will gain greater control of your life over time. We've talked about a number of them already in the book, but I summarize them here in the context of stress management.

Set Time Limits

If you don't schedule how you spend your time, someone else will. If you don't set limits to your workday, and draw clear boundaries around your personal time, your company won't acknowledge them. In Chapter 10, you'll learn more about how to better apportion your time.

Become Organizationally Savvy

Organizational savvy starts and ends with a clear understanding of power. It arms you with the skills to navigate internal politics and agendas, and increases your influence and impact, while enabling you to maintain your integrity and professional ethics. Savvy helps you accurately interpret what is going on around you, and improves your mastery over your environment and, thus, your sense of control. (More on this topic in Chapters 13 and 14.)

Maintain Networks and Upgrade Skills

It's critical that, as an executive, you recognize that it is possible for you to be a loyal and responsible leader in your company and, at the same time, acknowledge that you also "work for yourself." No company can or will guarantee a lifetime of secure employment to anyone in a senior position. Ultimately, your worth to your company and the market is determined by your skills and making others aware of them.

- Don't allow yourself to become complacent.
- Keep up with industry news, new technologies, and cutting-edge skills.

- Maintain your professional network.
- Improve and know your market value, so that you can negotiate from strength within your company.

By taking care of yourself in this way, if you do find one day that it's time to move on, whether by your own decision or the decision of your company, you will know you have other attractive options available.

Gain Financial Independence

Being financially secure is, of course, the pinnacle of control; it's what enables independence in many of life's arenas. When you have enough "money in the bank," you don't need to worry what your boss thinks of you, or whether you're vulnerable to the next company "reorg."

It's rare to find a business executive who doesn't list financial independence as one of his or her goals, but approaches to achieving this objective vary widely. Many executives have a generalized goal of achieving a certain level of net worth, and expect their stock options and salary/bonus trajectory to take them there. Others take a much more hands-on approach to their investments and financial endeavors.

Spending patterns, too, vary widely among execs. Typically, though, two patterns emerge as income increases.

- Expenses tend to rise with income. The good news is that it signals our lifestyle and standard of living is improving. The bad news is that, for some executives and their families, expenses *continuously* rise to meet the level of income without a concomitant rise in savings; and, in the worst case, debt is incurred, sometimes at high levels.
- As spending increases, the distinction between a luxury and a necessity blurs. Individuals begin to believe they *must have* this or that costly object or experience. They also may begin to compare what they have not to those who have less but only to those who have *still* more.

Sad to say, I've worked with many executives who found themselves at a tenuous point in their career without enough savings to be able to risk leaving their current job or start their own business. Financial insecurity is directly linked to the feeling of being trapped.

To ensure that you have the freedom, flexibility, and security you want and need, focus more intently on the goal of financial independence:

- Build your savings and net worth.
- Monitor your expenses so that they don't automatically rise to match your income.

In particular, pay attention to the last recommendation, for doing so will yield multiple benefits. If you regularly remind yourself what are *necessities*, the basic building blocks of an enjoyable, satisfying life, you will more readily realize that financial independence can be gained at lower levels of net worth, thus making it easier to achieve.

Self-Awareness

Arthur Rimbaud, the French poet, once remarked, "By the time a man is 30, he should be his own doctor." His point, in my opinion, was that we each should know ourselves well by that time in our lives. How much sleep do we need? What is our optimum diet? What are the signs that we are on the verge of a cold or getting run down? Rimbaud wasn't suggesting that we forgo doctors; rather that by knowing ourselves first, we will then know how best to care for ourselves—or even how to help our doctors help us.

I believe this same insight can be applied to stress management—that is, your most effective plan will be one built on keen self-awareness. Here are self-awareness areas I recommend you pay attention to in this effort:

- *Stress triggers*: What are the situations and who are the people that cause stress in you? In the Introduction, I mentioned that Steve

Milovich at Disney uses this knowledge to help him balance his calendar.

- *Stress signs*: What are early indicators that you are starting to experience stress? Consider changes in breathing and heart rate, physical agitation, muscle tension, inability to listen, and negative self-talk (see the next section). Once you know yours, you have a much better chance of (1) stopping yourself from making a stress-induced mistake and (2) moving quickly to reduce your stress.
- *Stress feedback*: Notice your impact on others. Tune in to the direct and indirect feedback you get from those around us. People in regular contact with us are often more aware that we have become "stressed out" than we are. Important information can be conveyed in comments such as, "When was your last vacation? Are you trying to pick a fight? Is there something wrong at home?"

Moving on, in the next section, I introduce a specific practice that can become an important part of your day-to-day and, sometimes, moment-to-moment, plan to keep you emotionally balanced and working effectively.

Self-Talk

There is a person with whom you spend more time with than any other, a person who has more influence over your growth than anyone else. This ever-present companion is your *own self*. This self guides you, belittles you, or supports you.

You engage this person in an ever-constant dialogue—a dialogue through which you set goals for yourself, make decisions, feel pleased, dejected, or despondent. In short, your behavior, feelings, sense of self-esteem, and even level of stress are influenced by your inner speech.

Pamela Butler, *Talking to Yourself* (HarperCollins, 1991)

This inner speech is Self-talk. Self-talk skills, including the ability to direct your focus and what you say to yourself, is an essential building block of any stress management plan. In Chapter 5, you learned that how you perceive events and circumstances, how you interpret the actions of others, and how you respond to situations in general all affect your stress level. In other words, your self-talk and your focus influence your level of stress whether you are aware of it or not. There are many techniques you can use to help you take charge of your self-talk and make it work *for* you.

Remember how John Galleteria, in Chapter 5, handled the airport delay when he was traveling with his family? He turned a potentially negative, stressful situation into a positive one for himself and his family. You can use similar skills to maintain your physical, emotional, and mental well-being. Self-talk can help you preserve your energy and stay focused on your goals.

I'll start by covering some basics about self-talk and describe how they can impact your feelings and behaviors.

We all talk to ourselves, regularly and rapidly, all the time. A normal conversation you have at work usually occurs at a rate of 125–150 words per minute. Your self-talk occurs at speeds of 400–600 words per minute. In fact, it is so quick that we often don't notice our mental patterns or habits. We don't think about what we think about. Hopefully, you are getting curious: What are those 400–600 words per minute and how are they affecting my moods and motivation?

The second, often invisible, action that we take is to direct our focus. At any moment there are numerous things we could focus on and we *choose* to focus on some and not others. Place yourself in John Galleteria's situation at the airport. What are some of the things it would have been very normal to focus on and say to yourself?

I'm so unlucky.

Why did this have to happen to me?

This is going to ruin the vacation.

We'll never get out of here.

These clowns don't know what they are doing.

My legs hurt, and I'm hungry.

I could have used this time to get important things done.

I can't even see the front of the line. There are probably people cutting in ahead of us.

Look at those airline employees. They act as if they don't have a care in the world.

I was stupid to go with this airline. Now I've spoiled things for everyone.

Sound familiar? We've all been there, done that. But now ask yourself: Does taking this approach help change anything? Does it solve any problems? Is it leading to any learning? Will it get you home quicker? You know the answer.

More likely it causes more anxiety, frustration, anger, stress, and probably unproductive behavior (cursing, criticism, conflict). Now recall the things on which John *chose* to focus on:

- The joyful aspects of his vacation and how lucky he was to have this family experience.
- Being a positive role model for his son.
- Reminding himself of something really serious—his sibling's serious illness.
- Using the time to have fun and engage in conversation with his family.

Without question, using effective, helpful self-talk and learning to redirect our focus take determination, commitment, and practice. But you can do it! And you will find you can apply the skill to all areas of life. Salespeople, athletes, and entertainers all use such techniques to enhance their performance (see my book *Super Selling through Self-Talk*; Price Stern Sloan, 1988). Religious people use this skill to stay on a spiritual path ("as a man thinketh . . ."). Parents and teachers apply such self-talk skills to building self-esteem and motivation in children (see my book *Performance without Pressure*; Walker Press, 1988).

When you apply these skills to stress management, you will reap benefits in three major areas:

1. Reducing worry and anxiety
2. Managing anger
3. Being grateful

Reducing Worry and Anxiety

"My life has been a series of terrible misfortunes, . . . most of which never happened," said Mark Twain. "Cowards die a thousand deaths, the brave man dies but once," wrote Shakespeare. Both these writers illuminate one of the more significant and pervasive aspects of fear and worry: When we worry, we picture in great detail what we *perceive* as a horrible event or situation, and our nervous system reacts as if it is happening. Worrying, most often, is simply a form of "dread rehearsal." And the downsides are considerable. Worry narrows our focus, depletes energy, and wastes time; and, as I pointed out in Chapter 5, it prompts our bodies to secrete high levels of stress hormones.

Clearly, it is more productive to use positive self-talk and focus skills than to spend time engaged in unproductive worrying. A good motto here is, "Improvement not perfection," because you won't be able to eliminate all anxiety, no matter how diligent you are. Nevertheless, you can make great strides. As a starting point, learn to ask yourself the key questions I provide here to begin to help you worry less often and for shorter periods, and to reduce your level of anxiety.

Key Questions

1. *Am I worrying or planning?* Worrying can deplete your time and energy, and reduce your effectiveness. If you find yourself feeling anxious, ask yourself, am I worrying or planning? Don't get bogged down in worry; instead, use it as a signal to anticipate, prevent, prepare, or plan more diligently.

2. *Is what I am worrying about a small possibility or a probability?* Mathematicians have shown that most of us often worry about the wrong things, from a straight probability perspective. We fear events that are publicized, even though they may have a very low probability of occurring (contracting AIDS, being the victim of terrorism). At the same time, we disregard actual dangerous situations—

---

such as applying makeup, talking on a cell phone, eating, or even reading while driving 60 miles an hour on a busy freeway. So when you find yourself worrying, ask yourself, what is the actual possibility of this happening?

3. *If what I'm worrying about does happen, will it really be a catastrophe? Or just an inconvenience?* This is probably the most important distinction to make to reduce your level of stress. Most of the things we worry about in our professional and personal lives do not fall in the catastrophe category. They are more accurately labeled inconveniences. True catastrophes are events like the genocide in Rwanda, 9/11, Hurricane Katrina, or serious health problems for you or your loved ones. Making a mistake during a presentation, missing a deadline, missing market share benchmarks during a new product launch, getting passed up for a promotion, or even losing a job are not true catastrophes. They are setbacks, disappointments, losses, and, in some cases, major inconveniences, but they are not catastrophes.

   To help modify your way of thinking about such setbacks, ask, "What is the worst thing that could happen?" Let's say you get fired or your job is "downsized". What would you do? First consider all the other setbacks, problems, and obstacles you've overcome in your life. Second, consider viewing this as an opportunity to focus on your own development. You could gather feedback about your behavior or skills or try to figure out how to prevent this from happening in the future. Third, explore the possibility that this may be an opportunity to go down a different path, take a different role, join a different sort of company or industry, or maybe start up your own business. There are many examples of people who went on to achieve great things after being laid off by a company, and in retrospect were glad it happened. Think about it; it is highly likely you will find another job, and highly unlikely you and your family will be out on the street. Your lifestyle may come down a notch or two, some luxuries may have to go, but *this is not a catastrophe*.

In summary, fear and worry don't help your performance. Preparation, planning, and giving your best effort does. Gathering feedback and learning from your mistakes does. When Eli Manning is throwing a football in the Super Bowl or Venus Williams is hitting a tennis ball at Wimbledon, fear and tension don't help. Practice, preparation, and training, followed by focus and execution, do. It is possible to have high motivation and exert full effort to achieve your goals and still see things from a true perspective. In fact, it can help your confidence and composure when you realize your self-worth is not on the line for each project or performance.

Useful Self-Talk

The following phrases, if you say them to yourself in the appropriate situations, can greatly reduce fear reactions. If you practice using them regularly, over time you will develop new, more useful, mental habits.

1. "I focus on creating positive results in any situation. Problems give me an opportunity to learn and use my skills."
2. "I'm disappointed with the results I'm getting so far. I'd better find out as much as I can about what is going wrong in this situation so I can improve it or at least get feedback to help me perform better in the future."
3. "Stop! Fear and worrying are a waste of my time and energy, and they block me from using my skills."
4. "I trust myself to acquire the knowledge and skills I need if this plan or approach does not lead to the results I want."
5. "I'm resourceful and I have the ability to bounce back. My trend is not my destiny because I can learn from my results and then change and adapt."
6. "My objectives in this situation are important. If I don't achieve them, I'll be disappointed and it will be inconvenient but it will not be a catastrophe or a horrible event. By thinking about negative results as a catastrophe, I'm creating tension and fear that actually reduce my chance of success."

7. "I create pressure in any situation by what I focus on and what I say to myself. I can remove pressure by concentrating on doing the best job I can right now and learning all I can."

Managing Anger

Anger can be a useful emotion, indicating to yourself and others what is deeply important to you. It also can be used as a way to say to others that you won't be mistreated or taken advantage of. Anger may also serve as a springboard to discuss issues and concerns so that disagreements aren't allowed to fester and lead to long-lasting resentments. And, needless to say, anger can be a source of physical strength when we are faced with threats or challenges. That's the plus side of this emotion. On the other side is the obvious damage—too much anger, expressed in the wrong situations, can cause to our health, equilibrium, and relationships.

As explained by Dr. Meyer Friedman and Ray Rosenman, authors of *Treating Type A Behavior and Your Heart* (Fawcett, 1985), anger results in a massive physiological preparation for action:

> If you become intensely angered by some phenomenon, your hypothalamus will almost instantaneously send signals to all or almost all the nerve endings of your sympathetic nervous system (that portion of your nervous system not directly under your control), causing them to secrete relatively large amounts of epinephrine and norepinephrine. . . . In addition, this same fit of anger will probably also induce the hypothalamus to send additional messages to the pituitary gland, the master of all endocrine glands, urging it to discharge some of its own exclusively manufactured hormones (such as growth hormone) and also to send out chemical signals to the adrenal, sex, and thyroid glands and the pancreas as well, so that they in turn may secrete excess amounts of their exclusively manufactured hormones.

Here are some key questions and self-talk phrases that can help you better manage and use your anger.

Key Questions

1. *Will being angry now help me or hurt me?* Review the discussion of positive uses of anger. Is this one of those situations? Remember that the caveman brain has its own vocabulary and its own set of goals. Once triggered, it crowds out signals from your frontal cortex, the logical, reasoning, problem-solving part of the brain. Ask yourself: Will being angry now help me perform this activity or make this decision? Is there a risk that I will say or do something I will regret (including confronting someone more powerful than me)? Will being angry detract from the energy and focus I'll need for my next meeting? If you realize that being angry now will hurt you, instead use techniques, including the self-talk phrases given here and relaxation techniques in the next section, to calm yourself.

2. *Will my anger have any impact on this situation?* In his seminars, my colleague Sandy Smith asks participants to name all the inanimate objects they get angry at. After some laughter, responses typically include the weather, cars, lawnmowers, golf balls, golf clubs, tennis racquets, alarm clocks, TVs, appliances, tires, computers, and vending machines. Sandy then asks, "Do any of these things care that you are angry?" Often, this humorous question jolts the participants into examining just what they are accomplishing when they get angry at "things." Again citing John Galleteria's situation at the airport: He realized that getting angry was not going to end the travel delay; it would only have a negative impact on him and his family. Similarly, if you are stuck in traffic and late for an appointment and let yourself get angry and upset, what happens? In addition to arriving at the meeting late, you are now also upset. You've let one problem cause another problem.

3. *Am I "stewing" or doing?* This is similar to the distinction between worrying and planning. Stewing does very little good and, potentially, a lot of harm. To go quickly from stewing to doing, ask

questions, such as: What can I do to turn this situation around? Is there anything I can salvage from this situation? What can I do to prevent this from happening again? What can I learn from this situation?

Useful Self-Talk

1. I can achieve my goals in this situation with firmness. I can assert myself without becoming angry or demanding.

2. No one can dictate how I will feel today. No one can "push my buttons" except me. I have a choice in how I am going to react to this person (or this situation).

3. The only person I can ever control is myself. I can never control another person; I can only influence him or her. If I expect to be able to control him or her I'll wind up angry or frustrated. If I accept that I can only influence his or her free choices I'll be calmer, learn more about the person, and be more effective.

4. This is a situation over which I have no control. My anger will have no positive impact.

5. I can calmly review and critique my performance and then make improvements without calling myself names or blaming my performance on someone else.

NOTE

If a situation occurs when your being too angry has clearly had a negative impact, it is an excellent opportunity for self-reflection. Usually, there is a lot to be learned.

Some Good Questions to Ask Yourself
1. What triggered me?
2. Why does this person bother me so much?
3. Did I try to communicate when I was tired or stressed?
4. What was my self-talk before I got angry?

Being Grateful

Gratitude is the state of being thankful and appreciative. I am fortunate to have learned about the healing and energizing power of gratitude relatively early in my life. When I was 20, I entered a monastery. The day-to-day living conditions fell somewhere between minimal and harsh; we had no beds, heat, or showers. Food was not plentiful, and my weight dropped from 198 to 138 pounds in a year. Despite the lack of many comforts, it was the most important and, in many ways, the happiest year of my life. Several monastery practices sustained me, and one of those was the practice of being grateful. It was built into every facet of the day. We stopped to be grateful many times a day, and were taught to be thankful to our parents, teachers, and the farmers who grew the food we ate. So even in the absence of many basic necessities or common comforts, I learned to appreciate, to be grateful for, what I had.

Thus, the essence of gratitude is focus. Focusing on what you don't have, or on what others possess that you don't, may be useful for goal setting, but it will not send you (or your nervous system) the positive messages and wonderful sensation that gratitude can deliver. Almost any system or religion you embrace would accept that simply being human is a miracle and a gift. Our basic senses and rational minds' capacity for feeling and creating bonds with people are gifts we sometimes take for granted until they are impaired or threatened.

Cultivating gratitude is one of the most effective stress management (not to mention, happiness) practices there is, providing tranquility and a balanced perspective. Many people, including myself, find that an excellent way to start every day is to focus on what you are grateful for. Say thank you for being alive, for your health and the health of those close to you, for your strengths and resources; extend your thanks to other people or a higher power. Leave no stone unturned in being grateful. Commuting to work, enhance your optimism and energy by focusing on what you like about, and are grateful for, at your job. For example, my work consists of writing, coaching, or teaching seminars. Before I begin any of these tasks, I take two minutes to remind myself how fortunate I am to have each opportunity to present my ideas and, possibly, have a positive impact on someone's life. A simple, but effective, gratitude exercise for the end of the day is to think about at least three good things that happened to you during that day. Then, to add to your learning (and for a change of pace) analyze how and why they happened.

Gratitude is a skill you can develop through repetition and practice. Like all the skills in this section, it is a blend of what we choose to focus on and what we say to ourselves. It is a basic building block of an effective stress management plan.

NOTE

To learn more about the scientific basis of the importance of gratitude to our well-being, see *Thanks: How the New Science of Gratitude Can Make You Happier*, by Robert Emmons (Houghton Mifflin, 2007).

Self-Talk Summary

I hope you've learned that self-talk is a core, multiuse life skill. You can use it throughout the day, in any setting. It is one of the Executive Stamina skills that increases your sense of control, because you *choose* what you say to yourself, thus enabling you to direct your focus in a positive direction. Begin your workday in a state of gratitude, and use positive, mental preparation to give yourself an excellent start to any endeavor. During the day, use self-talk skills to help minimize worry and anger, while maintaining your focus and balance. After work, use self-talk as a way to direct your reflections on what you've learned.

Tranquility: Prayer, Meditation, Relaxation

There is a variety of activities that encourage us to experience feelings of peace, tranquility, and relaxation. These practices help both to ward off and recover from stress.

Prayer

Prayer, in any form, and connected to a formal religion or not, is probably the most common way to practice stress management, even though many people who pray would not identify it as such.

Prayer can aid in stress management in many ways. Many people find strength and consolation in prayer and turn to it during their most stressful and painful periods. Research suggests that prayer can positively charge the immune system and help people heal. Additionally, prayer yields feelings of tranquility and calm, which dramatically reduce the damage stress can cause.

The study of theology suggests that many of the world's religions have three principles in common. The first is that there is a greater reality than that which encompasses the world in which we live. Second, this "higher power" is present for each and every human being. Finally, our purpose in life is to acknowledge and celebrate this higher power. Faith in these principles brings comfort and meaning to the lives of millions of people.

Praying is communicating with whatever divine power you believe in, through reciting texts or songs, or using your own words. You can pray alone or with others, in a church, synagogue, or other holy place, or at home. Some religions advocate praying all day, every day, throughout everything you do, whereas others set times for prayer.

There are many different types of prayer:

- *Petitionary prayer* involves asking God directly for something you desire. It is practiced most often in Christianity and Judaism. Adherents believe that God listens to their prayers, and that He (or She) answers them (the answer may be no).
- *Intercessionary prayer* means praying on behalf of others, as when you pray that a sick relative will get better. Intercessionary prayer can also be used solely to praise God.
- *Kabbalistic prayer*, found in Kabbalah, a mystical offshoot of Judaism, holds that praying affects the entire world and that your prayers can heal and repair reality.

- *Contemplative prayer* can be both intellectual and meditative. Christian, Jewish, Hindu, and Muslim scholars pray contemplatively by reading and analyzing religious texts. The more meditative form of contemplative prayer involves repeatedly reading a passage from a holy text, and then thinking about it until you come to realize new facets of its meaning and significance.

If prayer is a positive force in your life you may have certain times reserved for it. Another application to consider is taking prayer breaks during the workday. One of the major contributors to stress in our workday is the absence of breaks. We may rush from one meeting to another conference call to the point that the day becomes a blur. Time to reflect on events or restore balance is bypassed. Later in this chapter you will learn about meditation, breathing, relaxation, and yoga breaks. Many times a break of as little as five minutes can restore equilibrium. If prayer is helpful to you, you may want to try to discreetly use it to deal with stress during the workday.

Meditation and Measured Breathing

Historically, meditation was a practice of followers of Buddhist or Hindu traditions, but the practice prevails in various forms in the Christian, Jewish, and Muslim faiths as well. Today, the health, well-being, and performance benefits of meditation and measured breathing have become so widely accepted that many people meditate, separate from a religious context.

There is no one right way to meditate but there are guidelines common to most meditative practice.

- *Mental stillness*: A meditator is seeking to quiet the mind. That is why more accurate descriptions of this activity might be "concentration" or "absorption."
- *Single focus*: One path to this stillness is to attempt to focus the mind on one thought, word, or sound (a mantra), or simply on your breathing.
- *Measured breathing*: Meditation is accompanied by measured, controlled, deep breathing. Most of us, if we haven't just climbed some

stairs, breathe about 16 to 19 times a minute. In contrast, most meditators breathe five times or less a minute; and some, deep in meditation, breathe twice a minute. (As you can imagine, these are some pretty calm people.)

Let me describe a simple exercise that has been used for thousands of years to help beginning meditators.

Frozen Rope Breathing Technique

The frozen rope is one of hundreds of breathing and concentration techniques that are used to quiet the mind and achieve tranquility. I prefer the frozen rope because it promotes the ability to concentrate, as well as to relax. People have long used breathing as a way to achieve inner control because it is both a voluntary and an involuntary process. If we choose, we can direct the rhythm of our breathing and influence some of our inner processes, including our level of relaxation and calm.

1. To begin the frozen rope, sit comfortably with your back straight; loosen any belts or clothing that would restrict your breathing.
2. Your goal is to make your exhalations slow and even. Start by closing your eyes, breathing in deeply through your nose; then exhale slowly and smoothly through your mouth. As you exhale, imagine that your breath is extending like a frozen rope of air. Concentrate on the slow, even flow of air and the picture of the frozen rope.
3. At the end of the exhalation, wait a couple of seconds before you inhale. Initially, this will seem hard, so don't force it; later, as your breathing slows down, you will look forward to these very peaceful seconds, breathing neither in nor out but simply sitting quietly and concentrating on the frozen rope of air. When you inhale, allow your body to breathe as quickly and deeply as necessary to fill your lungs. Then begin the slow, even exhalation again.

Five to 10 minutes of this breathing and concentration will usually produce good results. An added benefit of the frozen rope exercise is that after you've done it regularly for a while, you can often trigger relaxation with only one to three breaths. Doing it 5 or 10 minutes a day is better than an hour one day a week. This type of breathing is a multiuse skill; once you become proficient, you can induce calm in almost any setting.

Benefits. The consistent practice of some form of meditation has been demonstrated to yield the following benefits:

- Alleviates depression.
- Stimulates parts of the brain associated with positive emotions.
- Lowers blood pressure.
- Speeds recovery from stress.
- Increases concentration and the ability to stay fully engaged in the present moment.

Additionally, for at least a few minutes a day, a meditator is receiving the internal message that simply "being" is a source of happiness.

NOTE

For more information on meditation, consult: *Meditation for Dummies*, by Stephan Bodian (John Wiley & Sons, Inc., 1999); *How to Meditate*, by Lawrence LeShan (Bantam, 1999); *8-Minute Meditation: Quiet Your Mind, Change Your Life*, by Victor Davich (Perigee Trade, 2004); and *Meditation for Beginners*, by Jack Kornfield (Bantam, 2005).

Relaxation Techniques

Dr. Robert Benson's ground-breaking book, *The Relaxation Response* (Harper Paperbacks, 2000) documented the specific physiological changes associated with relaxation. Benson found that many different activities could trigger this response (prayer, meditation, yoga), but he also discovered there were specific relaxation exercises that could produce it as well.

No matter how it is induced, the relaxation response not only reduces stress, but has many compelling health benefits. For those who are not comfortable praying or meditating, three relaxation exercises are described here. They are useful before and after work; and repeated practice will enable you to adopt them for use *at* work, during breaks or in stressful situations.

The Peaceful Place. In this very common technique, which most people are able to adopt, you simply imagine an ideal place of relaxation. This may be some place you've been, possibly a favorite spot from childhood; or it could be a place you've only seen in photographs or movies. For many, it is a natural setting—the seashore, mountains, meadows, or a wooded trail—but it could also be a certain room. Once you have your peaceful place in mind, do the following:

1. Settle into a comfortable position in a chair, or recline and allow yourself to let go. Then visualize your peaceful scene, as vividly and in as much detail as possible. Imagine yourself in the scene, and try to become aware of all your senses and how it feels to be in this place.
2. Simply allow yourself to relax and enjoy the quiet and tranquility and pleasure of being part of this scene. Five to 10 minutes is a good length of time to begin with.

Maltz's Relaxation Technique. Maxwell Maltz, in his classic book, *Psychocybernetics* (Pocket, 1989), recommends this relaxation technique. The first part of the exercise is similar to the peaceful place technique just described.

Once you have relaxed into the peaceful scene, you use your imagination to achieve deeper relaxation.

1. To begin, imagine that your body is made of lead. Focus on your arms, legs, torso, head, and so on, and imagine that each part is so heavy that you couldn't lift if even if you wanted. The dead weight is sinking deeper into the chair or bed. Continue in this way until your whole body feels very heavy and sinks into what you are resting on.
2. After a few moments, reverse it: begin to imagine that your body is becoming very light. Visualize little helium balloons attached to your hands, arms, feet, ankles, legs, head, and torso. Your body is so light that you being to float gently.
3. Continue until your body feels as if it is floating effortlessly, with no tension or stress, completely relaxed. Ten minutes is a good initial time period for this technique.

Jacobsen Relaxation Method. This technique, which involves alternately tensing and relaxing muscles, has been widely used for 70 years. It combines awareness of where the body is tense with an understanding of the opposing feelings of tension and relaxation. You alternately tense and relax each part of your body and each muscle group until relaxation spreads gradually to your entire body. An important benefit of this approach is that after you master the technique, you can often trigger relaxation by tensing and relaxing just one part of your body, such as your right hand or foot. In this way you can relax inconspicuously whenever and wherever you need to.

1. To begin, you need a quiet place, with a chair or a bed. Remove your shoes and loosen any binding or tight-fitting garments; sit back or lie down.
2. Starting with one hand, make a tight fist for five to seven seconds, then relax it completely. While you are tensing, be aware of how it feels. Then, when you relax, give yourself the command, "Relax,"

and feel the warmth and pleasure of doing so. After 10 seconds of relaxation, repeat the tensing-relaxing sequence.

3. Repeat this two-step process twice with your forearm, biceps, other arm, feet, calves, thighs, stomach muscles, back and shoulder muscles, neck, chin, and face. Occasionally, if you are tense when you start, you may have to tense-relax parts of your body more than twice to feel the positive effects.

4. Allow relaxation to spread throughout your body, and continue to heighten your awareness of the opposing feelings associated with tension and relaxation. It is important to cue your relaxation with the command, "Relax," because this will become a useful self-management device when you want to relax in challenging business interactions.

The Jacobsen technique takes 15 to 20 minutes.

Executive Profile

Melanie Macdonald, President and CEO, World Neighbors

Melanie Macdonald is a very effective executive and a delightful person, brimming with warmth and positive energy. For the past few years, she has devoted her talents to expanding the reach of an esteemed organization. World Neighbors is a powerful international development organization whose mission is to eliminate hunger, poverty, and disease in the poorest, most isolated rural villages in Asia, Africa, and Latin America. Unlike other charitable organizations that give away food, money, or material aid, World Neighbors invests in the people themselves, training and empowering them to implement life-saving and life-changing programs—agriculture, literacy, water and sanitation, reproductive and community health, natural resources management, and environment protection. Since World Neighbors' inception in 1951, it has helped to improve the lives of more than 25 million people in 45 countries. (Visit www.wn.org for more information).

Melanie began her career as a social worker in Canada. It was her personal experience of becoming a parent through international adoptions that led her to learn more about, and eventually pursue a career in, international development. Eventually, she became the CEO of CUSO, the Canadian equivalent of the U.S. Peace Corps. Unlike the Peace Corps, however, CUSO is not funded by the Canadian government, and at the time she took over the reins, it was struggling financially. Melanie worked long and hard for five and a half years, during which time she orchestrated a financial turnaround that put CUSO on firm footing.

Her success came at a high personal cost, however. In being so attentive to the needs of others, she neglected her own. Exhausted, on the verge of burnout, she became ill until, eventually, she was forced to take time to recover her health. When she returned to work, it was in a different role, as a consultant and coach to leaders and nonprofit organizations. Then she was offered the opportunity to lead World Neighbors in Oklahoma. It was a chance to work with wonderful people, for personally meaningful causes, but, understandably, Melanie was wary due to her CUSO experience.

She decided to take the role, but only after negotiating with the World Neighbors board for the establishment of her "personal health plan." Up front, she wanted to ensure that she had their support for the idea that her health and well-being had to be a priority (which it wasn't in her previous job). They responded by creating a CEO advisory board and providing a personal coach. Every year during her annual vacation, Melanie creates her next-year's health plan. She knows that at World Neighbors the "job is never done." Like other altruistic people, she knows she has a tendency to neglect herself. Her health plan is her way of protecting herself from this behavior.

Though Melanie's plan, of course, has elements unique to her, the concept behind it is useful to most of us. She agreed to share her plan for 2007–2008:

(Continued)

Melanie Macdonald, President and CEO, World Neighbors (Continued)

- Celebrate!
- Nurture me first so that I can then take care of WN and the staff team.
- Continue working with my coach.
- Follow through on my healthy food plan.
- Meditate, read, or make quiet time each morning for 15 minutes.
- Meditate in the ladies' room for five minutes midday.
- Walk most days for half an hour, and as often as I can at noon.
- Go to the fitness club or do weight exercises twice per week (do stretchy cord routine when I'm in a hotel room).
- Skate, swim, ride, when I can.
- Do stretching exercises most weekdays and at least once on weekends (three minutes each time).
- Keep riding and skating so that I can, one day, be a little old lady who is still riding and skating.
- Delegate, delegate, delegate to VPs—trust them; step in only when it's critical; keep my work at the overall, visionary level.
- Aim to work 50 hours per week, per my doctor's recommendations.
- Leave early whenever I can.
- Work at home on Fridays whenever I can.
- Limit U.S. trips to five-day runs, with weekends back in Oklahoma City.
- Limit field trips to two weeks, and take a family member at my expense.
- Revel in my weekend with Dave [husband].

Summary

You have just read about a number of techniques and practices that you can use as building blocks for your customized stress management plan. As we continue, keep in mind:

- Simplicity
- Enjoyment
- Control
- Self-awareness
- Self-talk
- Prayer
- Meditation
- Relaxation
- Melanie Macdonald's "health plan"

Think about which of these practices you might want to initiate—or reinstate—in your life, the ones that might work for you.

10

Yoga at the Office

In addition to the positive practices and techniques I've discussed in the previous chapters, in this chapter I want to add two more for your consideration: yoga and stretching exercises. Both can also be very effective in managing stress. There are, to be sure, many other excellent practices that can be very beneficial in stress reduction—tai chi, qi dong, massage, among them—but I'm focusing on yoga because it can more easily be integrated into the workday and workplace.

The Importance of Balance

To make this essential point—the importance of balancing one's executive "posture"—I will relate a bit of folk wisdom. This is a story about an annual log-sawing contest in a Midwest farm town. The reigning champ was a 70-year-old farmer of average height, with a lean, wiry build. His challenger was 22 years old, 6 feet 3 inches tall, and 220 pounds, with little body fat. The championship was an all-day affair and the challenger was confident that his opponent was no match for his youth and strength.

Early indications were that he was right. After a few hours, he was well ahead, and noticed that every hour the old man was taking a five-minute break behind the shed. He took this as a sign that the champ could not keep up the pace, and he pushed himself to keep the pressure on by sawing non-stop. The champ didn't vary his pace or his pattern of stopping for a few minutes every hour. As more time passed, things began to shift in his favor.

By midafternoon, he had caught up to the younger man in number of logs sawed; and as the day came to an end, he was decisively ahead. The 22-year-old was exhausted and clearly dumbfounded about what had happened. How could this old man have beaten him? He asked the champ about it; specifically, why he had taken so many breaks and what he had been doing behind the shed. He replied, "I was sharpening my saw."

Yes, power and persistence are forces we need, but not at the expense of effectiveness. Remember the discussion about self-awareness? It's a key executive skill, necessary to invoke especially when our emotions or attitudes are turning negative and our bodies are tensing in response.

Learning to notice such changes and then to restore your physical and mental balance is an important aspect of yogic practice.

Sharpening the Saw

> **NOTE**
>
> In this section I enlisted the help of Jnana Gowan, a yoga instructor who specializes in exercises and postures that alleviate the kinds of strains and stresses most likely to occur while sitting at your desk or in any office setting.

The material presented here is not, of course, intended to comprise a formal course in yoga; rather, it is to introduce some simple, quick techniques that don't require a studio, instructor, mat, or special clothing. These are techniques you can use discreetly while sitting at your desk or in the privacy of your office. Think of them of the equivalent of "sharpening the saw."

The 5,000-year-old practice of yoga, which began as part of the Hindu religion has become part of mainstream America. Yoga classes and studios are found everywhere today: in strip malls, local YMCAs, in gyms, spa retreats, even as part of corporate-funded health programs. This surge in interest has a number of bases: people are searching for ways to enhance the quality of their lives; they find that practicing yoga calms their minds and spirits; through regular practice, they are healing various body ailments. Yoga is also gaining acceptance among medical practitioners. Research by Herbert Benson, MD at Harvard Medical School, and Jon Kabat-Zinn, MD at the University of Massachusetts Medical Center has shown that yoga and meditation boost immunity and reduce stress. A number of prestigious hospitals, such as Memorial Sloan–Kettering and Columbia Presbyterian in New York City, as well as HMOs such as Kaiser Permanente, acknowledge the validity of such research by offering yoga classes to their patients and clients. What better proof that yoga works.

Yoga is a Sanskrit word meaning to yoke, or unite, specifically the mind, body, and spirit. It is the fragmentation of these aspects of self that typically get us off balance and/or cause illness or disease. However, what is called yoga in the western world is a very small component of a much larger holistic practice. What most of us are familiar with in this country are the physical postures, the *asanas*.

Basic Concepts

Tony Robbins, the internationally known motivational speaker has wisely noted, "People are not getting injured on football fields, they are getting injured in front of their computers." That is why, the primary goal of this chapter is to give you simple, easy-to-follow exercises you can practice throughout your workday. By doing these exercises regularly, you will, over time, create new, healthy, habitual patterns that will reduce stress and tension, and lead to better work performance and a deeper sense of inner peace overall.

Even if you currently practice yoga, you can use this program as a guide for incorporating yoga at work, in addition to your current program. If yoga is entirely new to you, this is an invitation to begin a regular, easy routine that will help you stay calm, focused, and more effective while working.

Breathe!

Begin by taking a slow even breath. Breathing is so underrated! In fact, it is the foundation of life, of every move we make. When the breath moves, the body moves. When you are stressed, generally you breathe too rapidly, and this upsets the body's pH level, a condition known as *respiratory alkalosis*, which can cause a host of aliments, such as nausea, muscle twitching, light-headedness, irritability, confusion, and anxiety. So by becoming acutely aware of your breath, and its inactivity or overactivity, you begin a new relationship to yourself and your good health. No matter how busy you are, there is always time to notice your breath. When you feel yourself spinning out of control, take a breath; it can make all the difference in keeping you from going overboard.

At the same time you're paying attention to your breath, begin to notice the tension in your body: where you hold it, how it makes you feel. As an example, clamp your jaw shut and grit your teeth as tightly as you can. Notice how it feels. You may feel tension in your upper back and neck; it may tense your facial muscles, such as between your eyes and around your mouth; your belly may tighten; perhaps it even triggers anger. Now, release your jaw and take a few breaths. Now how does it feel?

Once you begin doing the exercises in this chapter, you may learn there are places you hold tension that you were unaware of. That's great! How can you let go of something if you don't know it's there?

Move!

Another important action you can take is to simply generate more movement in your workday. Don't sit in one spot for hours at a time. That's an old habit that you are ready to replace with a simple, new, healthy one. By stretching your muscles, along with taking full cycles of breath, you will improve your circulation, increase oxygen volume, avoid repetitive strain injury (RSI), and improve your posture, as well as digestion. Go outside for some fresh air. Walk around the block to clear your head.

Make Friends with Yourself

Be kind to yourself. Treat yourself like a good friend, and give yourself a break. The last thing you need is an inner voice nagging you: "Your jaw is so tight; it's as if you have lockjaw!" Or, "Your shoulders are up to your ears again; you will never get this relaxation stuff; what an idiot!" This is not yoga, this is self-abuse. Being kind to yourself is an exercise unto itself. In other words, pay no attention to the "man behind the curtain;" just do the exercises and see how you feel afterwards.

Soften the Senses

One of the great yoga teachers of our time, B.K.S. Iyengar teaches that if the head and face are relaxed, the body will follow. Within the formatting of the program, you will be instructed to "soften the sense organs." Here's how:

- To soften the tongue, first do the opposite: press your tongue hard against the roof of the mouth, just behind your two front teeth. Hold for a moment, then release and let the tongue sit softly in the mouth.
- To soften the eyes, blink slowly several times, like a baby that is ready to go to sleep. Another approach is to look intensely at something in front of you, then release your gaze.
- To unclench your jaw, open your mouth wide and move your jaw side to side, and up and down. You make look a bit silly but this is a great way to remind yourself to release that tension. You may also want to give the jaw hinge a massage to help soften the area.
- Another good practice is to come onto your "sit bones," technically, the *ishial tuberosity,* the sharp bones of your backside on which you rest when sitting up straight on a firm surface. They are the base of the pelvic girdle. The reason it is so important to sit on these bones is that it keeps the spine erect, yet with its natural curve. If you roll back onto your sacrum, the spine collapses, impeding the internal organs,

making it more difficult to breathe. If you roll too far forward, you will create pressure in the lower back (the lumbar spine). You may have to experiment a bit, rolling forward and backward on your sit bones to find this natural posture. Be sure to place your feet hips width apart and parallel to one another. During your workday, remind yourself to come into this posture as often as you can.

Be Honest with Yourself

Finally, before we get started, I remind you, to thine own self be true. Maybe you have a bum knee, or neck problems; maybe it's been years since you've thought about stretching, much less done any stretching. That's okay; today is the perfect day to start, but do so with that knowledge and do not push too far too soon. A great way to determine whether you are overdoing it is to stay in touch with your breathing. Keep it smooth and steady. If you are straining to breathe, back off a bit and continue the pose; and if you need to stop altogether, do so. Take care of yourself.

Workday Yoga

To begin let's look at the top five tension hot spots, and how to release the tension in them:

1. The jaw: Unclench.
2. Shoulders: Drop them toward the floor.
3. Eyes: Soften by blinking often or closing for a moment.
4. Stomach/lower abdominal area: Soften your belly by taking deep breaths into the pelvic floor and by placing a hand on your belly or gently massaging/pressing in a circular motion.
5. Neck and upper back: Do the breath work and exercises detailed in this chapter.

Breath Exercise 1

You may start the breath work with this pose to help center yourself; it can be incorporated throughout the day as well. The placement of the hands, known as *anjali mudra*, may be used as a preventive against carpal tunnel syndrome and other RSIs.

1. Come onto your sit bones.
2. Place feet hips'-width apart and press them evenly into the floor.
3. Press your palms and fingers evenly into one another (see Figure 10.1).
4. Soften your sense organs: tongue, eyes, even the skin on your face; unclench your jaw; drop your shoulders away from your ears.
5. Draw your shoulder blades down toward the chair; keep them down, away from your ears.
6. Avoid jutting out your chest, as this will compress the lower back.
7. Reach the sides of your waist up toward your armpits, creating a long natural curve to the spine.
8. Hold for 5 to 10 cycles of breath; observe where you are breathing into your body.

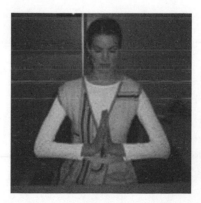

Figure 10.1   Breath Exercise 1, Position of Hands

Breath Exercise 2

Mom used to say, "Sit up straight!" She probably didn't say, "And breathe." But do both now: sit up and take a few breaths, and bring yourself into the present. Breathing into the belly can be very calming.

1. Bring your feet hips'-width apart, and sit on your sit bones.
2. Soften the sense organs: tongue, eyes, facial skin; unclench your jaw; drop your shoulders away from your ears.
3. Take a few breaths and notice where in the body you are breathing (upper chest, throat, belly?).
4. Inhale through the nose, directing the breath down to your belly.
5. Exhale through the nose.
6. Continue for 3 to 5 minutes.

> **TIP**
>
> It can be helpful to think of the inhale as filling a glass of water, from bottom to top, and the exhale as pouring the water out, from top to bottom.

To extend the breathing session, you may start with the first exercise add the next one.

Breath Exercise 3

You really *aren't* tied to your desk, so why not get up and go outside to do this next one, which has three parts? Equalizing your inhales and exhales can help regulate your mood, especially if you are feeling as though you need an emotional uplift. Note that turning the palms upward in part 2 is a preventative to carpal tunnel syndrome; however, if you are experiencing any RSI issues, be careful not to overstretch.

Six-Count Breathing

This may be done standing with your feet hips'-width apart, parallel.

Part 1

1. Have your eyes softly opened or closed.
2. Sit up on your sit bones; relax your shoulders away from your ears.
3. Breathe, and notice where in your body you are breathing.
4. Inhale through the nose, directing the breath down to the belly.
5. As you inhale, begin counting from one to six, directing the breath to the belly, diaphragm, base of lungs, and so on.
6. Exhale, beginning at top of lungs, to midlungs, lower lungs, then belly.

Breathe into the backside of your body, not just the front. It may take some practice to be able to get to six counts, so be patient with yourself. It takes time to train the breath.

Part 2

1. Continue counting; inhale, stretch your arms out to the side of your body and up above your head, with the palms parallel to one another.
2. Draw your shoulders down, away from your ears, even your arms up.
3. Continue counting to six as you exhale, arms down.
4. Synchronize the movement with the breath—inhale, arms up; exhale, arms down.
5. On last inhale up, interlace your fingers over your head; bring your palms toward the ceiling (see Figure 10.2).
6. To release, continue slow steady breathing as your arms come to your sides.

Figure 10.2   Six-Count Breathing, Part 2, Position of Arms

Part 3

1. Stand up, with feet hips'-width apart, parallel.
2. Continue six-count breathing.
3. Repeat several times.
4. Inhale, arms up; on exhale, bend at the hip crease and tip the upper torso toward the floor. If you are experiencing discomfort in the lower back, bend your knees slightly.
5. Bend your elbows and cross your arms, hanging upside down. If this feels like too much, rest your hands on a chair or desk and allow the spine to lengthen.
6. While releasing upside down, use the weight of your head to lengthen the spine; relax the neck.
7. Reach your sit bones to the ceiling as your head releases to the floor.
8. Breathe, smoothly and evenly.
9. Stay for several breaths
10. Place your hands on your thighs; draw your belly back toward the spine and use the strength of your arms to help press yourself back to standing.

Over time, this purposeful breathing will become easier. The more you practice, the more enriching it will become. Once you feel more comfortable doing it, you may want to experiment a little. For example, to calm anxiety, lengthen your exhalations; to alleviate dullness and fatigue, lengthen your inhalations. And, as instructed in the six-count breathing exercise, to help lift you from a dark mood, equalize the lengths of your inhalations and exhalations.

There are many classes, books, and Internet sites devoted to breath work, describing the difference it can make in your life, I encourage you to explore this subject and find what works best for you.

Eyestrain Relief

Exercise 1

This helps reduce eyestrain, which is it is related to neck and jaw tension and headaches.

1. Be aware of your breath and posture.
2. Close your eyes.
3. Rub your hands together until they feel warm; place the palms of your hands over your eyes, gently (see Figure 10.3).
4. Keep your shoulder blades down; rest your elbows on a desk if you wish, being mindful not to collapse your posture.
5. Soften the belly and breathe as your eyes relax.
6. Repeat as desired.

Exercise 2

1. Be aware of your breath and posture as you come onto your sit bones; sit erect.

2. Relax your jaw and neck; drop your shoulders away from your ears and soften your eyes.

Figure 10.3 Eyestrain Relief, Position of Hands

3. With your eyes closed, circle your eyeballs clockwise: look upward toward the forehead, then to the right temple, down toward the chin, to the left temple, back up to the forehead.
4. Repeat three to five times.
5. Go in the opposite direction.
6. Repeat three to five times.
7. Relax in a neutral position.
8. Open your eyes gently.

Healthy Eye Tips
- Change your point of focus several times within each hour.
- Blink often; this will release tension and keeps your eyes moist.
- Massage your forehead, temple, and cheekbones to relax your face and eyes.

Shoulder Rolls

These can be done in front of your desk or in an empty conference room or other space, seated or standing. Remember, your shoulders are not part of your ears or heart. This exercise helps to keep them where they belong: down and pressed outward. This posture will help release tension in the upper back and neck area, and increase circulation in the upper torso.

1. Be aware of your breath as you come up onto your sit bones.
2. Inhale; bring your right shoulder up toward your right ear. Slowly rotate it back, drawing the shoulder blade down, making a full circle.
3. Repeat action on the left side.
4. Do both sides three times.
5. Now reverse the action, going forward; do both sides.

Mountain Pose

The posture of most people is to stand too far back on their heels or too far forward. The mountain pose navigates you to a proper stance, where you can hold steady and strong, like a mountain. Kick your shoes if you can for this one, to help you feel your position more fully.

1. Stand with your feet hips'-width apart, with the outside of them almost parallel.
2. Press and spread your toes into the floor. Feel the weight of your body distributed evenly through your feet, from the toes to the heels.
3. Lift your kneecaps up by contracting the front thigh muscles, but do not lock the backs of the knees.
4. Pull up from the back of your thighs.
5. Lift your frontal hip points slightly, and draw the tailbone down slightly toward the floor to level the pelvis.
6. Keep your hips directly over your knees, and your knees over your ankles. This gives a stable foundation; and positioning the pelvis properly keeps the spine healthy.
7. Extend the spine—slowly inhaling. Lift up through the legs as you raise the ribcage; open your chest and drop your shoulders down.
8. Extend your neck upward, keeping the sense organs soft.
9. Breathe smoothly and evenly for 5 to 10 cycles.

Figure 10.4   Standing Lunge, Leg Extension

Standing Lunge

1. In front of a desk or table, stand with your feet hips'-width apart.
2. Inhale; lengthen upward.
3. Exhale; step your right foot back three to four feet, toes facing forward (see Figure 10.4).
4. Ideally, keep your heel on the floor; but if it is up, that's okay.
5. Keep your hips parallel, facing forward; roll your right hip forward and down.
6. Reach your tailbone into your right heel, keeping back leg straight.
7. With every exhale, go a bit further into the stretch.
8. Keep your front knee above the ankle.
9. Draw your shoulder blades down the back and reach your collarbones into your armpits, to open the chest.
10. To go deeper, bend the front leg more.
11. To come out, step right leg forward.
12. Stand in mountain pose for several breaths and then repeat on the left side.

Chest-Opening Stretch

Remember: Don't hover over your computer all day. This exercise is a little backbend, which will energize, refresh, and invigorate your body. It also

Figure 10.5   Chest Opening Stretch, Position of Arms

will improve your posture, help decrease rounded shoulders, and release tension in mid-/upper-back.

1. Sit on the edge of a chair, on your sit bones, with feet hips'-width apart.
2. Reach behind to hold the backside of the chair (see Figure 10.5).
3. Lift your chest and keep your chin level with chair seat.
4. Draw your shoulder blades down the back, and lift up your chin. (Note: If you have neck problems, keep your head level with the chair seat.)
5. If your arms are straight, squeeze your elbows together; if your elbows are bent, work on straightening your arms.
6. Relax into the pose for three to five cycles of breath.
7. Exhale; release and repeat one to three more times.

Seated Twist

Take your time to move carefully into this pose. Do not push yourself—literally; instead, allow the breath (on exhale) to guide you further. Twists can stimulate the kidneys and the liver, as well as assist in more productive

Figure 10.6   Seated Twist, Position of Hands and Body

digestive function. This pose can also help to release tension in the entire back, particularly the midback.

Using Chair with Armrests
1. Sit on the edge of a chair on your sit bones, with your feet hips'-width apart, calves vertical to the floor.
2. Inhale; lengthen the spine toward the ceiling.
3. Exhale; reach both arms to the right, gently holding the armrest (see Figure 10.6). Stay for one or two breaths.
4. Pay attention to the sit bones; rest them evenly on the chair.
5. Deepen the twist on the exhale, lengthen on the inhale.
6. If you are able to move your right hand to the back of your chair, do so; but instead of pulling, keep your palm open, as if you were pushing the chair up. This action opens the upper back; pulling will jam it.

Using Chair Without Armrests
1. Sit on the edge of a chair, on your sit bones, with feet hips'-width apart, calves vertical to the floor.

2. Swivel to the right so your right shoulder is next to the back of the chair.
3. Inhale; lengthen the spine toward the ceiling,
4. Pay attention to the sit bones; rest them evenly on the chair.
5. Deepen the twist on the exhale, lengthen on the inhale.
6. Open your hands, pressing the palms upward into the back of the chair. This action opens the upper back; pulling on the chair will jam it.
7. To come out, release the twist of the torso; bring arms down.
8. Switch sides and repeat.

Spinal Release

The following three-part pose helps improve your posture, decrease rounded shoulders, and reduce tension in the mid- to upper-back. Be sure to go one step at a time; if at any time you feel dizzy, come up carefully. Often, dizziness occurs when the breath is not moving, so be sure to breathe.

Part 1

1. Sit on the edge of a chair, on your sit bones, with feet a little wider than hips'-width apart.
2. Inhale; lengthen the spine toward the ceiling, keeping your head and neck in alignment with your spine.
3. Exhale; bend at the hip crease, resting your forearms on the inside of your inner thighs (see Figure 10.7).
4. Press both feet evenly on the floor, focusing on the inner heels and balls of the feet.
5. Stay for several breaths, keeping the spine straight.

Part 2

1. Exhale; keep your sit bones connected to the chair. Bend your elbows and cross your arms, letting the weight of your head release

Figure 10.7   Spinal Release, Part 1, Position of Forearms

the spine toward the floor (the spine will round). A less intense way to do this is to support the armpits with the knees, resting with your thighs holding you (see Figure 10.8).

2. Stay here for several breaths. Make sure to keep your breath moving. If you feel dizzy, slowly come up, using the strength of your arms to press yourself upright in the chair.

Part 3

1. Bring your hands to floor, placing them a little wider than shoulder-width apart.
2. Reach them as far away from you as you can.
3. Plant your feet evenly into the floor.

Figure 10.8   Spinal Release, Part 2, Position of Head and Arms

Figure 10.9 Spinal Release, Part 3, Position of Head and Arms

4. Exhale; reach your knees away from your centerline, sit bones on the chair, arms stretching forward (see Figure 10.9).
5. Inhale; bring your hands directly under your shoulders, let head hang, softening your eyes jaw, and tongue as you rest in the pose.
6. Repeat several times.
7. To come up, bring your hands onto your thighs, using the strength of your arms to help press yourself into a seated position.

Ending Your Practice

If there is a space at work where you can put your legs up a wall as you lie on the floor, I highly recommend this pose, a variation of *viparita karini*. Benefits of this pose are: blood pressure regulation, relief of indigestion and nausea, as well as relief from stress-induced headaches and migraines. But most important is that you'll find this pose very relaxing. And if you can't do it at work, try it at home to "come down" after a long, hard day.

1. Sit on the floor, with your right shoulder four to six inches from the wall.
2. As you exhale, begin to bring your legs up as your torso moves down, until you are lying back on the floor.
3. Keeping your legs straight, rest both feet on the wall comfortably. Do not stretch your hamstrings (back of thighs); if they are pulling, push yourself further into the room.

4. Make sure both shoulder blades rest evenly on the floor, with your arms at sides, palms up.
5. Stay for 5 to 15 minutes.
6. To come out, push yourself into the center of the room a bit, keeping your belly soft.
7. Roll onto your right side; stay for two to three breaths.
8. Use the top of your arm to help press yourself up.

Take a few moments to integrate the good the stretching and breathing did for your body before jumping back into your work.

Suggested Exercise Minisequences

The following minisequences will help get you started with your yoga-at-work practice. They have been designed to give you time to complete each pose, and move between the poses. Feel free to mix and match your own sequences.

5-Minute Program (recommended hourly)
2 minutes: Six-count breathing, parts 1 and 2, finishing with palms upturned toward ceiling
1 minute: Chest-opening stretch
1 minute: Standing forward lunge (15 seconds each side, two sets)
1 minute: Eye relief

10-Minute Program (recommended for break time)
4 minutes: Six-count breathing, parts 1, 2, and 3
1 minute: Mountain pose (will feel long!)
2 minutes: Standing forward lunge (15 seconds each side, four sets)
1 minute: Chest-opening stretch
1 minute: Eye relief

20-Minute Program (recommended for lunchtime)

4 minutes: Six-count breathing, parts 1, 2, and 3

1 minute: Mountain pose (will feel long!)

3 minutes: Standing forward lunge (30 seconds each side, three sets)

2 minutes: Chest-opening stretch

4 minutes: Spinal release, sequences 1, 2, and 3 (stay about 30 seconds each step, including 30 seconds to slowly come out and rest before doing second set)

2 minutes: Seated twist (practice each side 30 seconds, two sets)

2 minutes: Eye relief

Summary

To conclude this chapter, review the hourly check-in list here. Once you begin to sit with a natural curve of the spine and to notice your breath, you can dramatically change your life. It will not happen overnight, but over time you will find that you are feeling better. And, remember, practicing yoga daily for short periods of time is better than a lengthy session once a month—and definitely better than never practicing. Start with the five-minute sequence hourly and see what happens.

Hourly Check-In List

1. Be aware of your posture, sit up on your sit bones.
2. Be aware of your breath; take time to notice where you are breathing. Guide the breath to your belly and the back of your body. Breathing in the upper chest triggers the fight-or-flight reflex.
3. Locate your tension spots and breathe into those areas, or do a few poses to relieve the tightness.

The yoga postures and stretches described in this chapter can bring more calm and balance to your workday, and can easily be incorporated to your weekly flexibility workouts.

PART III

OPTIMIZING JOB PERFORMANCE AND RESULTS

11

Identifying High-Payoff Activities

The old adage, "Work smarter, not harder," is actually very sound advice for executives. Though the concept resonates with everyone, we often forget to apply it in our daily lives. Most executives already expend a significant amount of energy thinking of ways to optimize their time. So, why devote a chapter to pointing out that you should spend your time on the activities that yield the highest payoff for your specific objective? Three reasons:

1. *Reflection*—World-renowned psychologist and physician Edward de Bono poignantly summarized the importance of spending time wisely: "No amount of hard work in the wrong direction ever takes you in the right direction." Because many executives work at a hyper pace, allowing little time for reflection, it is often the case that they are spending too much time on noncrucial activities and neglecting others that are essential.
2. *Habits*—In conjunction with an absence of reflection, most of us have formed habits and established patterns that have us spending valuable time on low-payoff activities. And as we all know, habits are easy to make but difficult to break.
3. *Increased Urgency*—I am hoping that the previous chapters have increased your sense of urgency about choosing wisely where you

focus your time and energy. Activities that don't vigorously advance our goals or, worse, waste our efforts, carry two risks. First, extending the length of the work day actually increases the chances of our reaching the point of diminishing returns before we achieve our objectives. Second, every time we say yes to something, we may also be saying no to a more important business or personal activity.

Unless you are able to function on four hours of sleep a night or have wide gaps of unfilled time in your calendar, then it is useful to see each obligation you commit to as a tradeoff. The extra time you spend at an unproductive meeting may be even more costly than you realize. That could be time better spent strategizing for the next quarter or talking with your top saleswoman who is being heavily recruited by your competitor. That meeting might cause you to miss a dinner at home or a workout or the opportunity to help a child with homework.

What Is the Best Use of Your Time?

Only you can answer that question, and it will be different for everyone, and will change with circumstances. Nevertheless, there are some guidelines you can follow to help you identify those activities that should be a priority in your current role. To begin, ask yourself:

- What is my unique position on the team?
- What are the factors necessary for me to succeed in this role?
- What are the current risks and priorities of my role?

Unique Position

A starting point in helping you decide which activities are essential is to examine your specific role on your team and your organization. Which tasks are you in a unique position to accomplish? Which key activities, if not completed by you, will not get done? Some examples of essential activities include:

- *Representing team interests*: As the leader of a team, you represent the team at certain meetings: budgeting, operating plan reviews, talent reviews, project updates with senior management. Could other people on your team go to these meetings and do a credible job? Probably, but even if they could they are not invited. You are tasked to represent your team in very important settings that impact the team's resources, reputation, and individual team members' careers. Are you fully prepared for these meetings?
- *Resolving conflicts*: Conflicts between your team and other functions are inevitable. Members of your team may have important information and useful ideas about resolving the conflict, but you may be required to intervene at higher levels.
- *Attending top-to-top meetings*: Your salespeople may be excellent and credible but many times, a key customer wants to establish a strong relationship with you as the head of the division. If you don't make this a priority, or don't do it well, it could undermine many people's efforts.
- *Spotting national or global trends*: If your team is geographically dispersed, individual members will be reporting to you about important trends they are seeing in their regions. It is up to you to connect the dots, to determine what is a regional situation or the beginning of a national or global trend. For example, certain consumer preferences or trends might emerge in California that may have resonance across the country (e.g., nonsmoking policies, organic food trends, environment-friendly companies). You must capture this kind of input, share best practices, and think strategically if your organization is able to profit from this information.

These four examples are just the tip of the iceberg; obviously, there are many others that will apply only to you and your current role. So, the first step in answering the "best use of time" question is to look at the important tasks that only you are in a position to accomplish.

Key Questions

- Which tasks am I in a unique position to accomplish?
- Which key activities, if not completed by me, will not get done?

Success Factors

The fact that you have reached an executive position means you already have developed valuable skills, knowledge, competencies, practices, and systems that enable you to add value at the top level of an organization. That doesn't mean you can't always learn more, and a good place to start is with other people who perform or used to perform roles similar to yours. Network with predecessors or peers, or even pick up one of the many books on the market by or about executives you admire (e.g., Larry Bossidy's *Execution: The Discipline of Getting Things Done* [Crown Business, 2002], Jim Collins's *Good to Great* [Collins, 2001]). In expanding your reach in this way, you may come to realize you want to emphasize, or minimize, the importance you currently assign to certain activities.

It can be particularly useful to explore topics for which there is no straightforward formula, such as:

- How much time should I devote to planning, preparation, and reflection?
- How much focus should I place on motivating people?
- What are the right levels of internal and external communication?
- What are the key relationships I should always maintain?
- How much time do I need to spend nurturing my top performers?
- What is the right balance between internal and external focus?
- How do I keep my pulse on the organization? The consumer? The competition?
- How do I get feedback about my leadership practices, and accurately gauge how I am perceived?
- How much time should I devote to self-development?

By seeing how others approach their roles and the responsibilities they entail, you can better evaluate your own and, likely, pick up useful tips you want to incorporate going forward.

Current Risks and Priorities

Establishing priorities may seem a no-brainer; after all, you are being paid to identify opportunities that will add value to the organization, and then to determine the appropriate level of effort necessary to take full advantage of these opportunities. Similarly, other priorities will originate from identifying risks or threats to the organization, which you or your team are in a position to prevent or contain. If you are in a middle management position, these priorities may even be determined for you.

Examples of priorities might include establishing or implementing:

- Ethics guidelines and controls
- Pricing systems
- Brand image
- Supply chain strategy
- Talent management
- R&D/marketing collaboration
- Six Sigma practices
- IT transformation
- Responses to competitive threats

Paying Attention to Subtle Clues

In addition to the more straightforward process of determining "best use of time" activities, there are other, more subtle clues to which you should pay attention.

Longer-Term Planning

The pace of the workforce today is fostering short-term thinking. We are expected to be available 24/7, technologies keep us in touch no

---

(*Continued*)

Paying Attention to Subtle Clues (Continued)

matter where we are, and we all multitask in an effort to keep up. As a result, important tasks, but those perceived as less urgent for the moment, are pushed onto the back burner. Good examples are training, systems implementation, strategic thinking, and other creative activities.

Gradual Change

The Law of Gradual Change applies to all aspects of business, internal and external. Often, the greatest risk is the one unseen—thus the lament, "I didn't see it coming." That means monitoring gradual changes must be a priority in itself, and as such is a very good use of your time. The information you gather while doing this may lead you to reprioritize and react in a timely manner.

Near Misses

A very good source of information about prioritizing your activities can be obtained by analyzing a "near miss" situation. Unfortunately, many of us don't do this in much depth. We are often so relieved that a negative event wasn't too costly ("I dodged a bullet") that we quickly move on, rather than revisit the situation in detail.

In our personal lives a near miss could be an auto accident that doesn't do much damage, an episode of road rage that endangered you or your family, an incident where a child is suspended from school but not expelled, or a serious infection that lingers longer than you would expect. In business a near miss might refer to a product launch that was delayed multiple times, a new system implementation that was marred by miscommunication, or a competitive threat that did damage but was eventually overcome. If you analyze your near misses you will uncover vital high payoff preventative action steps that warrant a greater investment of your time.

Spending Time Effectively

At this point, you should have developed very solid ideas about your high-payoff activities, so now I want to introduce other guidelines, which, if followed, will help to ensure you are spending as much time as possible on necessary activities.

- Put it in your schedule.
- Hire the best.
- Fill holes in the organizational chart.
- Create three "buckets" of priorities—nice to do, good enough, need to do well.
- Delegate.
- Regularly ask: Is this the best use of my time?
- Combine priorities—multitask effectively.

Put It in the Schedule

If something is a priority, it is imperative that you allot the appropriate amount of time to it. One of the simplest and most effective ways of doing this is to, simply, put it on your calendar and set aside the appropriate amount of time each week to it. If you don't put it on the calendar, any number of factors could conspire against your completion of this priority task:

- You may just forget to do it.
- Other people may place demands, which seem more urgent, on your time.
- You won't have an accurate perception of committed time versus available time and so may make suboptimal decisions about future commitments of time.

Bottom line? Schedule any high-payoff activity, especially those with longer-term importance, immediately.

Hire the Best

The most consistently successful (and often least stressed) executives I work with are relentless about hiring the best available talent for their teams. This initiative applies to everyone, from the administrative staff to the number-one "go to" person. These execs find people who excel in areas that they don't, and then they delegate accordingly. They don't just "make do" with marginal performers, and so are less likely to be heard uttering the all-too-familiar refrain, "I should have moved on this person sooner."

Fill Holes in the Org Chart

Most executives at some point in their careers will have a space in the organizational chart that goes unfilled for a period of time. The smart ones, who are thinking ahead both about themselves and their team, are aggressive about filling those positions. Currently, the demands of most positions in any company push people to their limits. Why tempt fate and expect one person to do two or three jobs, with no consequences?

Create Three Buckets of Priorities

A common expression many people have heard since childhood is "If something is worth doing, it is worth doing right." While I don't want to directly contradict something your mom or dad or favorite teacher told you, if you are a busy executive, I strongly recommend that you modify this advice. A clunkier but, I think, more effective version might be, "Some things worth doing are worth doing right and some are worth doing 'good enough.'"

The main message is that effective executives divide things into three buckets: nice to do, good enough, and need to do well. While this sounds logical, if you tend to be a perfectionist you may blur these lines. If you know how well a task can really be done then it may be hard for you to do any less. My question to you is, "Do you have the time?" If you work too hard or, sometimes, even work at all on a lower payoff activity, what activity loses out? A high payoff activity, a workout, a nature walk, a networking lunch or a family event?

Let's look at some concrete examples of activities whose importance could be categorized into these three buckets and how to address these activities.

Nice to Do

This category includes activities that would add some value to you or the organization, but they are not crucial. If you don't get around to completing them, nothing bad will happen and you will not feel guilty. If you are unable to address them, nice-to-do activities are excellent candidates for delegation to, or to serve as developmental opportunities for, other people on your team. Examples of nice-to-do activities might include certain trips, meetings, conferences, reading materials, task forces, or lunches, depending on your current priorities and scheduling.

Good Enough

The activities that fall into this category are usually perceived as those that deserve maximum effort, but this is often not the reality. Remember, there is still another bucket, "need to do well," where the most important activities will fall. The difference between these two categories is that there is a variety of tasks that are important and need to be accomplished but, given other priorities, tight schedules, and personal needs, do not need to be done perfectly.

This is a difficult distinction for perfectionists to make. If "good enough" is not a phrase you're comfortable using, I suggest you learn to say it more often, for the good of your overall performance. You *can* write "good enough" reports, give "good enough" presentations, be a "good enough" participant on a task force, and even be a "good enough" mentor. If you tend to dedicate the same intense effort to all your activities, it can be a beneficial to evaluate your schedule and determine which activities belong in this bucket. You can commit to performing these tasks but make sure that the effort you devote to them matches their importance, not your standard of how much better you could do it.

To all my perfectionist readers, I acknowledge that you could make the report better if you revised it one more time. But you must decide if the improvements you could make to this report are worth the time and effort. Some of my clients tell me, "Marty, I am not a perfectionist. You don't understand my job. My whole calendar is filled with 'need-to-do-well' tasks." If this sounds similar to how you perceive your role here are some points to consider:

- Consider the three-bucket system while planning the activities of your upcoming workweek. I've rarely met an executive who couldn't pull some nice-to-do and good-enough items out of their need-to-do-well buckets.
- Read Chapter 12, which will point out ways to increase your control over your calendar. Most executives have greater flexibility, the ability to say no, and more authority to set limits than they realize.

"Something has to give." If your entire schedule is packed with "need-to-do-well" tasks, and you are seeing signs of reaching the point of diminishing returns, then ask yourself, Is this pace sustainable? What am I willing to trade off? Am I consciously making these sacrifices?

Need to Do Well

Obviously, this is the bucket in which the high-payoff activities and success factors you have identified belong. These are the activities worthy of attention to detail and optimum effort, the activities that have the potential to pay huge dividends by saving you time later. Planning, preparation, and systems implementations are clear examples of tasks that fall in the need-to-do-well bucket; less obvious ones might include communicating or building relationships that, for reasons only you can determine, belong in this bucket. A word of caution here: I have seen many individuals who spent hundreds of hours developing a new system and then neglected to dedicate two hours to stakeholder communication that would have ensured a smooth launch. Similarly, individual and team efforts can be short-circuited if key relationships are not cultivated or maintained.

Once you have identified the priorities most deserving of your time and effort, it is important to be realistic about the amount of time that you need to devote to each of them, and schedule them accordingly, *before* filling in the rest of your schedule. And while doing this, don't forget to reflect on the activities you've spent time on over the past month. Make note of some preliminary thoughts about which buckets you put them in and which, in retrospect, you should have put them in. You can use this table to begin your list. It may help you make decisions about the current use of your time, and even if you make no changes now, it will help you if a crisis or new opportunity causes you to reprioritize.

THREE BUCKETS LIST

Nice to Do	Good Enough	Need to Do Well
_____	_____	_____
_____	_____	_____
_____	_____	_____

Delegate

One of the best ways to improve your delegation skills harkens back to an earlier guideline: hire the best. When you hire highly qualified, responsible, low-maintenance people in the first place, it will be easier for you to do your job, delegate accordingly, and manage a successful team.

What should you delegate to others? Good-enough and nice-to-do tasks are good choices. The best activities are ones that are important, but that you don't like to do and/or that someone on your team is more skillful at than you.

What are the most important factors to keep in mind when delegating?

1. Explain the task as clearly as possible. Take the time to explain in specific detail what you are delegating. Are you delegating a task, an overall function, or a goal that you want to achieve?
2. Explain the scope and responsibilities, and assign the appropriate decision-making authority.
3. Be clear about how much communication you expect regarding progress and decisions or issues that arise.

Another key to effective delegation is accurately assessing the competence of the person you are assigning to the task. Ideally, he or she will have the ability to do the task well or learn quickly from mistakes.

Ask: Is This the Best Use of My Time?

In addition to following the guidelines and exercises in this chapter for assessing your schedule and identifying high-payoff activities, it's important to check in with yourself on a regular basis. A simple way to do this is to regularly ask yourself, "Is what I am doing now really the best use of my time?"

When you focus on optimizing your time and energy, an important factor to consider is when during the day you are more proficient at certain tasks. For example, I find my most creative ideas come to me lying in bed from 5:30 to 6:00 in the morning, so I keep a pad and pen next to my bed. My best writing hours are between 8:30 and noon.

You need to figure out which times of the day are optimal for you to complete tasks that involve, for example, planning, reflecting, doing creative work, making phone calls, writing and answering e-mails, resolving conflict, completing performance reviews, and so on. If you notice a marked difference in your output at different times, factor this in when you ask yourself, "Is this the best use of my time?"

Combining Priorities

With so many priorities, roles, and commitments, looking for ways to advance two or three of our objectives at the same time always makes sense. You have read about examples of accomplishing two goals at the same time in the fitness chapters (e.g., reading business-related materials while riding a stationary bike, or walking while thinking creatively about possible business solutions, and so on). In the chapter on relationships we will revisit this concept and look at ways of combining relationship goals with other priorities. Some of the most meaningful and motivational activities combine our business goals and our deepest personal values. Many executives have a strong desire to strengthen their communities. Some are searching for a way to be charitable, give back to society, or leave a legacy. For others, the path is to accumulate wealth and donate to a cause that inspires them. More and more executives and organizations today are finding ways of integrating societal goals with their business endeavors. Examples include:

- Indra Nooyi, PepsiCo's CEO, has "turbo-charged" her company's expansion into the "better-for-you" aisles of our supermarkets. In addition to achieving strategic objectives, she has stirred the aspirations of thousands of PepsiCo's employees by appealing to their higher motives. Her leadership banner is "Performance with Purpose," and she has aggressively revamped product offerings, focused on innovation, and is insisting that PepsiCo adhere to environmentally-sensitive practices.
- Monitor, a highly successful management consulting company, used its resources and skills to partner with *Fast Company* magazine to identify and reward social entrepreneurship. Social entrepreneurs use their business acumen to address social and environmental issues. In this way, Monitor's employees can "live their values," at the same time it enhances their respect for and loyalty to their organization. And, obviously, the program is a good source of positive publicity.
- Habitat for Humanity retreats: Today, more and more corporations are combining off-site meetings and retreats with Habitat for

Humanity building projects. Dee Danmeyer, executive director of the Orlando affiliate, says demand is so high that they are fully booked a year in advance. Tamla Olivier, a human resources executive at T. Rowe Price in Baltimore, has organized several of these projects for that firm's employees. She finds that, in addition to the contribution to the community, these activities bolster camaraderie, networking, and teamwork skills and practices.

NOTE

According to a 2004 Cone Corporate Citizenship Study, 86 percent of American consumers indicate that they are somewhat likely or very likely to switch to a brand associated with a cause, if product and quality were on par.

As you analyze your schedule, your priorities, and all the objectives you are trying to achieve, it is beneficial and rewarding to be creative and look for useful ways to integrate them with your personal value system as well.

Executive Profile

B. Ramalinga Raju, Chairman and CEO, Satyam Computer Services

Satyam is a global consulting and IT services company that has experienced phenomenal growth, from 100 associates in 1992 to over 42,500 in 2007. It now operates in 57 countries, providing a wide range of expertise to 570 companies. Raju, and his brother Ramu, founded the company and infused it with a strategy and leadership philosophy that emphasizes entrepreneurship, innovation, and learning. They have created the Satyam School of Leadership under the direction of Senior Vice President Ed Cohen. In 2007, Satyam won the

American Society of Training and Development (ASTD) BEST award as the number-one learning company.

Satyam's success and visibility has made Raju one of the most respected leaders in India. I was fortunate to work with him and his top 25 executives, and was impressed with their curiosity and openness to learning. I was interested in Raju's personal leadership approach, particularly how he deals with the challenges of growth, change, and complexity. I learned that he places a very high priority on reflection. This is so important to him that he embeds it in his schedule and has made it a vital aspect of leadership at Satyam.

On a personal level, he practices a form of contemplation and meditation in the morning, and often at another point in the day. He believes that because executives are confronted with so much new information each day they need to reflect upon, sort out, and assimilate the implications. Raju is also a voracious reader, and credits the learning he gains from this activity with shaping his leadership values. Although Satyam's associates are very practical and fast-paced, Raju encourages them to divide their time between thinking, doing, and communicating. He also emphasizes the importance of asking good questions, staying in touch with reality, and thinking about the interest of stakeholders, investors, and clients.

I asked Raju how he maintains his balance while leading a company that has been growing at a rate of 35 to 40 percent a year. He explained that his religious practice and family bonds are the foundation, and that he also regards his efforts to build Satyam as connecting to a higher purpose. He does not separate work and leisure into unenjoyable/enjoyable categories. He loves his work—he has found his "sweet spot."

Summary

Executives often remark that time is their most precious commodity. Building on this premise, the insights and techniques in this chapter can guide you to be able to add the maximum value in your role. My goal was to help you identify where your efforts will yield the biggest rewards and to free up time to devote to these activities. When you achieve this, you will still need to be vigilant. There are many factors, both internal and external, that lead us to spend time on low-payoff activities. In Chapter 12 you will learn how to prevent this.

12 | Taking Control of Your Calendar

While eliminating unproductive activities is something most people strive to do, I'm hoping that now it has acquired some increased urgency. The most fundamental of priorities and commitments already account for a large part of your schedule, and most executives will acknowledge that they don't have the luxury of participating in unproductive activities. Yet established habits, a lack of certain skills, and a prevalence of outdated systems allow this misuse of time, talent, and resources to persist. Despite these organizational shortcomings, individuals must scrutinize their habits and patterns to determine when time is either not being optimally spent or, in some cases, being wasted. This chapter will outline crucial skills you can develop that can help you increase the control you have over your calendar.

For those of you who are already feeling symptoms of burnout, the questions you may have are, "Is this just an inevitable price I have to pay if I have this role, at this company, in this industry? Does this have something to do with how I do my job and can I be better at setting limits, boundaries, and controlling my schedule?" In other words, is it you (and your ability to control your behaviors) or is it the role you fulfill? This chapter can help you answer those questions because it will equip you with the skills and techniques for gaining more control and reducing stress. One important factor to consider is that your company may be more flexible than you realize. You may have more power to set limits and protect your personal time than you realize. A recent Hudson time-off survey, conducted by

Rasmussen Reports, found that many employees were reluctant to take advantage of opportunities their companies offered (e.g., vacation days), despite the fact that they were available to them.

To begin, I want to introduce the key principle underlying all the messages in this chapter: If your plate is full, realize that every time you say yes to something, you are saying no to something else. With that in mind, I want you also to consider the implications in your life of:

- Spending time on low-priority activities.
- Not having a plan for your time.
- Engaging with toxic people.
- Wasting time in unproductive meetings.
- Failing to overcome procrastination.
- Becoming addicted to technology.
- Traveling unnecessarily.

Spending Time on Low-Priority Activities

This is an easy trap to fall into, especially if the activity used to be a high-priority one; you simply continue to do it, long after you should have moved on—delegated it to someone else, for example. You may also continue to engage in an activity that's comfortable for you, or you're good at, or that was, at one point in your career, a wise use of your time. I've covered this before—the importance of evaluating all your activities and determining which are high priority and which need to be "downsized." Whenever you're "running on empty," take the time to ask yourself the hard questions. Here are some examples:

- If you are now vice president of sales, should you still be following the "player-coach" model of keeping a few clients?
- If you are the president of the commercial loan division, should you still be scrutinizing all the loan approvals? Similarly, should you still be doing the analyses, presentations, or field trips that you used to do?

Only you (sometimes in consultation with your boss) can answer these questions. If your schedule is out of control, reevaluate and start eliminating tasks or responsibilities that are no longer the best use of your time.

Not Having a Plan for Your Time

Simply put, if you don't have a plan for your time, someone else will. And you can't blame them for trying, especially if it has worked in the past. There you are, an easy target, an open door, a good listener, someone with lots of ideas and resources. You must expect and prepare for it. Expect the interruptions and the meetings, the calls and task force requests popping up on your calendar. If you are lucky, once in a while someone else's agenda dovetails with yours, but I wouldn't count on this happening too often. Here are some essential ways to protect yourself from the inevitable requests.

Limit Interruptions

Interruptions lower your productivity beyond the actual time you spend responding to them. Even if you were engaged in a routine activity before the interruption, it will take time to reestablish your focus and get back on track; and depending upon the nature of the interruption and what you were doing when it occurred, you may be diverted even longer. If, say, you were involved in systems planning, strategic thinking, presentation preparation, analysis, or writing, an interruption can set you way back in terms rhythm and creativity. If you were "in the flow" when an interruption occurred, it can also affect your mood negatively, causing you to become frustrated or angry.

Also, become aware of the tendency some of us have to interrupt ourselves—usually by way of technology: cell phones, pagers, and the like. By keeping these devices on all the time, it is more tempting to distract ourselves.

It is not realistic to think we can eliminate all interruptions, but a reasonable goal is to reduce their number, thereby establishing greater control over our schedules. Improvement is the goal. How? You've already taken the first step by reading this: recognition. Here are other suggestions that may help.

Control the Setting

When you are engaged in a key activity that will be negatively impacted by interruptions, close the door; instruct your assistant to tell others you are unavailable for the next X-amount of time; position yourself away from the window; shut off your tech devices.

Relocate Entirely

Certain tasks call for relocation to a place where you can't get interrupted or distracted. For example, you may want to hold an important feedback session or a performance review in a conference room. Training sessions or meetings may require an off-site setting. For key creative or reflective activities, find a place that's right for you—and most executives will tell you that their office is *not* that place.

Resist the Quick Yes

Don't commit to taking on new activities or responsibilities without thinking it through and consulting your calendar. If you don't follow this rule, it will be very difficult for you to gain control over your calendar. David Allen, a productivity guru and author of *Getting Things Done* (Penguin, 2002), agrees. "A basic truism I have discovered over twenty years of coaching and training is that most of the stress people experience comes from inappropriately managed commitments they make or accept." Remember, "If you don't have a plan for yourself, someone else will." Other people will make both routine and unexpected requests on your time. It is at these moments that you must make decisions about what goals are most important. Are you a nice person who likes to help others? Are you afraid of conflict or making someone else upset? Do you think it will hurt your career to say no? Being in any of these scenarios might predispose you to say yes.

It's also good to remember in this regard that "we train other people how to treat us." You have, no doubt, already done this. People know how to approach you—whether you respond best to pressure, to name-dropping, or to flattery. Whatever the reason and whoever the source, my advice to you is to never say yes quickly. This is easier said than done, of course, when someone is standing in front of you waiting for an answer. Be strong. Few of us can judge accurately how long an assignment or project will take based on someone else's description of it. Even after close scrutiny, we underestimate the time required to complete a task. Needless to say, the person asking for your help is likely to lowball the estimate of your time involvement, to persuade you to take on the project. You must take the time to consider what is already on your plate and how this new commitment will impact those current priorities. Ask yourself: Is this a best-use-of-my-time activity? It may be, but you can't know that without investigating the matter thoroughly. Follow these guidelines:

1. Listen politely. Try to determine as accurately as possible the urgency, objectives, and time commitments involved.
2. If the request has some merit or interest for you, tell the person that you will need to check your schedule and current commitments before making a decision. Give the person a specific date and time when you will get back to them.
3. If this is not a project or task you can take on now, for whatever reason, make use of the "soft no," the polite but interested refusal. Here are some examples:

   - "I don't have the time right now to attend the meetings that will be required if I join the task force. I agree with you that I have some relevant experience. I might agree later to review the findings of the task force and give you feedback before the final report is published."

- "My team and I are fully committed to two projects that are high priorities. But I can recommend an excellent consultant who could provide the support you are looking for. If this project is really urgent, maybe you can find the funds to hire her."
- "Given what is currently on my plate, the only thing I could do is to have lunch with you on Tuesday and brainstorm some design ideas. If I get an unexpected cancellation, I will reconsider working on the project; otherwise, my schedule is full for the next 60 days."

What if the request comes from your boss or senior management? In such a situation, the techniques you've just learned become even more useful. Here are some very important points to consider before you frame your response:

- Your boss usually is not aware of your current commitments. If this is the case, let him or her know: "We are all working at full capacity right now so taking on this project would require making some adjustments, either making a current project a lower priority or getting some help (e.g., outside consultant, increased head count or borrowing someone from another department)."
- There is an even greater chance that your boss is unaware of your personal commitments. If, say, his or her request will cause you to renege on a promise to be at a family event, or take a vacation, mention as well. You might say, "I want to help get this done, and I understand the urgency, but I scheduled this vacation and promised my family, and I don't want to change that. Let me brainstorm with the team and I will get back to you with a plan on how we can proceed."

In the end, you may need to shift priorities, work longer hours (depending on the importance and urgency of the request) and leverage your team; but you often can find a way to meet your commitments to your company, your personal relationships, and yourself. Whatever the outcome, you need to send an important message to your boss: I am a flexible, responsible, can-do person, but I will continue to set limits and boundaries in my role. Setting limits in this way may be the most important rule to begin implementing for all executives but especially if you tend to put other people's needs first and have a difficult time saying no.

Engaging with Toxic People

We all know so-called toxic people. They're the ones who deplete you; they waste time in meetings or conversations, and often are the cause of conflicts that seem to have no resolution. You notice after interacting with them that you feel drained and, often, angry. Toxic people come in many guises: some are bullies; others are naysayers, masters at putting down people and projects. Some are straightforward, while others are more subtle. Some toxic people tend to love melodrama, and setting it in motion. Whatever form toxic people come in, one thing they all have in common: They waste your time and energy

> **NOTE**
>
> One thing toxic people can do for you, however: They can add to your self-knowledge, if you take the time to figure out why they have such a powerful impact on you. Conversely, once you understand their effect on you, you may develop the skill to turn them around.
>
> This topic is beyond the scope of this book, however; if you want to learn more about how to handle toxic people, refer to *The No ***hole Rule,* by Robert Sutton (Business Plus, 2007) and *Survival of the Savvy* (Brandon and Seldmen, Free Press, 2004).

So what's the smartest, easiest, and most effective strategy for dealing with toxic people? Simply, minimize your contact with them, as much as possible. Obviously, this may be easier said than done, depending on their relationship to you at work. But by setting boundaries, limiting interruptions, and governing what you say yes and no to, you will effectively reduce your interactions with toxic people, which will result in an immediate improvement in your productivity.

Wasting Time in Unproductive Meetings

How many meetings have you have attended in your career? Hundreds? Thousands? How many of them would you consider to have been productive, a good use of the collective time spent? Most of us would cite a low percentage. Without an effective structure, adequate preparation, attentive participation, and expert facilitation, most meetings never accomplish what they're called to do. Here are two tips for making meetings more productive.

Use a Facilitator

To conduct effective meetings, the most important factor is facilitation. I called on Kevin Wilde, the chief learning officer for General Mills, to provide valuable input for this section. Kevin is widely respected in his field for many reasons (he was named by *Chief Learning Officer* magazine as "CLO of the Year 2007"), but at General Mills one his most important contributions is to serve as facilitator for Mike Peel, Executive VP of Human Resources, and Steve Sanger, CEO, at some of the company's most important senior management meetings.

According to Kevin, a good facilitator prepares and distributes a clear and comprehensible agenda for every meeting. Low-priority items or topics that apply only to two or three attendees are not included; they are reassigned to a different agenda. At the meeting, the facilitator ensures that all attendees are informed of the purpose and parameters of the discussion at hand. Is this an information-sharing session? Is the team expected to reach a conclusion, make a decision? Are they providing input regarding a decision that their CEO will ultimately make?

Most important, the facilitator keeps the discussion focused, and ensures that the appropriate amount of time is devoted to each issue based on its relative priority. Finally, a facilitator documents the outcome of the meeting: who has agreed to do what, and when. This makes it easier for the team's leaders to "inspect what they expect," thereby assuring accountability.

If you or one of your colleagues is a good facilitator, you may not need to bring in someone like Kevin. That said, you may prefer the freedom using a facilitator provides; it enables you to participate freely in the meeting. Or you may want to consider a "rotating facilitator," whereby alternating members on your team take on this role. Just be sure anyone performing this function has, or is willing to learn, facilitation skills. You spend so much time in meetings, it's important to make it time well spent.

Encourage Interaction, Not Passivity

One of the most common time wasters and energy deflators at informational meetings is when the speaker reads verbatim from a PowerPoint presentation. Typically, in these meetings, participants are all given a copy of the presentation. They usually scan the pages at a faster rate than the presenter can speak. In addition, they are reading the slide, again ahead of the presenter's recitation of it. If the presenter reads the presentation, word for word, the audience is now processing the information for the third time within a span of minutes. The audience is likely composed of bright, creative, highly compensated executives. This one-way repetitive monologue rarely fosters a setting conducive to asking questions or citing concerns. Compounding the problem, many presenters squeeze way too much information onto the slides and too many slides into the presentations.

Almost always, what happens is the presenter barely gets through all of his or her slides. The net result is a suboptimal use of time and a passive role foisted on the audience that leads to boredom, frustration, and a minimum of team building.

If you use slides, as most people do, decide in advance the key discussion points on each slide. Leave some time for questions and discussions with your colleagues. Put less on each slide and use fewer slides overall. While it might require more skill and preparation on your part, and more effort to manage time and keep the discussions on track, your audience will be more energized and participants will learn from each other. You will also get a much better gauge of how receptive the audience is to your idea.

Failing to Overcome Procrastination

For our purposes, I will define procrastination as a behavior that involves engaging in a lower priority or time-wasting activity while avoiding a high-payoff activity that you know you should be doing. The emphasis here is on the fact that you know that a certain task is a "best use of your time" and that completing it would help you reach your goals, yet you find yourself avoiding the task. Most executives procrastinate about something. We probably procrastinate even more in our personal lives, but this chapter will focus on procrastination during business activities. However, the insights and techniques you will learn here will help you overcome procrastination wherever it is occurring.

Procrastination is more likely when we are faced with:

- *Large projects:* These are projects that are time consuming and costly—These could include IT systems transformation, facilities upgrades, or the need for strategic thinking. The reasons we usually put off getting started are either (a) the task seems overwhelming, or (b) we've had a negative experience with this kind of project that hurt our confidence or (c) the task seems vague, like "strategic thinking."
- *Tasks we are afraid of:* Yes, even CEOs have fears: speaking in public, having a "tough love" conversation, firing people, developing media contacts, or making mistakes. Fears in any of these scenarios can

trigger avoidance behaviors that ultimately delay or sabotage their accomplishment.

- *Tasks we don't like:* We may not like building and maintaining networks (if this is the case, you probably refer to this task as schmoozing), writing reports, number crunching, tracking our expenses, going to training classes, or even reading and reflecting. If these tasks are simply "nice to do" and you put off doing them there is little consequence. However, if some of these activities are success factors then avoidance will hurt you.

How does procrastination hurt your effectiveness? In addition to the obvious, if something important to your productivity doesn't get done, here are some other effects:

- *Loss of peace of mind:* If we could blissfully procrastinate this negative would be eliminated. In fact, we are rarely settled and relaxed while procrastinating. In some corner of our minds, a nagging thought detracts from our serenity. We may think about the important unfinished task on our "to do" list and be distracted, or feel guilty.
- *Loss of self-esteem:* Over time, the process of acknowledging something is important. Committing yourself to tasks and then putting them off erodes our self-respect. You may doubt yourself. "Why don't I do what I say I'm going to do?"
- *Upsetting Others:* Some of the tasks you delay make it harder for other people to be productive. If they are waiting for you to complete a report, make a decision, or start a certain task force and you don't deliver, over time procrastination will hurt your relationships and even your reputation.

The most likely reasons you will put off tasks are:

Fear of change
Fear of the unknown
Fear of failure
A large project

Not being clear about what you are supposed to do or not knowing
how to get started
Having done it before and experienced failure
The task is boring or unpleasant

Before I offer techniques for overcoming procrastination, take a few
minutes to list those tasks or activities that send you into procrastination
mode, along with the reasons why.

PROCRASTINATION LIST

Tasks or Activities I Avoid   **Reasons I Avoid Them**

1. _____   1. _____
2. _____   2. _____
3. _____   3. _____
4. _____   4. _____

Tips and Techniques for Overcoming Procrastination

The suggestions I offer here for overcoming procrastination are based on
the common causes for avoidance behaviors I listed above.

- If the task you're avoiding makes you uncomfortable or fearful, consider these options:

  1. Seek training and coaching in the area in which you lack confi-
     dence. None of us is good at everything; if you need help, ask for
     it, then practice your new skill until you gain confidence.
  2. Balance the risk you may be overfocused on the cost of making a
     mistake or a poor decision by also focusing equally hard on the risk
     of being slow or not acting. When you see that there is a signifi-
     cant downside risk to *not acting* in a timely way, this may motivate

you to move forward. Remember, your competitors may innovate, install the next generation IT system, hire a top talent, or make a strategic acquisition before you.

- If the project seems too vague or overwhelming:

1. Break down the project into incremental steps. Start small, but get going. Sometimes the biggest hurdle in these situations is to simply get started.
2. Schedule minimums. This is a very useful application of the minimum system. Even if you tell yourself, "I am going to work on this for 30 minutes today," you will notice a positive shift in you attitude, motivation and, eventually, execution.

- If the task is unpleasant:

1. Do it now and get it over with. One proactive habit to get into is to identify the tasks that you are likely to put off and do them first. Your self-esteem and sense of control will rise almost immediately.
2. Schedule it immediately. If you don't, you know what will happen: Something else will take your attention or you'll find an excuse to put it off.
3. Focus on the positives. Remember what you learned about self-talk. You can control your focus by what you say to yourself. If you focus on how boring or unpleasant a task will be, you are effectively demotivating yourself, making it less likely you will devote full effort to completing it.
4. This is the converse of the first suggestion here. That is, don't allow yourself do something you love until you complete that important task you have been avoiding—and don't cheat. If you are staring at four months' worth of travel and entertainment expenses that you have allowed to accumulate, and your favorite sports team or movie is going to be on TV in an hour, make a deal with yourself that you won't turn on the TV until you have completed at least two months' worth of expenses. It may be a good idea to get

support for this: make an agreement with someone in your family to hold you to this.

Everyone procrastinates about something. If you are avoiding something important, use any of these techniques to cut down on your procrastination time. Using them in a disciplined way will have the added benefit of heightening your sense of control.

Becoming Addicted to Technology

As we all know, we human beings can become addicted, or at least very strongly attached, to many things. One of them is stimulation; and in this day and age, that stimulation often comes in the form of now-ubiquitous communication technologies—cell phones, pagers, BlackBerries, e-mail, the Internet. Yes, these technologies and devices are tremendous aides to our productivity; some of us wonder how we got by without them in the past. But too much of anything, no matter how valuable, can be detrimental to our well-being. The warning signs that you may be addicted to "being in touch" include:

- Checking e-mail and voicemail incessantly.
- Interrupting yourself or others to answer your cell phone.
- Spending time online unnecessarily.

Checking E-Mail and Voicemail Incessantly

Over a century and a half ago Henry David Thoreau wrote in *Walden*, "Hardly a man takes a half-hour's nap after dinner, but when he wakes he holds up his head and asks, 'What's the news?'" Imagine what he'd say today if he saw us checking our voicemail and e-mail. Ask yourself: Am I checking in more than I have to? Do I become anxious when I can't check in? Are the devices constantly stimulating me?

If you answered yes to any of those questions, monitor your behavior in this regard for a day; or ask people who work or live with you, and listen to what they have to say.

Interrupting to Answer Your Cell Phone

Remember the discussion about the impact of interruptions on productivity? Do you interrupt yourself when writing a report or planning a presentation to answer your phone? Do you interrupt a conversation with someone else because it rings?

Doing so is not only counterproductive, others can perceive it as disrespectful. You know how it feels when you are saying something important to an individual or a group and someone interrupts to answer a cell phone or to look at his or her messages on a BlackBerry device. It is important to develop clear boundaries about when to use these devices and when to turn them off—and it's not just when you're at the movies or a concert.

Spending Too Much Time Online

Maressa Hecht Orzack, a Harvard-affiliated psychologist who helped establish the Computer Addiction Service at McLean Hospital, admitted this about her own computer use: "Initially, I noticed I was spending too much time on computer games . . . I became so absorbed that I neglected or delayed meeting various personal obligations. I stayed up too late. This led me to realize that behavior of this kind could be an addiction."

No question about it, the Internet and the Web have become invaluable tools for most of us; the danger comes when we let ourselves get caught in a web that is hard to extricate ourselves from. And this is tricky because it is easy to lose track of time while online. Make it a practice when you're on the computer to ask yourself regularly, "Is this the best use of my time?" Could I instead be exercising, stretching, doing yoga, meditating, spending time with family or friends, or getting started on that project I've been avoiding?

Traveling Unnecessarily

Think back to the last time you had a meeting at an out-of-town conference center. You woke up, did your morning activities, but something was missing: commuting. You didn't have to drive to get your coffee, go to the gym, or get to your meeting. While traveling to the conference center may have involved some hassles, few of us mind missing our commute once we are there. It is definitely possible and desirable to make our commutes more productive and less stressful but consider some possibilities for simply cutting down on our travel time.

Telecommuting and Videoconferencing

In April 2007, a freeway meltdown in San Francisco's East Bay caused the region's residents to have nightmares about traffic chaos, but very few of the expected problems occurred. John Grubb, vice president of communications for the Bay Area Council, speculated that telecommuting might be one of the reasons that larger problems were avoided.

Millions of people telecommute already but technology is making it much easier to be very productive at a home office, at least for part of your week. In addition to the communication tools we've already mentioned, there has been a dramatic improvement in videoconferencing or creating virtual meetings. For example, Cisco Systems developed "TelePresence" so that users appear life-size on the screen and sit around a virtual table. Second Life, created by Linden Labs, uses collaboration tools to allow multiple users to share and edit documents online.

While these are cutting edge developments as I write this book, many months before you are reading it, there are undoubtedly even newer vehicles for video and virtual meetings available to you now.

Daily commutes for many executives are arduous and, if you live near big cities like New York or Los Angeles, increasingly unpredictable. Business travel (unless you have use of the corporate jet) is increasingly more time consuming and often less comfortable. So, a quick way to save a lot more time and reduce your stress is to take full advantage of these technologies, your company's flextime, and your own degree of control over your schedule and reduce your business travel.

Location Neutral Careers

Increasingly, lawyers, consultants, software developers and designers, architects, and investment advisors are able to pursue their careers and live where they choose. This is one reason why places like Steamboat Springs, Nantucket, the Upper Peninsula of Michigan, and Teton County, Idaho have up to 10 percent of their residents in these types of careers. Japan, which has invested heavily in technology infrastructure, is expected to have 50 percent of its workforce operating from home by 2010.

You may not be able to effectively contribute in your current role from Steamboat Springs, but perhaps you can determine what part of your job is location neutral. You may be able to make the case that without commuting time and office distractions, you will be more effective on certain projects. Ask your manager and/or team if they are willing to allow you to pilot or test this possibility for a specific assignment.

Summary

The core concept of this section is worth repeating. Whether you do it yourself, or allow others to do it for you, spending time on less important activities increases these risks: You may extend your day, pushing you closer to the point of diminishing returns. A more important issue or activity may not receive the time and focus it deserves. You may sacrifice a personal priority relating to your health, relationship, or renewal.

PART IV

CAREER
MANAGEMENT

13 | Reaching Your Full Potential

The last two chapters focused on ways of giving ourselves the best chance for outstanding job performance and business results. At this point you may be asking, " (1) Isn't that the best way to manage your career?, (2) If I get consistently good results won't I be fine?, and (3) Why these extra chapters on career management?" Here are the answers:

- Getting results is extremely important and the number-one thing to focus on. It is a good way to manage your career but, without additional practices, it is not the optimum way.
- If you get consistently good results you probably will be fine, but there is no guarantee that you will reach your full career potential.

These additional chapters on career management will address these deeper issues.

If you have a strong track record of results within your organization, odds are you have moved up or are being considered for a broader role. Ideally, your results will speak for themselves and the selection process will be fair and objective. Most big companies have formal processes to document performance, gather feedback, and perform appraisals. In addition, there are talent reviews, human resource planning, "bench strength" and succession planning, and so on. Most of the time, personnel decisions involving higher-level positions culminate with the decision makers sitting around a table discussing the candidates being considered.

Some obvious but important facts to point out about this event: You are not in the room. You won't be there to provide additional information or correct any misperceptions. You are relying on at least one person there (who has influence and is willing to use it on your behalf) to accurately recount your achievements and potential. This discussion is between human beings, not an exchange of data by computers. Human beings strive to be objective but often are subjective in our assessments. Strong results will not guarantee the decision will go your way. There is a variety of factors that can influence this decision.

Decision-Making Factors

New Skills Requirements

If you've been a consistent top performer in your current role, you have already demonstrated your value to your company. But what if the new role calls for different competencies (e.g., strategic thinking, building teams, cross-cultural sensitivity, running a P&L operation, fostering innovation, and so on)? Without some indication that you're talented in unproven areas, the company may be hesitant to give you the new job. That's why sometimes the best salesperson fails to become head of sales; the best controller is not made the CFO; or the head of R&D is not promoted to lead new product development.

Faulty Attributions

People may agree about an event and its outcome, yet disagree as to how it all came about. Social psychologists call such interpretation differences *attributions*. In attempting to explain results, different people will attribute them to different factors. What effect does this have on a personnel situation? Consider these sample comments:

"He had a very good year. I heard he has a bright marketing guy who provided most of the strategic thinking."

"Her track record in Brazil is excellent. I would attribute most of her success to being in the right place at the right time."

"Let's not confuse genius with a bull market. Everyone did well these past two years, so I would put her results in context."

"I know he had a good year. I just think he had the potential for a great year. My experience tells me he 'left money on the table' despite these results."

I think you can see how attributions can redirect attention from one person to another, and if they go contested, can influence the trajectory of a person's career—and in the wrong direction.

Faulty Comparisons

When being considered for a new position, your achievements often will be compared to those of other candidates in a different company, division, market, or regulatory environment. The point is, rarely will a direct comparison be possible; rather, what ends up happening is an "apples to oranges" comparison. Thus, decision makers then tend to fall back on subjective, less quantifiable, factors to make their final choice, such as personal relationships.

Lack of Direct Knowledge

Edward Hallowell wrote a book called *Crazy Busy* (Ballantine Books, 2006), which, as you've no doubt noticed, is an underlying theme of this one. A good assumption is that the decision makers responsible for determining your career path are extremely busy. What are the implications of their being busy? They rarely directly observe who does the work or provides the innovative thinking. In collaborative efforts it is hard for them to sort out who did what. Because they don't always feel they have time to check things out, they may be too reliant on the perceptions and feedback of the few people who get access to them. They can be "sound bite"- or "incident"-driven. This means that they may not get that many impressions of you and may give a lot of weight to the few interactions they have. Performance in meetings, attendance at conferences, and participation in visible projects can impact your career more than you realize, and more than they should.

Political Maneuvering

In all organizations, there are people who try to shape perceptions of themselves and others by "managing the airwaves." They are the "politicians," who seek to promote themselves at the expense of their colleagues. We've all seen them at work, taking undeserved credit, blaming others for their shortcomings, and attempting to undermine the reputation of someone they see as a competitor (e.g., "That Marty is a good guy. He gets things done—if you point him in the right direction. Yes, you have to call the plays for him, but then you can count on him."). If one of these political types is on your case, he or she can seriously detract from your getting the credit and recognition you deserve.

Relationship-Based Decision Making

Although corporations strive for a transparent objective process when evaluating people it is almost inevitable that personal feelings will influence decisions about who will fill leadership positions. You may feel you have clearly demonstrated the talent and potential for a key role but three relationship factors can impede the eventual outcome.

1. *You're an unknown.* A corporation may have an established process for scanning the entire enterprise for qualified candidates to fill important positions. However, often when a leader departs unexpectedly,

the process is short-circuited. The call goes out, "Who do you know who is available?" Being known is always an advantage, but in these situations it can be the key qualification. If those responsible for filling the position don't know you well you may not be considered for a role you are qualified to fulfill.

2. *You're known but they are more comfortable with someone else.* Of course people will elevate leaders they like and with whom they are comfortable. The problem for you (and eventually for the shareholders) arises if close relationships and loyalty are rewarded over competence. The media is replete with examples of the "loyalty over competence" decisions in corporations, nonprofits, and government agencies. In addition, if an executive has a very strong relationship with someone, this person often will benefit from the "halo effect." The halo effect refers to the undeserved credit that someone amasses because he is liked or has bonded with someone. These individuals tend to receive high marks in areas that they do not deserve. If you are competing for a position against someone who benefits from the loyalty factor or the halo effect, the chances for an objective decision are greatly diminished.

3. *You're known, but you have "wounded the king or a queen."* A famous piece of advice is, "If you are going after the king, kill him, or don't go after him at all." If you wound the king, he is alive and he knows who did it. A corporate equivalent might be, "In business, friends come and go, but your enemies accumulate." In the next chapter we will focus on the key skills necessary (executive vocabulary, power analysis, verbal discipline, emotional management) to avoid unintentionally "wounding the king." This is another prevalent reason behind why decisions are not always about results. If you have criticized, challenged, or made assertions that threaten someone in a higher position of power, and they are not the type of executive who tolerates this well, it may come back to haunt you.

These six factors can often influence the decisions made by senior management. While achieving results is a key building block in establishing successful careers, being unaware of these detrimental factors can cause you to top out before reaching the levels you aspire to. These six factors can lead to decisions that are not always fair or objective. Therefore, in addition to results, integrity, and leadership, another important component to reach the professional level to which you aspire is organizational savvy.

Organizational Savvy

Organizational savvy refers to a set of skills that combines personal integrity with sound judgment regarding corporate practices and human nature. It has many applications, which include improving influence and persuasion, maintaining high integrity organizations, and fostering effective collaboration. But here we will focus on the importance of Org Savvy in career management.

In *Survival of the Savvy* (Free Press, 2004), I and my coauthor Rick Brandon wrote in depth about the wide variety of practices associated with being organizationally savvy. Here, I will review the fundamental behaviors that can give you a better chance of reaping the rewards of all your hard work.

Based on the definition I just gave, you won't be surprised when I tell you that becoming savvy can take some time; specifically, honing these skills may require you to allocate or reallocate some of your time. In fact, I strongly urge you to put the development of these skills into the "best use of my time" category. In short, they are critical career success factors. Not developing or employing them can offset years of sustained effort.

Often I'm asked, how savvy to I need to be? Or, how much time do I need to devote to becoming savvy? Without sounding glib, the only answer is, you need to be as savvy as your situation demands. That said, there are general categories of savvy skills to use as guidelines. These include:

- Studying power
- Networking wisely
- Learning the culture
- Promoting yourself effectively

- Knowing who to trust
- Knowing the requirements of your next role
- Creating and maintaining an accurate perception of your talent and potential
- Using self-management skills proactively

Studying Power

Being savvy means knowing who has power and how it is used in the organization. This requires understanding:

- How decisions are really made in the organization.
- Who has access to, and influence with, senior executives.
- Who, in meetings and on projects, is "heard;" who gets credit and attention; who gets interrupted, minimized, or marginalized.
- What the top priorities and core values are of the people in power.
- What the key close relationships and competitive relationships are among the senior staff.

Networking Wisely

The day you need a network it is too late to build it. It's never too soon to build a network of supporters and like-minded colleagues—savvy leaders start on day one. And once you've got a network in place, don't forget to tend to it, for you never know when you'll need it. In terms of developing organizational savvy, the people in your network can:

- Inform others about your accomplishments.
- Defend you against misrepresentation.
- Support and sell your ideas.
- Keep you up to date on company "buzz," including how you are being perceived organizationwide.
- Recommend you for a new role.

Learning the Culture

As in social cultures, corporate cultures have norms, core values, and taboos, as well as prescribed or preferred ways of getting things done. Savvy executives understand the power of culture to shape individual behaviors and attitudes. Even if one of their goals is to ultimately change the company culture, they know that, first, they must learn, and have respect for, the one currently in place. Thus, they identify those individuals who are the most astute about the culture in which they must operate, and then they depend on those people to bring them up to speed on how it functions.

Promoting Yourself Effectively

Unless you "blow your own horn," you run the risk of being overlooked when opportunity for advancement knocks. Remember what I said earlier about people at the top of the corporate ladder often being too busy to notice individual accomplishments. You also leave yourself vulnerable to political types who are masters at taking credit for the achievements of others. That said, take care not to go too far with this, or you run the opposite risk, of turning people off with your overt bragging, which will give the impression you are not a team player, but want to be the "star."

Savvy executives find ways to make their accomplishments known in modest, yet effective, ways. One good approach is to emphasize the learnings and applications of their best practices, as opposed to just stating their results.

Knowing Who to Trust

To protect the company's resources and reputation, as well as their careers, it behooves savvy leaders to determine from the outset who they can trust. In this regard, you should become familiar with a concept referred to as "working trust," which involves taking an observational stance when working with someone. For example, does John keep confidences, share credit, and take responsibility for his mistakes? Or does he tend to exaggerate, overcommit, give incomplete or superficial explanations, refuse to admit mistakes, and so on? Savvy executives are better able to detect deception and then can take appropriate action to protect themselves or the company.

Knowing the Requirements of Your Next Role

In his autobiography, *My American Journey* (Ballantine Books, 2003), Colin Powell described how he would focus on the "scorecard"—the key competencies—for the position he wanted next. That knowledge told him what skills he needed to develop or demonstrate to the "powers that be."

This is one of the most straightforward and beneficial savvy practices. If the scorecard for the job you want is significantly different from that of your present role, your current success will not necessarily make you the right person for the new job. Use your network, contact the human resources department, or ask your boss what you will need to know and be able to do for the role to which you aspire.

Creating and Maintaining an Accurate Perception of Your Talent and Potential

An apt saying for this section is: "The difference between reality and perception is that people make decisions based on perception." Rarely are any of us perceived accurately or the way we would like to be, whether professionally or personally. So many influences come into play here, many out of our control. Thus, savvy leaders operate on the premise that people often make decisions based on perception, as opposed to fact. Being savvy in this area doesn't mean creating false perceptions; rather, it means, to the best of your ability while functioning in the all-too subjective business world, making sure that the impression people have of you is as accurate as possible. Here are some guidelines for doing this:

- Be vigilant; find out how you are currently perceived. Even if what you hear is disappointing, listen carefully.

- Identify which of your attributes and characteristics need to be improved.
- Design a development plan to shore up those negative areas. If the feedback indicates you need to be a better listener, or a more strategic thinker, direct your focus there. If you feel that the "buzz" on you is not accurate, determine how to go about changing that.

Using Self-Management Skills Proactively

Being savvy means being a good communicator, particularly in situations involving conflict or debate. Given the pressures and passions surrounding important projects, it is easy for our emotions to get triggered in these situations. In the next chapter, you will read about how easy it is, unfortunately, to damage our careers when certain emotions take over. Therefore, savvy leaders develop an essential set of skills: verbal discipline, vocabulary to respectfully challenge ideas, and emotional self-management.

Savvy Summary

Use the table provided here to help you assess your own savvy behavior. For each of these areas just discussed, and listed in the left-hand column, indicate whether you feel you are doing enough or need to do more.

We learned in Chapter 11 that if something has long-term importance but may not seem urgent, we need to schedule it on our calendar. If not, time for it will be squeezed out by the press of the day's challenges, crises, and requests. If I've convinced you that being savvy is a priority but you think you are already fully committed, then you probably need to revisit the calendar. Are there some items that can be transferred to the nice-to-do bucket or can be delegated? Do you have more urgency to eliminate the time wasters or master the art of saying no? Be sure to make room for being savvy. It will increase your effectiveness and impact while saving you time in the future.

ORG SAVVY CHART

Savvy Skill	Doing Enough	Need to Do More
Studying Power		
Networking wisely		
Learning the culture		
Promoting yourself effectively		
Knowing who to trust		
Knowing the requirements of your next role		
Creating and maintaining an accurate perception of your talent and potential		
Using self-management skills proactively		

Executive Profile

Mike White, CEO, PepsiCo International and Vice Chairman, PepsiCo

Four years ago, PepsiCo created PepsiCo International (PI) by combining its food and beverage businesses outside the United States. Under Mike White's leadership, PI has become a $13 billion division, charting the highest growth rates and profit contribution at the company. Mike has maintained his friendly, modest, and approachable leadership style throughout the 16 years I have known him; and in all those years, I have never heard anyone say a negative word about him. How does he manage such consistency and stability, even now as he handles businesses in 180 countries, across every time zone, and against competitors such as Coca-Cola, Nestlé, Procter & Gamble, and many others? Here's what he has to say:

(Continued)

**Mike White, CEO, PepsiCo International and
Vice Chairman, PepsiCo (Continued)**

- *He takes time off.* Mike could be up at 6:00 A.M. every day and work until midnight and still never run out of business issues to deal with. But he is disciplined about setting aside time when he cannot be reached. In addition to spending time with his family, Mike enjoys playing the piano, sailing, and attending concerts.
- *He hires the best and then lets people do their jobs.* Mike hires, develops, and retains excellent leaders, and knows how to delegate effectively. Mike also makes sure that everyone on his team is clear about his or her role, which enables them to perform at top level. This also precludes misunderstandings and reduces conflict.
- *He is curious.* One of the reasons Mike performs so well in cross-cultural settings is that he goes into new situations assuming he has a lot to learn. He believes a vital part of his job is to ask the right questions, look for the interconnectedness of information (systems, patterns), and eventually figure out how to get to the heart of an issue.
- *He is organizationally savvy.* Obviously, Mike can't be everywhere at the same time and so he must rely on his field staff and functional experts. Using targeted questions and his ability to read people, he evaluates not just the information he receives, but the "messenger" as well.

Summary

How your career advances will be based on more than just your desire and your track record; it will be heavily dependent on the input of others, which may not always be to your advantage. That is why developing organizational savvy is vital to your success.

In the next chapter, we'll expand on this idea, looking specifically at how to avoid making career mistakes.

14

Avoiding Career Management Mistakes

This chapter addresses the phenomenon whereby tremendous professional effort and the best of intentions can still lead to career management mistakes. There are many variations of this phenomenon, but in each case, going past the point of diminishing returns increases the risk of derailment or "topping out." The best way to describe this concept is with an actual event that occurred to a client of mine.

Steven L. was the head of the Northern Latin America (NOLA) division of a multinational consumer products company, headquartered in Rio de Janeiro, Brazil; Steven, however, was based in Ft. Lauderdale, Florida. In his position, he was required to take part in an annual company conference held in Rio and attended by the entire senior leadership of the Latin American division, along with the top three executives of the International group.

About two weeks following the event, which comprised a series of meetings and presentations, including an annual operating review, I received a call from James O., the company's chief human resources executive for the International division. He said, "Marty, I want you to coach Steven. He gave a disappointing presentation in Brazil, and senior management now has some questions about his leadership capabilities."

255

I replied, "James, I would be glad to help, but could you give me more specifics? I talk to him regularly and, from what I understand, he and his team are hitting their numbers this year."

"Yes, he is hitting his numbers, but he made a bad impression last week. His presentation was flat—no energy or enthusiasm. And, more, he seems to have lost his passion for the business. We don't see the 'fire in the belly' anymore. Who knows? If he had led his team with more passion and urgency, they might have blown away the numbers, instead of just hitting them. Several people left the conference feeling NOLA left money on the table this year."

After gathering more specific information about Steven's behavior in Brazil, I called him to set up a meeting. When we met face to face, I asked him how he had prepared for the meetings in Brazil. Here is what I learned:

- Steven had worked until the last minute on several projects.
- He had taken an all-night flight to Rio, timed to arrive the morning of the first meetings. All of his peers and other senior managers had come one or two days early, and in that time had been enjoying the sun, sea, and spa facilities at the hotel.
- In addition to appearing at the last minute, Steven arrived sick, having developed a cold as a result of the late hours he'd been keeping and lack of sleep. So his usual fair-skinned appearance looked paler than usual, especially in comparison to his rested, tanned peers.
- He acknowledged that his presentation was less than inspiring and that, in general, he had not demonstrated his usual enthusiasm and optimism about the future of the business, but he was surprised, and angry, that this one incident could have resulted in so many negative assumptions about him and his leadership capabilities.

Anyone who believes in fairness and meritocracy might see this situation in a way very similar to how Steven saw it. Why should his being off his game at one conference offset all the good work that he and his team did over a year? In my coaching and work with clients, I try to correct these perceptions. But it happens quite often. It may not be fair but incidents like this can definitely influence decisions about your career. Because senior management is usually very busy, they may see you only once or twice a year. They often pride themselves on being good judges of people and being able to size up leaders quickly. And, like everyone else, they are inordinately influenced by what they see. Steven had great values (dedication to the company, putting the company's interests over his own) and good intentions. But by working too long, jeopardizing his sleep and not allowing for recovery time, he risked undermining his career aspirations.

Recall my discussion of the Law of Diminishing Returns in the Introduction. There I pointed out that your health, key relationships, long-term goals, and religious and even ethical practices could suffer when you ignore this "law." For most executives, these are important considerations and provide reason enough to take this inflection point seriously. Even if these personal tradeoffs don't matter to you, even if you only care about accelerating your career, it is still advisable to respect this "law." Over time, your career risks and mistakes accrue, and based on another law, the law of probability, you become a career accident waiting to happen. When, instead, as detailed in the chapters on fitness, nutrition, and stress management, you take proper care of yourself, you build your capacity, enabling you to be more productive each workday and, longer term, throughout your career. Also recall, from Chapters 11 and 12, the importance of spending your time on high-payoff activities while eliminating or reducing the number of tasks that are not a good use of your time or that add to your stress. Readers who are sports fans recognize how many championships or races are won by teams that demonstrate good fundamentals and eliminate fumbles, errors, penalties, or crashes. This also applies to executives.

When you spend more time working in your career "sweet spot," you are, in effect, extending your capabilities. We all have a limit to how much we can do in 24 hours; and when we go beyond that limit, we naturally get tired and begin to make mistakes, mistakes of omission and commission. That's why it's critical to recognize when you are reaching your limit, so that you reduce the potential for making unnecessary business and career mistakes.

Career-Limiting Moves

In this chapter, I want to delve into what I call *career-limiting moves* (CLMs) that are clearly linked with being overworked and overstressed:

- Impact issues
- Mistakes of omission
- Mistakes of commission

Impact Issues

Confidence, high energy, clear focus, relaxed alertness, and looking fit add to your executive image. Developing a sound approach to fitness, nutrition, and stress management will help you perform better. These practices will also improve your appearance and personal impact. While these factors don't outweigh intelligence, hard work, creativity, or business acumen, they do play a role in whose ideas get implemented and who gets promoted. Success in executive roles is seen to be more and more dependent on stamina and discipline. Although it may not be fair, if you appear to tire easily, seem discouraged, get ill frequently, or are slow to recover you may be vulnerable to what happened to Steven L.

Here are some savvy tips for preventing this from happening to you:

- When preparing for key meetings, conferences, and presentations, remember it's about more than "just the facts, ma'am." Don't neglect the personal aspect. Prepare yourself as well, which includes getting plenty of rest.

> **WARNING**
>
> Do not automatically disregard negative feedback you receive because it makes you uncomfortable or because you feel it is inaccurate. Instead, pay attention, and accept that the impression you're giving is not the one you intend; then work to change it. Ask for help if you need it.

- Use self-talk skills when composing your thoughts and, subsequently, your words to express all that you need to—how your team is performing, the progress you are making, the challenges you have overcome, and what you are most excited about.
- If you are sick or fatigued, use it to your advantage, to "humanize" your situation. Say, for example, "I welcome the opportunity to discuss our business with you today, and to hear your feedback and suggestions. But I must warn you I am fighting a cold and so apologize in advance if I seem a little off my game. But I can assure you, I've never been more excited about the prospect. . . . " You get the idea.

Now that you're fully aware of the dangers of overworking and failing to take care of yourself, it's time to move on to another common type of mistake: of omission.

Mistakes of Omission

Major mistakes also come as the result of our neglecting to do things that are important for the purpose of advancing our careers. These I classify as mistakes of omission. Here are some true-to-life examples:

Failing to Network

Francoise, a very conscientious fashion executive, attributed her career progression in large part to the fact that she had mastered all facets of the business. She took pride in her deep knowledge of the industry and her track record in it; in addition, she had the division president as her main sponsor. But beyond this relationship with the division president, she did not have a strong network of other colleagues, either in her division or in the company at large. Often, she remarked that she didn't have time for "schmoozing." Unfortunately, when the division president was forced out of the company, essentially, Francoise's "network" walked out with him. Her new boss, who had won a power struggle with Francoise's former champion, did not know Francoise. She quickly saw that she had little credibility with him. Over a period of months, she was increasingly marginalized by her new boss, and she had no other sponsors in her company who were willing to support her.

Narrowing Your Focus

Stress tends to narrow our focus, putting the blinders on the peripheral vision we need to recognize key signs and signals that we are being undermined by others around us. I have seen many executives whose careers were short-circuited because they weren't paying attention to the activities of their subordinates; they "didn't see it coming."

Consider the case of Roberto G., who joined his company as the VP of manufacturing. He was told that though the organization preferred to promote from within, his key competencies won him the job over the internal candidate, Allan—who, though bitter about the decision, stayed with the company. Roberto immediately launched himself into a large systems transformation project, and was soon too busy to take much notice when two other employees approached him to let him know that Allan was making negative comments about Roberto and his project. Roberto chose to overlook the information, assuming that Allan had not yet come to terms with being passed over. Roberto continued to home in on the transformation project, believing it was what the company desperately needed and, moreover, would establish his credibility in the firm.

He also did not think much about Allan's long history with the senior team and his very strong internal network. Over time, however, using his network, Allan began to systematically "manage the airwaves," hinting that Roberto was not providing leadership, that the team had become divided, and that Roberto didn't respect the history or the culture of the company. Roberto, of course, heard these rumblings but told himself, "I don't have time for this political BS. I know I'm doing the right thing, and I know that I am the only one who can pull this off." Eventually, however, Allan's comments reached the CEO, who did pay attention to them. After one senior team meeting, the CEO essentially echoed the negative commentary that had been circulating; he told Roberto that he was out of touch; that his team was in disarray, and he was not even aware of it. He added that without the confidence and support of his team, Roberto couldn't be effective in the company.

Roberto's reputation never recovered, and he left the company three months later. With good intentions, Roberto had immersed himself in a worthwhile project but ignored the key signs and signals indicating that he needed to take action to protect himself.

Ignoring the Buzz

Krishna, an executive in the IT industry, had been educated in India, where everyone he knew took the same rigorous tests, and the smartest, hardest-working students won the awards and were accepted at the best schools. Understandably, he carried over this approach when he began his career in software development. And so he became known throughout the company for his dedication and long hours he devoted to projects. And it seemed to be working for him: Within two years he was assigned to lead the company's team in Spain, an assignment he viewed as a possible stepping-stone to becoming the president of the European division. He took on this new role with his usual laserlike focus, and it seemed to be paying off, although many of his associates at headquarters remarked that they had little contact with him.

Not surprisingly, then, when the Spanish team demonstrated excellent results for two consecutive years, Krishna expected to be promoted to president of the European division. Instead, he learned that a peer, whose results were not as stellar as his, would be getting the job, and would be Krishna's new manager. Krishna reached out to an ally in human resources and asked her if she knew why he didn't get the job. What she told him was that the "buzz" on him was that though was a tireless worker and an excellent executor, he was not the kind of strategic thinker that could lead Europe; in fact, many people at headquarters gave credit for the strategic thinking in his department to his VP of marketing.

At that moment, Krishna realized he had been completely unaware of the "buzz" about himself. When you are not aware of the buzz, you can not take action to correct it. The company may make decisions about your career based on these perceptions. Like Krishna, you may only discover the buzz after the decision is made.

Not Studying Power

Lorraine W. was the chief financial officer at a biotech company that had been started 15 years earlier by two cousins, currently the CEO and COO. The company had gone public the year before Lorraine came on board, though the two cousins retained 20 percent ownership. Lorraine had been brought in because the organization now needed a CFO with public company experience—board members were understandably concerned about SEC scrutiny, meeting Sarbanes-Oxley requirements, and addressing less-than-ideal accounting practices that had taken hold during the start-up years.

Lorraine believed she had been given a clear mandate for change, along with the necessary power to install new systems and controls. She attacked these objectives assiduously, working long hours to design change management projects. After 90 days at the company, she held an off-site meeting with her financial directors, the head of treasury and the controller. During the discussions about her proposed changes, the financial director who supported the Information Technology function challenged Lorraine, saying the changes would take away decision-making power from the head of IT, and therefore he couldn't support the plan. Initially, Lorraine was surprised, and then irritated. She told him that the changes were standard business practices, even if they were new to this company; and she reminded him she had been brought in to make such changes and that, as CFO, it was her call to make. End of discussion.

What Lorraine had neglected to recognize, due to her single-minded approach to her job, was that even though this was a public enterprise it was still run like a family business. Worse, the two founders had a very close personal relationship with the director of IT; so close in fact, they had a history of ignoring his weaknesses and not scrutinizing how he ran his group. As it turned out, this man had so much derived power that no one in the company dared to challenge him. Needless to say, the fallout of the meeting was almost immediate:

- The IT finance director informed the head of IT about the proposed changes, adding that Lorraine was arrogant, power hungry, an empire builder, and disrespectful of him, IT, and the company's culture and history.
- Those comments were embellished further in a discussion between the head of IT, the CEO and COO.
- The CEO and COO met with Lorraine and expressed their displeasure and disappointment with her behavior. They backed the head of IT 100 percent, telling her that she had no idea of his contribution to the company. They then announced they were seriously questioning whether she was a good fit for their company.

Lorraine had been too busy to study power. She assumed she had a mandate she didn't really have. Her actions threatened the "turf" of someone who had more power than she had and wound up damaging her standing in the company.

Mistakes of Commission

To reach executive levels and achieve a long, successful career requires discipline. Discipline is needed to reach performance goals but it is also necessary to avoid the many potential mistakes that can damage careers. Here are some of the types of discipline that are essential at the higher echelons of the corporate ladder:

Verbal Discipline

The more power an executive has, the more he or she needs to learn how to monitor what he or she says and, just as important, doesn't say. Verbal discipline includes:

- Keeping information confidential.
- Not sharing certain thoughts and feelings with people you don't trust (verbal discipline is not being dishonest; it is simply not saying everything you think or feel).
- Refraining from telling sexual, ethnic, or religious jokes, or using curse words.

Alcohol Discipline

Sometimes you will hear references to an event as a "social business" get-together. However, this moniker in not completely accurate. Any meeting, dinner, conference, fundraiser, or retreat should be treated the same as a meeting at headquarters. They are all business meetings and the same practices and disciplines should be followed. This includes the use of alcohol. It is very easy for executives to hurt their careers in these social settings. Alcohol discipline means knowing yourself and knowing what level of alcohol in your system will loosen your inhibitions. After that point, the normal control you have not to say or do certain things is no longer there.

Sexual Discipline

Our sexual appetites don't disappear when we arrive at work. You could make the case that working closely on challenging projects or differences in power and status actually increases it. It takes discipline not to act on your sexual attractions and impulses. This is even more difficult for executives that come from cultures where staring, touching, flirting, or making suggestive comments is more commonplace in an office setting. These same behaviors, or, even worse, sexual contact, in a U.S. enterprise or U.S. multinational can quickly derail an executive's career.

Decision-Making Discipline

Good decisions often rely upon a participative information-gathering process, analysis, weighing of options, and some due diligence after an alternative is chosen. When this discipline breaks down, there can be negative consequences to companies and careers. Executives lose patience or make impulsive decisions. Some examples can include acquisitions that had uncovered tax liabilities, consultants hired who claimed experience in a project that they were actually doing for the first time, and joint ventures entered into with partners who were later discovered to have a criminal record. Stress, time pressure, or burnout can lead to this type of poor decision-making.

Ethical Discipline

Temptations abound in the business world for several reasons. There is a lot of money and status available. Business executives often have considerable power. There are many conflicts of interest in business. A conflict of interest means your self-interest may conflict with doing the right ethical or legal thing. There can be conflicts of interest between board members, top executives, and shareholders (e.g., compensation, stock options, stock buybacks). There are many potential conflicts of interest between executives and their consumers in varied industries. An executive's self-interest can lead to hiding bad news, misrepresenting results or forecasts, or sweetheart deals with vendors. In addition, a corporation's self-interest can deviate from the interest of society or the community in which they operate. Unless you have achieved some very high level of religious of spiritual attainment, it requires rigorous discipline not to act in your self-interest in these circumstances, especially when there seems to be evidence that you can get away with it. If you have been reading the business section of your newspaper the past seven years, you will have noticed that many executives have been derailed by going down this slippery slope.

Emotional Discipline

People don't leave their emotions at home when they come to work. Having a wide range of feelings, including anger, sadness, anxiety, or discouragement, over a period of time during working hours is not unusual. Being aware of what you are feeling can actually be very useful. Expressing or showing your feelings can be risky.

- Displays of nervousness or discouragement can lead others to lose confidence in you.
- Crying can be labeled as overreacting or being too sensitive.
- Communicating when your caveman brain is in charge, or going "limbic," as we've read about in Chapter 5, can simultaneously "wound the king" and give that person ammunition to retaliate.

There are many people I have coached who can point to a five-minute confrontation or an angry e-mail as damaging events in their careers. It is not possible or desirable to eliminate emotions. It is certainly useful to acknowledge them to yourself and to people you trust. But in most business settings achieving enough control over your emotions to display what is appropriate for your environment is a useful discipline.

Discipline Summary

There is an undeniable connection between discipline and career progression. The areas of discipline I just covered point to the importance of leveraging certain attributes in the pursuit of our objectives. Alertness, mental clarity, agility, and patience become more and more important as executives are forced to move quickly from crisis to challenge to opportunity. This also has implications in regard to the impact of stress and fatigue. Fatigue can fog our thinking, interfere with our ability to be disciplined, and, ultimately, impact our behavior. We make poor decisions when stress increases our impulsivity and lowers our patience, when we fail to think through options or consequences, and due diligence is given short shrift. Stress also tends to weaken our listening skills, and we begin to interrupt and stop paying attention, which discourages participatory decision-making.

The latest research on sleep deprivation points to an even more basic liability. If you are overtired, you may become unable to properly process new information. Dr. Michael Chee, a neuroscientist at the National University of Singapore Graduate Medical School, working with Duke University, found that "When people are sleep-deprived, they may not be seeing what they think they should be seeing. If the information is not properly handled by the visual system, either as a result of a failure to direct attention appropriately or a failure of visual areas to process what is seen, you can forget about the later stages of information consolidation and storage."

Without question, excess stress and fatigue make it more difficult to maintain the disciplines we've discussed. We simply lose the inhibitors we need to stop us from, for example, making a joke we shouldn't, taking that extra drink, or behaving inappropriately to a colleague. When we are stressed and tired, our resolve weakens. It becomes easier to cut corners and rationalize our behavior ("Look how hard I work for this company." "Everyone else does it." "I'll just do it this one time.").

Executive Profile

Michael C. Feiner, Professor, Columbia University Graduate School of Business

Michael Feiner is a professor and Sanford C. Bernstein Ethics Fellow at Columbia University's Graduate School of Business. His classes on leadership are among the most well attended in the Columbia MBA

(Continued)

Michael C. Feiner, Professor, Columbia University Graduate School of Business (Continued)

program. Mike is a firm believer in the connection between leadership success and fitness. He has been an avid runner for 37 years, typically running 7 to 8 miles every morning—though now, at age 65, he "only" covers 5 to 6 miles on his daily runs.

I asked Mike to share his thoughts about the link between leadership and fitness. He says leaders need four types of energy: intellectual, emotional, moral, and physical.

- He believes that the physical energy attained through fitness is the foundation for the three other types of energy a leader needs.
- Intellectual energy is required for information gathering, problem solving, and decision making. Fitness enables clear thinking and the ability to concentrate. Fatigue leads to poor decisions.
- Emotional energy is necessary to manage disappointments and surprises, and to address relationship issues and conflicts.
- Moral energy is crucial to remain steadfast in the face of business pressures. A leader may feel pressure to hit targets and cut corners, and be faced with conflicts of interest. The discipline and strength obtained through regular exercise can help a leader avoid going down this slippery slope.

In addition to these benefits, Mike treasures his "run time" as time for himself. It is a rare time when he has no role, not as father, son, spouse, boss, or professor.

Summary

For many of you, this may be the most important chapter in the book, for working past the point of diminishing returns is a serious problem for a lot of executives in today's multitasking business environment. We are all more prone these days to making mistakes that, in a single minute, can undermine years of hard work and diligence. Learning how to avoid these mistakes is essential to a long and successful career. I am also hoping that learning about the potential cost of these mistakes increases your urgency to develop your fitness, nutrition, time, and stress management plans.

PART V

PERSONAL RELATIONSHIPS

15 | Maintaining Positive Relationships

This book, as you know by now, is about career success and how to design a healthy, sustainable path to achieving that goal. The topic of this, the final chapter in the book, is one I've touched on throughout: the importance of positive relationships. Forming and maintaining positive personal and professional relationships is at the core of everything you do, which is why I've left my in-depth coverage of this topic until the end.

I want to start with two questions. First, do we need loved ones, friends and family, to be successful in business? No. There are many examples of high achievers in the corporate world who are basically loners with very low need for affiliation.

Second, do we need close personal relationships to be happy? Most people will answer yes and research supports the association between positive relationships and reported happiness. Tim Kasser, associate professor at Lenox College, in a study on intrinsic values, found that people who focused on being connected to friends and family, exploring interests and skills, and "making the world a better place" were happier than those who focused mostly on material goals. Marriage, at least for men, is also linked with higher levels of health and increased longevity.

And who among us would argue that good relationships can't provide a source of support, empathy, listening, sharing, laughter, love, and even meaning? In addition, family objectives are often a key motivator for an executive's strivings. As wonderful as this sounds, a business career can present challenges to relationships, and relationships can present challenges to a business career. The first reason is time, something I talk about in each chapter. Forming and maintaining good relationships requires time.

The second reason is the potential for relationships to deteriorate. Relationships are particularly prone to being impacted by vicious cycles. These cycles can eventually consume large quantities of time and energy and distract our focus from other goals and priorities. So the irony is that, if relationships don't receive the time, energy, and focus that are needed to support them, they can become major consumers of your time, energy and focus. The flip side of those wonderful attributes (empathy, laughter, love, etc.) I described earlier is that relationships have the potential to bring out some of the worst feelings we may ever experience. Guilt, resentment, insecurity, humiliation, abandonment, and abuse can be, and are, experienced in relationships.

In a study of 9,011 British civil servants, most of them married, those with the worst close relationships were 34 percent more likely to have heart attacks or other heart trouble during 12 years of follow-up than those with good relationships. Those relationships could be partners, close relatives, and friends.

Our goal is to maintain positive relationships but, first, we need to understand how vicious cycles operate and why they can occur easily. Then, we will look at the skills and systems you can use to prevent these cycles or quickly extricate yourself from them.

Vicious Cycles

A vicious cycle, as depicted in Figure 15.1, is a series of linked events that become self-perpetuating. As the cycle is repeated, the conditions

deteriorate and the people enmeshed in the cycle find it increasingly difficult to find a way to put a stop to it. In a worst-case scenario, it can become
a "death spiral," leading to the collapse of an enterprise (bankruptcy) or of a
marriage (divorce). The media are replete with the consequences in our
society of being caught in a vicious cycle.

　Poverty is one such vicious cycle we, sadly, see played out every day in all
parts of the world. When, for example, a child grows up in a poor family, he
or she will not have had the advantage of good nutrition, leading to developmental weaknesses, which have implications for long-term cognitive abilities. Likewise, children of poverty often go to school hungry and hence
cannot concentrate, thereby interfering with their ability to get a good education, which will, of course, limit their career opportunities down the road.
Disadvantaged children also, often, have to go to work at an early age, forc-
ing them to forfeit their education in order to help their families. You can
clearly anticipate the cycle perpetuating for such children as they become
adults.

　Sectarian violence is another vicious cycle we're all too familiar with.
One killing, for example, sparks revenge killings, which trigger more ha-
tred and more revenge. And on it continues, until entire neighborhoods,
even countries, become unlivable.

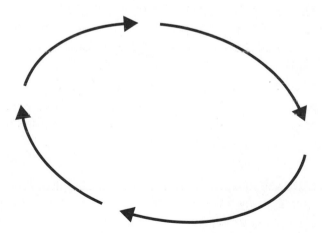

Figure 15.1　Vicious Cycle

In short, vicious cycles become self-reinforcing and more and more destructive. Therefore, the best way to avoid them is to learn to spot their early warning signals and pay attention to those signs so that we can put a stop to them before they become entrenched in our lives.

Spotting Vicious Cycles in Relationships

In relationships, the two most common types of vicious cycles are avoidance and attack cycles.

Avoidance Cycle

An avoidance cycle commonly occurs when the people involved in a relationship are uncomfortable addressing problems; they prefer to deny what's going on, or so fear being confrontational or getting into conflict, they do nothing. Doing nothing is, essentially, fuel for a vicious cycle. The example here illustrates how such a cycle happens.

Edward is a partner in a successful management consulting company. His multiple responsibilities include delivering services to existing clients, bringing in new clients, and developing new consultants. His wife, Ellen, works part-time from home as a marketing communications consultant. They have two children, a boy 9 and a girl 11 years old.

When Edward took this job, both he and Ellen accepted that, to make partner in the firm, he would, for a certain period, have to devote most of his time to his work. Thereafter, they expected he would be able to spend more time with the family.

But after reaching this professional milestone, this never happened; in fact, from the point of view of Ellen and the children, Edward seems to away from home even more, with out-of-town travel added to his job description. Ellen, nevertheless, does her best to continue to be supportive, and to avoid overt conflict. But there is no

---

denying that she and the children are becoming more sensitive to, and focused on, Edward's absence, as well as the changes taking place in him as a result of the long hours he is keeping. In particular, it troubles them that:

- He has very limited time for them.
- When he is home, he is often stressed, distracted, and too tired to really interact with them.
- He doesn't give them his full attention, and rarely shows genuine interest in their lives.
- He occasionally breaks promises he's made to attend family and school events.

Nevertheless, Ellen and the children don't confront him with their concerns and hurt feelings, instead only making snide comments or jokes. Edward is too tired and too preoccupied to notice the shift in their feelings. Over time, and without being aware of it or making a conscious decision to do so, Ellen and the kids start to withdraw from Edward. They essentially give up expecting that he will be there to meet their needs for fun, attention, or intimacy. In giving up, they also become resentful, and this is demonstrated in subtle ways. For example, when he comes home from work, they barely respond to his "How was your day?" inquiries or to his hugs.

The cycle begins to accelerate when Edward, Ellen, and both of the children start seeking other ways to meet their relationship needs. Like so many executives who become disengaged at home, he gets involved with a single woman that he worked with on a cross-functional task force; though it has not become physical, it is intimate. They share long business dinners, travel together, and frequently exchange e-mails. Their relationship makes Edward feel younger, admired, and less lonely—he's found someone he can share all his feelings with, and someone who understands the pressures of his job.

Ellen, too, has found a way to fill in the emptiness left by Edward's absence. She has developed a close friendship with two single women she met at the gym. She spends a lot of time with them, joining them for dinner and drinks at a café in a nearby town that has music and dancing. She now regularly leaves the children in the care of babysitters.

Edward and Ellen's 9-year-old son, who has always been somewhat awkward socially, begins to withdraw even more. He spends most of his free time playing games on the Internet. And though he feels isolated at school, he doesn't share his feelings with anyone, and no one notices. Their daughter, who is much more outgoing, lately has been spending time with a clique of kids who think themselves very funny, especially in their irreverent and somewhat contemptuous behavior toward authority figures; they are all overtly cynical about their parents.

Where is this cycle headed? Affairs, divorce, children alienated from their parents and developing emotional problems or getting into trouble? It is hard to predict but the warning signs are there. The warning signs may not be there to Edward and Ellen. Remember the Law of Gradual Change, and they are both distracted enough that they may not notice the signals. Without knowing the final resolution we can still predict that this family will have to devote a lot of time and energy to repair the damage or deal with a messy rupture. In addition it is easy to imagine some very unpleasant feelings that will eventually emerge.

Attack Cycle

An attack cycle has many of the same elements as the avoidance cycle; the difference is that at least one person in the relationship is confrontational, more vocal about addressing perceived slights, broken promises, and unmet needs. This type of individual obviously is going to make a relationship more combustive; therefore, more "fireworks" and drama characterize this cycle. Yelling, name-calling, threats, and, worst of all, physical abuse may occur. Case in point: Recently, a top media executive was suspended from his job for allegedly hitting his girlfriend in a parking lot. He eventually resigned.

Of course, as in all vicious cycles, as more confrontations occur, in whatever form, the relationship deteriorates further. The ties that bind loosen, and eventually become totally undone. People may find ways to retaliate; and/or they withhold affection. When this occurs in a family with children, cliques or subgroups may form as children side with one parent against the other. And for the parent who is an executive, family stress is piled on top of job stress. When both parents are executives, as is more often the case these days, you can imagine the result. Home is no longer a sanctuary from the rest of the world, no longer the place to find support and to unwind. Communication, even in the form of body language, becomes painful. Participants begin to exhibit all the symptoms of stress, including sleeplessness and the tendency to look for quick fixes, in alcohol, drugs, gambling, illicit liaisons, and so on. The executive(s) may find more reasons to stay late at the office or be on the road more of the time. All these behaviors accelerate and prolong the cycle.

Vicious Cycle Summary

There are many variations of the two types of relationship vicious cycles I've just described. Some start out as an avoidance pattern, but eventually grow to include attack elements, and vice versa. These patterns may also play out between grown siblings, over issues such as perceived favoritism, conflicts with in-laws, or fights over money. It is not uncommon for previously close sibling relationships to deteriorate to the point of irreconcilability.

A major element in any type of vicious cycle is the breakdown of trust. Once we start to distrust someone, our attitudes and behaviors change. We no longer give them the benefit of the doubt; in fact, we may unfairly attribute negative intentions to their behavior, having thoughts such as:

- "He meant to do that."
- "She is trying to make me look foolish."
- "He purposely came home late even though he knew how important this was to me."
- "There is no way she simply forgot; I told her twice."

Once trust is lost, we can no longer be as open or vulnerable as is necessary to maintain a positive relationship. We no longer feel we can rely on them. We refuse to accept their explanations or excuses. Sadly, once trust is broken, it is very hard to rebuild. Think about a time when you lost trust in someone, because he or she betrayed you in some way, lied to you, didn't fulfill a commitment, or didn't keep a confidence or promise. Were you able to reestablish a trusting relationship with that person? How much effort did you make? If you were able to do it, how long did it take?

The bonding that occurs in relationships is a foundation of happiness, and may be our most effective weapon against stress. But these bonds are not unbreakable, and should never be taken for granted. They must be nurtured and supported by some basic practices, for once broken, they are hard to repair.

With that admonition in mind, I want to introduce basic, core skills that will help you to maintain relationship bonds and prevent vicious cycles.

Executive Profile

Edward Betof, PhD, Senior Fellow and Academic Director, Executive Program in Workplace Learning Leadership, Wharton Business School; and Nila Betof, COO, The Leader's Edge

This is a relationship profile, rather than an individual profile. In it, I highlight the careers and positive practices of a couple, Ed and Nila Betof, to illustrate how two people can succeed at supporting one another professionally, raising a family, and enriching a marriage (they celebrated their thirty-eighth anniversary in 2007).

Ed is a national expert in talent management, leadership develop-ment, and corporate universities. Senior managers at his former em-ployer, Becton Dickinson (BD), attest to his pervasive, positive impact on BD's success. It is no surprise that when the Wharton School of Business created the first doctoral program of its kind for chief learn-ing officers (CLOs), Ed was asked to be its director.

Ed has many admirable traits, but for the purpose of this chapter, I have chosen to spotlight his approach to health and career choices.

Whenever Ed and I have worked together at off-site seminars, he always makes it to the gym before me and often leaves after me. He never loses sight of the fact that many of the men in his family have a history of cardiovascular disease; some have died prematurely as a result. So early on, Ed decided health would be a top priority in his life. He works out to maintain his fitness, and then takes it to higher levels through participation in sports. For example, though now over 60, he competes in open tennis events against players in their twenties. Other priorities for Ed are his marriage, Nila's career, and his role as a father; so, in any decisions he makes, these issues are important fac-tors. In the past, for example, he chose to turn down jobs that might involve moving, even at the risk of slowing his career progression.

Nila, who earned a PhD in organizational development, has had a diverse, successful career in consulting, operations, and as COO of a start-up. Her background has prepared her well for her current role as coach and advisor to senior female executives. When asked for in-sights she has gained from her own career development and the ex-ecutives she has coached, Nila said women tend to take on more roles and responsibilities then men, and have higher expectations of themselves—in an attempt, she says, to try to "take care of everyone else first," leaving too little time to address their own needs. In addi-tion to regular business challenges, she adds, women face greater stress because they are often operating in a predominantly male culture, and so must walk a line between projecting strength and

(Continued)

**Edward Betof, PhD, Senior Fellow and
Academic Director (Continued)**

maintaining their femininity and sense of self. Thus, overextended and overcommitted, they become vulnerable to many of the problems described in *Executive Stamina*. In helping women address these issues, Nila takes a multifaceted approach, appropriate to the individual situation, but two points she always emphasizes are:

1. *Carve out personal time.* If female executives don't make this a top priority, and protect this space in their schedules, their numerous responsibilities will begin to erode it, until it disappears entirely.
2. *Get help.* For executives who are also mothers, it's critical to find reliable child care, and back-up assistance, to allow for flexibility and peace of mind.

Jointly, Nila and Ed think carefully through decisions regarding financial and career impact; and each, at different times, has put the other's career ahead of his or her own. They also took turns completing their doctoral programs, and waited for 10 years to become parents.

Relationship Practices

Similar to the other tips and techniques I've presented throughout the book, I approach relationship practices from the standpoint of my theory of *minimums*, always cognizant of the time pressure executives, as a rule, function under. Of course, you may want—or at times, need—to do more than the minimum I recommend, but my objective here is to give you the basic ingredients you need to take care of the important relationships in your life.

These practices are described in the framework of seven guidelines.

Don't Take Relationships for Granted

This may seem like stating the obvious, but it bears repeating, for we humans are prone to do exactly that: take things for granted, including our health, our financial situation, and our relationships. By resisting the tendency to put your relationships on "autopilot," you safeguard the bonds you have made and treasure.

Remember the Law of Gradual Change

This law is especially critical in the realm of relationships. Marriages don't suddenly deteriorate, and parents and children don't become alienated overnight. The best defense against gradual change is to include your key relationships in your Shifts/Drifts chart. Later in this chapter, I'll explain how to apply the Minimums and Shifts/Drifts systems to maintaining relationships.

Be Predictable

If you are an executive, your romantic partner and friends, extended family, and children (if you are a parent) know how much time your career consumes. They probably have adjusted their expectations about how available you are or when you will be present. What is very difficult for most of them is when you don't show up when they do expect you, you break promises, or you make frequent changes because of work demands. Some of these things are out of your control but this lack of predictability probably impacts children the most. They often can adjust to seeing you on a more limited basis than they like, but adjusting to unpredictability often means a kind of giving up. They stop expecting you to be there, and build a life and support network that does not include you.

A good practice is to be very careful about commitments and promises. The ones you make should be met except in genuine crises. This will go a long way to ensure that the people around you maintain their trust in you and dependence on you.

JoAnn Deak, PhD, describes how important this is to the father-daughter relationship in her groundbreaking book *Girls Will Be Girls* (Hyperion, 2003). "Unless the two have developed special ways of sharing time outside the ordinary, a father's constant absence or tardiness has meaning to girls. The fifth time he misses the game or isn't there for the school play, it is a huge hurt that girls don't just 'get over.' They get sad, they get discouraged, they get self-critical, they get angry, they get icy; but they don't *not* feel about it."

Make Time for Listening

Human beings have a need to be listened to. This means for another person to give them his or her attention, show an interest and curiosity about their thoughts and feelings, and demonstrate that they have been heard and understood. This experience requires time and a setting where people won't be interrupted too often. It is also necessary that the listener not be too distracted by his or her own issues or behaviors (watching TV, reading a newspaper, working on a computer). When we listen to someone we reinforce our connections with them. Listening gives us a chance to show empathy and the like emotionally. Listening also helps the speaker go deeper, "peel back the onion" several layers, and indicate needs, concerns, or feelings that otherwise wouldn't be expressed. This is especially true of children, who are expert at picking up real attention and interest. If you don't provide those things you may miss important issues that are stirring inside them.

When you add up the importance of listening and the requirements for good listening to occur, you see that it is probably wise to be intentional and planful about listening to all the key people in your relationship world.

Communicate Clearly

The flip side of being a good listener is being an effective communicator. People can't read your mind, no matter how close they are to you; and body language can never tell them enough, even if they are good at picking up wordless clues you're sending. When appropriate, be willing to share:

- *Inner thoughts:* You are a dynamic being, as we all are. You change, evolve, grow all the time. It's important to you and the people close to you to know what's going on with you. Don't make them guess.
- *Important feelings:* Sharing feelings is one of the primary ways we form bonds with the important people in our lives.
- *Constructive feedback:* If someone close to you is disappointing or frustrating you in some way, tell that person, or he or she will continue to upset you. Eventually, this could lead to an inappropriate reaction on your part. So address the issue promptly, patiently, and with compassion. Don't "make a problem out of a problem" by waiting. Give timely, specific feedback that focuses on improvement, not criticism.

Resolve Conflict Effectively

Many marriage experts say that the most important indicator of the quality and longevity of a romantic relationship is the ability of the two parties to effectively resolve conflicts. Conflicts are inevitable, even between the best of friends, family, and "soul mates." But when the people involved are willing to listen to each other's opinion and perspective, to search for win–win solutions, or to reach a reasonable compromise, it builds their confidence to handle future concerns. In contrast, conflicts left unresolved escalate or smolder underground, eventually becoming triggers for a vicious cycle. For couples, a wise practice is to hold preventative discussions about common areas of conflict—financial decisions, in-laws, religion, parenting practices, children, and so forth.

The best approach to conflict resolution is to stay aware of your *limbic system*, in order to maintain control of your emotional brain, which has the potential to put your health and career at risk. When you "go limbic," you not only escalate conflicts, you sometimes want to initiate them. So, if you pay attention to the signs that this part of your brain is taking over, take a break before you do or say something you will regret. Likewise, if you are already in this overemotional state of mind, resist the urge to initiate conversations about sensitive subjects.

Pay Attention to "Tells"

A *tell* is a sign or signal. It is information that people reveal about themselves through their verbal or nonverbal behavior or changes from their normal patterns. The term originated with Mike Caro, a poker professional and coach, because a big part of success in poker is attributed to "reading" the other players.

We give off "tells" about our interest or disinterest, impatience, surprise, frustration, embarrassment, resentment, hesitancy, anxiety, confusion, excitement and guardedness. If we are too busy or tired or distracted, or too tethered to electronic devices, it is highly likely that we will not be noticing the cues from the people with whom we are in a relationship. This potentially hurts the relationship in several ways:

- We fail to pay attention to important issues—what matters to the people in our lives, their inner feelings, or what is changing in their lives.
- We miss the signals alerting us to the beginning of a vicious cycle. (Remember that preventing these cycles is the first goal, but next in importance is to notice the early signs and prevent their escalation.)
- We fail to recognize our impact on others. Maybe we talk too much, and dominate conversations. Maybe we are not as funny as we think we are. Maybe what we regard as light-hearted teasing is actually hurtful to someone's feelings. You can't count on people telling you these things, no matter how close they are. Humans are notoriously uncomfortable about giving this kind of feedback. They may want to avoid conflict, or to avoid hurting your feelings or provoking anger. Sometimes they aren't even aware themselves of how much something is bothering them. So if they aren't giving you direct feedback

and you aren't noticing the "tells," then you probably will repeat your behavior.

If you are a parent or have responsibility for the development of a child, being present enough to notice "tells" is possibly even more important. This is due to several factors. Children may not know exactly what they are feeling or how to express it, or may be fearful of how you will react. For example:

- Your daughter's friends might be pressuring her to do something against her values, or what she's been taught.
- Your son might be the victim of verbal or physical harassment at school, or over the Internet.
- Your nephew might be questioning his sexuality or gender identity.
- Your niece may be concerned about some aspect of her appearance.
- Your daughter might have a poor self-image.
- Your son misinterprets something you say. For example, "Well, somebody's got to work hard to pay for all these lessons and this equipment," causing him to feel guilty or responsible because you work so much.

In each of these circumstances a tell side comment ("There's a boy at school who . . ."), facial expression, or change from usual behavior may be the only clue that something is bubbling inside.

Relationship Practice Summary

Of course, there are many other important relationship practices—including rituals, religious or spiritual practices, fun, vacations, and so on. In this chapter my goal was to highlight some basic practices that can diminish the chance that vicious cycles will impact your relationships. In addition, I wanted to reinforce that some of these basics, like listening, being predictable, communication, conflict resolution, and noticing tells, take time, attention, and, in some circumstances, scheduling.

Using Minimums, Recognizing Shifts and Drifts, and Combining Activities to Maintain Relationships

In this, the final section of the chapter, I'll describe how to apply to relationships the systems I introduced earlier in the book: setting and scheduling minimums, recognizing shifts and drifts, and combining practices for greater effectiveness.

Minimums

The minimum approach works best in situations that have the following elements:

- You have identified a key priority or objective.
- The priority or objective, though important, doesn't qualify as urgent, so it is at risk of falling prey to the Law of Gradual Change.
- You are aware of your current inability to take action to advance or maintain your goals in meeting this priority or objective.

Not all priorities require minimums. For example, assume you work for a financial services company and have been selected as one of three finalists (out of 12) for the placement of a $2 billion investment from the United Auto Workers pension fund. The presentation to the pension investment board is next month. In a situation such as this, you will almost never need minimums. Why not? Consider: This is a huge opportunity; you have worked hard to reach the top three finalists, and clearly there is urgency—you have only a month to complete the project. This is potentially your biggest "win" of the year. You are a professional, and you will be ready. Truth be told, if you can't prepare for this kind of opportunity, minimums won't help you.

In contrast, as I've mentioned earlier in the book, there are many other types of situations that have longer-term importance. And it is their long-term nature that sometimes leads us to fail to give them the attention they need in a timely fashion. It is for these situations that we need minimums. Previous examples I've cited include maintaining our health, conducting a spiritual practice, and financial planning. But probably the number-one example that falls into this category is our relationships. This is the area where lack of attention, combined with gradual changes, can weaken our connections with the people to whom we are closest. So in this section, I'm going to explain how to apply minimums to help you make sure that other demands and commitments don't cause you to lose touch with the people in your life.

In my coaching experience, I've come in contact with people who resist the idea of scheduling time with their family and friends. It seems to them too businesslike an approach to something so personal. They ask, "Why should I have to schedule romantic time with my spouse? Shouldn't it just happen spontaneously?" Or "Why do I need to schedule time alone with each of my children? I'm there for them if they need me." And I agree—in an ideal world, where none of us is under such pressure, and we always have time to meet these needs without planning. But we're not living in an ideal world. That's why the minimums system is necessary.

Here are my two guidelines for deciding when setting relationship minimums is necessary for you:

1. You recognize that a relationship is precious to you.
2. You are likewise aware that you are not doing the minimum necessary to maintain it.

A useful example is family dinners. I place family dinners in the category of important but not urgent, and so believe they can benefit from applying the practice of setting and scheduling minimums. Consider that Columbia University's National Center on Addiction and Substance Abuse has launched an annual program called "Family Day: A Day to Eat Dinner with Your Children," in September, in response to two telling research findings:

1. Fewer than one-third of American children sit down to dinner with both parents on any given night.

2. Children who eat dinner regularly with their parents have fewer instances of substance abuse, show less obesity, and cheat less at school.

My point is, setting minimums is most useful when you take an honest look at how you are actually spending your time and, as a result, have to acknowledge that if you don't block out parts of your schedule, there is a high likelihood that you will not live up to your word or your intent in your relationships. Remember, scheduling minimums can help you in one of two ways.

1. *You meet your minimums*. This is the ideal result. You demonstrate to others their importance to you. You do what you say you will—you keep your word. And by making time to communicate and listen effectively and attentively, you are more likely to see the signals telling you what needs more attention, and thus you need to raise your minimum.

2. *You don't meet your minimums*. Not doing the minimum is a loudly ringing alarm bell. This is a relationship you believe is valuable, you set the minimum activity to maintain it, and you are not finding time to do the minimum. While, of course, this is not a good result, the fact that you set the minimum and, at the time you set it, planned to follow through forces accountability. You now would need to take a hard look at yourself, to analyze what has happened. Was it on the calendar? Did you say "yes" to something else? Are you and the other people in the relationship overcommitted?

This last point is a very real possibility. Many families today are overcommitted—not just executive parents, but their children, too. Sports teams, lessons, volunteer activities, time with friends, hobbies, and so on, all sound good, and, of course, are good, if not taken to extremes. Problems arise when good things become too much of a good thing. That's why it's critical to accurately assess how much time each commitment will take, to monitor the overall impact, and to identify what might be getting lost in the shuffle. If you are having difficulty meeting your relationship minimums, then it's time to examine why.

Keep in mind that setting relationship minimums is different from setting professional minimums or personal long-term goals. In these latter areas, you need to consult only yourself, possibly with the help of a credible advisor. When it comes to relationships, however, you should arrive at the minimum through a dialogue with the other person or persons involved. Depending on the nature of the relationship, you may need to discuss the following:

- Would this minimum meet the other person's needs?
- Would he or she set the minimum higher or lower?
- What is his or her idea of fun or romance?
- Does he or she have creative ideas about achieving the minimums?
- Does he or she have insights into the specific scheduling issues you face?

If you are a parent, or are responsible for the development of children, I strongly recommend setting a minimum of "alone time" with each child. Why do I emphasize this? In a household or group of three or more, there is a high likelihood that one person may dominate. And that person's need for greater control or more attention can inhibit the participation of another member of the family. Moreover, the most important issues facing a child may be difficult for him or her to broach unless you are alone together. Unless given some uninterrupted, private time with you, the child may not discuss inner "rumblings," and you may not pick up the "tells" the child is sending.

How to Set Relationship Minimums

So, if I've convinced you to review your need for minimums, here is how to get started.

1. Focus on your key relationships. Review the seven positive relationship practices in the chapter. Are you below the minimums?

2. Review the discussion of vicious cycles: Are you seeing signs of either the avoidance or attack pattern in your relationships?
3. If you are in a romantic relationship, ask yourself if you're doing what's necessary to "keep the romance alive."

Once you've answered these questions, engage in a discussion with the people involved to help you set the minimum necessary to maintain or improve each relationship. To help in this, let me share the most common needs I've noted among the executives I've coached.

- *Need for romance:* When it comes to romantic relationships, alone time between partners is vital. Too many commitments, coupled with stress and fatigue, will crowd out romance. And when either of the partners has unmet romantic needs, the possibilities increase that he or she will consciously or unconsciously seek other ways or people to meet these needs, thus escalating the chances of further alienation, arguments, feelings of betrayal, and, ultimately, divorce.
- *Need for personal communication:* When the communication between two people in a relationship has become little more than an exchange of checklists, of to-do lists, they inevitably will lose the connection to the other person's thoughts and feelings. Being overtired, distracted, or tethered to communication devices are all enemies to effective personal communication.
- *Need for time alone with children:* I've already made my case why this is so important. I remind you here because I have seen so many well-intentioned, busy executives neglect to make this a standard relationship practice.

Shifts and Drifts

When I explained this system in Chapter 3, I mentioned that it is useful to include a section in your shifts and drifts chart for your relationships, where you list each person important to you on a separate line. Each month (or more often, if you want), you would make note of any change on the chart. Here are some of the things you should be looking for.

Drifts

By now you're well aware that relationships are especially vulnerable to the Law of Gradual Change, so focus on any signs of slippage. If you have set some minimums that you didn't meet in the last month, take note and make it a high priority to reinstitute them next month.

Shifts

To reiterate, shifts are discrete changes that we may notice but often fail to think through their implications; thus then we also neglect to make adjustments or reprioritize. In a relationship with another person, it is useful to look at shifts in two ways.

- *First, identify any key shifts in your life.* For example: Are your corporate assignments or pressures increasing or decreasing? Have you taken on more responsibility at your religious institution? Have your commitments to other relationships (e.g., care of older parents) changed or increased? Are you recovering from an illness or injury? Have you been presented with a "once in a lifetime" opportunity you want to take advantage of? All these shifts will impact your time and availability, and you may need to reconfigure how you plan to maintain your relationship in light of these changes.
- *Second, identify key shifts in the life of the other person.* Any or all of the previous questions might apply. It can be useful to both of you to try to determine your respective needs. Given the shift(s), will they need more or less of your time?

In many families and relationships, what happens is that people may acknowledge on some level the shifts in their lives, but they don't take time to reflect upon the impact those shifts might have; thus, they don't make the necessary adjustments until the impact is felt. That is why, when one person in the relationship takes on new responsibilities or commitments, it is a good practice to allow for "digestion" time. I caution you to be wary of "adding on" until you adapt to this change; you may even need to pull back in other areas. This may mean monitoring how this change will affect your existing routine and schedule.

Combining Activities

Earlier, I defined the "good" kind of multitasking, that is, combining priorities into one activity; and I explained how you could apply the practice to help you meet business or fitness goals. Here I want to demonstrate how this approach can be used to optimize relationship time. The key is to think about creative ways of advancing two or more of your goals. Some examples:

> **Goals:** Fitness; being in touch with nature; raising your children's awareness about environmental issues
> **Activity:** A nature walk in a forest or along a stream being impacted by climate change

> **Goals:** Learning home-building skills; fitness; shared family experiences; teaching children to give back to the community
> **Activity:** Spending a long weekend with your family on a rebuilding project in New Orleans

> **Goals:** Fitness; time for communication with a romantic partner or child
> **Activity:** A walk; slow-paced jogging or moderate-paced bike ride

> **Goals:** Personal development (arts, languages, dancing); time with family or friends
> **Activity:** Generating mutual interest in family or friends, and participating with them

Goals: Business travel; time with family

Activity: Taking family members on business trips (Note: According to the National Business Travel Association, 62 percent of U.S. business travelers said they add a leisure component to at least one business trip per year. Among those travelers, two-thirds say they bring along a family member or a friend.)

Another way to free up time is to "outsource" more of our personal chores. We already outsource business activities regularly, and we are also used to hiring others to, for example, clean our houses, do home repairs, prepare our tax returns, and so on. Of course, before you make the decision to pay someone to do something you could do yourself, you must weigh the cost against what you can afford and how precious your time is. For most executives, time is the scarcest commodity, so it is worthwhile to consider making the time/money trade-off.

TIP

Did you know that vast talent pools of skilled but relatively inexpensive workers in India, China, Bangladesh, Romania, Ukraine, and other places are now accessible through your computer? Tasks like landscape architecture, kitchen remodeling, math tutoring, and travel planning can now be sent out to bid by Internet-proficient folks in the United States. There is even an Indian-based concierge service, Get Friday, that fulfills many of the roles of a personal assistant.

Even after you have applied the time optimization techniques described in *Executive Stamina*, if you find you are still too busy, consider the outsourcing option. The money you spend may be worth the time you save.

Summary

Relationships are highly vulnerable to the negative impact of cycles, so it makes sense to do all you can to prevent these patterns from occurring, or to address them as early as possible if they've already taken hold. To help you maintain these positive practices:

- Implement the minimum system to protect against the Law of Gradual Change and the tendency to take relationships for granted.
- Monitor your relationship connections by putting them on your monthly shifts/drifts tracking chart.
- Creatively combine activities to meet multiple priorities and goals in the minimum amount of time.

Conclusion

I and Joshua have attempted to provide you with dozens of tips and techniques to help you personally and professionally. We have emphasized progressive change and improvement, not perfection, so try to get started with simple changes in the areas that are most important to you. Our focus is on the long term. Set yourself on a path that is realistic and sustainable. We simultaneously hope that you can expand your capacity while learning where your limits are.

Since self-awareness is central to our message, we hope that you have learned some things about yourself. And since we are always interested in learning, please contact us with your feedback, comments, or questions. For information about Executive Stamina seminars, speeches, or coaching, please go to our web site: www.executivestamina.org.

Index